TALES FROM THE SHARP END

Also by Natascha Scott-Stokes

Travel

An Amazon and a Donkey

The Amber Trail: From the Baltic Sea to the Aegean

Chickenbus Journey: False Paradise in Guatemala

Biography

Wild and Fearless: The Life of Margaret Fountaine

Travel Guidebooks (as coauthor)

The Cadogan Guide to Belize

The Cadogan Guide to Central America

The Cadogan Guide to Guatemala

The Cadogan Guide to Guatemala and Belize

The Rough Guide to Germany

The Rough Guide to West Germany

Praise for *Tales from the Sharp End: A Portrait of Chile*

"*Tales from the Sharp End* is a genuine pleasure to read. If you haven't yet visited Chile, you will want to after reading this book. Natascha Scott-Stokes has an engagingly personal writing style, and her portrait of Chile is rendered evocatively in a series of unforgettable stories about the nature, people, and history of the land she has come to feel a part of. There is humor and beauty here, as well as bittersweetness. In the end, this is Natascha Scott-Stokes's ode to the place that she has chosen to live in and to love. Reading her, one cannot help but feel that she has given over a part of her soul to Chile, but that—delightfully for us—it has been a reciprocal exchange."

—Jon Lee Anderson, author of *Che: A Revolutionary Life*

"Natascha Scott-Stokes offers readers the rare gift of combining an outsider's skeptical peek into a foreign land with an insider's keen grasp of Chile's cultural quirks and politics, dramatic turning points and unparalleled landscape. *Tales from the Sharp End* is a witty, richly colored gaze at Chile from within."

—Pascale Bonnefoy Miralles, author of *The Investigative Brigade: Hunting Human Rights Criminals in Post-Pinochet Chile*

"A most welcome addition to the literature on Chile. Natascha Scott-Stokes gives us a broad overview of this remarkable land, weaving together natural history, Spanish explorers and colonizers, as well as the country's troubled recent history."

—Mary Helen Spooner, author of *The General's Slow Retreat: Chile after Pinochet*

tales from the sharp end

Natascha Scott-Stokes

A PORTRAIT OF CHILE

University of New Mexico Press — Albuquerque

Printed in the United States of America

ISBN 978-0-8263-6662-7 (paper)
ISBN 978-0-8263-6663-4 (ePub)

Library of Congress Control Number: 2024938893

Founded in 1889, the University of New Mexico sits on the traditional homelands of the Pueblo of Sandia. The original peoples of New Mexico—Pueblo, Navajo, and Apache—since time immemorial have deep connections to the land and have made significant contributions to the broader community statewide. We honor the land itself and those who remain stewards of this land throughout the generations and also acknowledge our committed relationship to Indigenous peoples. We gratefully recognize our history.

Cover image adapted from Alain Bonnardeaus via Upsplash
Part openers and chapter openers adapted from images by Powel Nolbert and Jake Weirick via Upsplash
Interior images courtesy of the author unless otherwise stated
Designed by Isaac Morris
Composed in Alegreya, Nobel, and Utopia

Dedicated to the sisters Berta and Nicolasa Quintremán, defenders of Pehuenche land and their ancestral rights in Chile, and all the environmental campaigners and writers around the world who have been murdered.

Impossible usually means only "nearly impossible" and the "nearly" is the adventure.

Rosie Swale in *Back to Cape Horn*

Contents

Acknowledgments

First and foremost, I must thank Michael Millman, without whose enthusiasm for this book I would be unable to share my work with you.

I am deeply grateful to my friends and family who have acted as critical readers and listeners or have allowed me to tell their stories. Some are listed here in alphabetical order, and the others know who they are:

Karen Anderson; Iain Ballesty; Hernán Blanco; Ruth Bradley; Ann Davenport; Riet Delsing; Gianna Devoto; Anya Doherty; John Ewer; Rodolfo Follegati; Waldo García; Erica Gardner; Sergio Gaymer; Verónica González, Helen Hughes; Rémi Leblanc; Sascha Leblanc; Cat MacFarlane; Virginia Ortiz; Heather Philipp; Lucila Recart; Caroline Richards; Howard Richards; Shelley Damaris Richards; Philip Sanders; Charity Scott-Stokes; Lezak Shallat; Mary Helen Spooner; Gerardo Vidaurre; and Kathleen Whitlock.

All photographs are by the author except where otherwise stated.

Please note: some names in the text have been changed to protect privacy.

Introduction

Chile is the dagger in the back of South America. A country born of greed and desire, with a long history of destruction, mirrored even by the forces of nature that regularly shake human constructions to the ground in massive earthquakes and smother all life in suffocating smoke and ash from hundreds of volcanoes, of which 105 have erupted at some point over the past five centuries. Insecurity and violence is always the dominant theme in this country.

This was not the context uppermost in my mind when I persuaded my family to emigrate to Chile in 2006. Instead, I was focused on bringing my depressed husband into the sunshine and returning to the bewitching world of Latin America, where our relationship had blossomed almost two decades earlier.[1] Admittedly, that was in the exquisite setting of eighteenth-century Antigua Guatemala, but we both agreed our beloved Central America was not a safe or practical place to live with two young sons. Nor were other culturally enticing destinations like Colombia, Brazil, or Peru. And so we agreed on Chile, one of the most highly developed countries in Latin America, characterized by modern infrastructure, a strong economy, and political stability—at least, it was between the return of democracy in 1990 and the social uprising of October 2019.

My impression during a research trip was favorable. The country felt like an old-fashioned Spain, and while colorful Indigenous markets and the exhilarating unpredictability of elsewhere in South America were generally missing here, public transport was comfortingly punctual and you didn't seem to have to worry about crime either.[2] With a young family, we were not looking for anything exotic or the thrill of danger. What we wanted was a safe place to bring up our children and give them the chance to become bilingual in Spanish and English; we also sought to open their eyes to a wider world without risking malaria or a gun to the head. And so we arrived at Santiago's airport on a crisp October morning, with eight laundry bags and no contacts. Within weeks a 6.3 earthquake shook us from our beds, but the locals insisted it was just a *temblor* (a tremble) and, in time, we learned to accept that attitude. Today, I don't even bother getting out of bed unless plaster starts falling off the wall.

Chile is an extraordinary 4,300 kilometers (2,670 miles) long but never more than 350 kilometers (217 miles) wide, lined by the Andes Mountains to the east and the Pacific Ocean to the west. So on a transverse route you are either heading to the mountains in the *oriente* (east) or toward the sea in the *poniente* (west), while the Pan-American Highway gives you just two choices: up or down, north or south. Traveling along that dusty road is one of the great thrills of this part of the world, where you can access both the driest desert on earth and impenetrable cloud forests barring the way to Patagonian ice fields. In fact, that is the true magnet of this jagged knife-edge of a country: the unique landscape born of its geography and the gorgeous plant and animal life you can find there. Few things are more thrilling than climbing the coastal mountain in my valley to see both the Andes and the Pacific Ocean at the same time, or to set eyes on the mighty Baker River churning through southern Patagonia. European conquerors did not value the views nature has to offer, but this was and remains the country's greatest treasure.

The portrait of Chile I have sketched in this book comprises self-contained themed chapters you can read in any order you wish, though they are set in the timeframe of my specific experience of living there from 2006 onward. They range in theme from history to travel, geography, and flora and fauna, and from society to art and culture. They also address the politics and violent conflict that are as complex and thought-provoking as the country itself.

Over the years I have been presented with many reasons to wish myself elsewhere, and yet I cannot bring myself to leave this heart-breaking land at the sharp end of climate change and human folly. What keeps me here is the wonder of a grassroots desire for change pushing through the concrete of oppression, and the timid hope that I am witnessing one of the most unequal countries in the world becoming something more just and humane. The storyteller in me is riveted by the human drama here, as intense and violent as the landscape I love. It may well end in tears, but the best stories often do, especially in Chile.

San Francisco de Limache

1

Heart of Darkness

The Conquistador Legacy

Joseph Conrad's *Heart of Darkness* is not just to be found in the Congo. It has always existed wherever men (for it is usually men) have gone to chase their dreams, especially ones involving wealth and possessions and power. Latin America is no exception, but Chile is unique in the sense that it was the bottom of the barrel, as far as riches were concerned during early colonial times. Located at the southernmost tip of the Inca Empire and the South American continent, it was the least desirable commission for Spanish conquistadors who had missed out on the fabulous riches of gold and silver in Mexico, Peru, or Bolivia.

The region that became known as the Realm of Chile was where you went if you were too late or stupid or badly connected to cash in elsewhere, and the resentment and inferiority chip on the shoulder lingers in Chilean culture to this day. It shows itself in a brittle pride and profound suspicion of outsiders, best exemplified by one of Chile's favorite jokes: *How does an Argentinean commit suicide? He jumps off his own ego*. The fun is to poke a stick in the eye of the oh-so-cosmopolitan Argentineans, who sometimes treat the insular Chileans with a certain condescension, but the bitter note is a clear sign of an undercurrent of resentment toward anyone who seems to be lording it over the locals.

Foreigners who come to make a life here need to step very carefully, even to this day, if they want to avoid causing offence by appearing too confident, too rich, or too clever. On a small scale, that means making every effort to speak Spanish and respecting local conventions. On a large scale—such as the famously controversial conservation trust founded by Doug and Kris Tompkins—it means trying to balance national pride against environmental protection, political agency against foreign intervention. It can even apply to much smaller efforts of well-intentioned help, as happened to the Filipino woman I knew who was thrown out of the Chilean Translators' Association for trying to mount a campaign to blacklist unscrupulous companies without clearing it with the association first; and to the South African woman in my hometown who tried to mount a campaign to clean up the local river but ended up being vilified as the bossy gringa telling other people what to do. Finding the fine line to tread between local sensibilities and trying to be a good citizen according to Western liberal ideas is very hard indeed in this part of the world. To be fair, intervention by outsiders has a bad reputation here, particularly since the American CIA helped to destroy Salvador Allende's democratically elected government in the famous coup of September 11, 1973, which resulted in seventeen years of vile military dictatorship under Augusto Pinochet.

Chile really does have an astonishingly dismal heritage, especially dating to the early colonial era, even by the cruel and avaricious standards of the sixteenth century, not least because it is the only country in Latin America where Spanish military forces failed to conquer the most significant Indigenous population, despite the tiny army of warriors the Spanish faced, compared to the vast armies of the Aztecs in Mexico or the Inca forces in Peru. In fact, the Mapuche are the only native people of South America who were never conquered by a colonial army (though they were finally defeated by the republican Chilean army in 1881), and they carry on doing battle to this day, still fighting for their land and the survival of their culture against a cruel and violent government that continues to attack, imprison, and even arbitrarily execute them.

The man celebrated as the founder of the Realm of Chile is Pedro de Valdivia (1497–1553), a high-ranking professional soldier who gained his royal commission to become the first governor of Chile by outstanding service to imperial forces all over South America. But this is a sanitized version of events, because the first European to set foot in what was to become Chile was actually someone called Gonzalo Calvo de Barrientos, who started his career as a common criminal in Seville, where he avoided prison by being shipped off to South America instead. The next time he shows up in the history books is when he was caught stealing items from the Inca Atahualpa's gold ransom in Peru. This time his punishment was to have an ear cut off, leading to his becoming known as El Desorejado (the un-eared one) and also being banished to the remotest part of Atahualpa's empire, the region beyond the Atacama Desert to the south. And so he set off for his banishment in 1533, three years before an actual conquistador headed in that direction.

Barrientos traveled over the Andes and along the eternal desert coast facing the Pacific Ocean, where he found a home at last, in the lush valley of Quillota, near the mouth of the Aconcagua River, almost three thousand kilometers south of Cuzco. He was lucky to be allowed to become a pastoralist among the local Indian population and was even permitted to take several wives, so his main claim to fame is as the father of Chile's mixed mestizo race. Over five hundred years later, I was shocked to be told by my gardener that the reason Chilean society is so hopeless is because they are from such poor genetic stock, though it was the Indian blood he was lamenting, not the Spanish.

The un-eared one's new life ended abruptly, however, when the famously brutal conquistador Diego de Almagro turned up in 1536 and began killing the locals. He and his army of mercenaries were particularly belligerent by the time they encountered Barrientos, because hundreds of their number had already died during a terrible winter crossing of the Andes near Lake Titicaca (on the borders of modern Bolivia and Peru) and because all their suffering during the agonizing march south appeared to have been for nothing. They found neither gold mines nor other riches and certainly had not come all this way to be farmers.[1] Almagro's expedition was deemed a failure, and he returned to Peru full of resentment against his former partner Francisco Pizarro, very soon going to war against him for control of the much more lucrative territory around Cuzco. But this, too, was a failure, and Diego de Almagro was first strangled and then decapitated after losing the Battle of Las Salinas in 1538.

By the time Pedro de Valdivia was granted a royal charter to explore the lands south of Peru, a couple of years after the events just described, the reports about that region were so negative that (according to his first letter to the Spanish king) men avoided the expedition "like the plague," and he was forced to sell his Bolivian silver mine to finance the project. Even offering exorbitant wages, he could only muster 150 Spaniards to accompany him, of whom a good number died during the agonizing journey over the Andes and through the Atacama Desert. History does not record how many of the several thousand Indigenous slaves they took with them survived.

The expedition took eight months to reach what is now central Chile. Upon arrival, Valdivia had to spend more precious funds persuading the local Indian leaders to leave the Spaniards in peace long enough to build wood-framed houses and stockpile food supplies. But his project was a struggle every step of the way, with even his business partner plotting to kill him, to the point where he was forced to hang five of his own men before he could officially establish Santiago on January 24, 1541. Nor did his gifts to local chiefs ensure the peace. The Spanish settlers were soon known by the local Picunche people as *cupais* (devils), and the first version of Santiago was burned to the ground before the year was out. In truth, Valdivia's gifts were nothing compared to the brutal methods he employed to gain control over the region, and retaliation was bound to come. His enemies were many, not least the Picunche leader Michimalonco, whom Valdivia had forced to hand over his best gold mines in return for his freedom, which he inevitably took advantage of to unite competing chiefs against the Spanish.

Valdivia's report of the disaster of Santiago's burning is full of pathos, recording that his men were left with just one fork, a single hen, and one cockerel. But there is no mention at all of the person who saved the day: namely his mistress, Inéz de Suárez, who was the exception that proves the rule in terms of Chile's bloody male-dominated history. Not only is she recognized as the only female conquistador of Latin America but she matched her male counterparts for courage and ruthless violence, most famously exemplified by her actions to save Valdivia's forces during the battle that took place while he was busy quelling an uprising elsewhere.

According to eyewitness reports, the Spanish were vastly outnumbered—130 men, women, and children to 10,000 warriors—and close to capitulation after an entire day of fighting, when Inéz intervened to suggest a dramatic gesture was needed to destroy the enemy's courage and turn the battle in favor of the Spanish. The men listened with respect, given that she had proven herself many times during their long march from Peru, but they thought her strategy was too risky. Namely, she proposed killing the seven Indian leaders, including the Inca governor Quilicanta no less, whom the Spanish were holding hostage, and throwing their bodies over the battlements. What if they really did lose that day? Revenge was bound to be even more gruesome.

"How should we do that?" the men asked.

"Like this," she said, ending their timid discussion with one fell swoop of her sword that took Quilicanta's head straight off.

Quickly, the other hostages were decapitated as well, and their heads were thrown among the attacking forces, where they immediately had the desired effect. The warriors retreated, turning their backs on certain victory, and the story goes that Inéz even donned armor and mounted a white horse to charge after them. At least that is the heroic pose in which she is depicted in historical paintings.

Unfortunately, that (in)glorious military success could not change the fact that Valdivia's enterprise was a truly miserable one, in which his men were forced to work as hard as the slaves on empty stomachs. Hunger was a constant problem, and Valdivia records that fifty grains of corn and some onions were the standard daily ration in the early years. The Spanish also suffered unusually severe winters, during which heavy rains plagued their reconstruction efforts, grain stores, and health, while the threat of Indian attack never abated. Only massive increases to Valdivia's men's allowance prevented them from deserting, and he begged his royal patron for both money and reinforcements. But communication between the Spanish court and the Americas could take years, so he was forced to send a handful of men to Peru, with a commission to bring back as many men as gold could buy. But of the five men sent with Captain Alonso de Monroy, four were killed before they had even got halfway to their destination.

A gruesome footnote to this history is what happened to one of the men of Captain Monroy's party, who happened to be a Black African: The Indians, who had never set eyes on anyone with skin like his, washed him in boiling water and scoured his flesh with dried corn cobs until he died "a cruel death."

It took de Monroy three years to return to Santiago, by which time the new recruits were also starving, due to the horrific journey south and the many combat situations they had had to face along the way. Those who arrived by galleon from Lima were the lucky ones, but they hardly amounted to the several thousand men Valdivia needed to secure his claim, especially south of the Bio-Bio River, where the Mapuche armies were not only devastatingly brave but also highly skilled at beating back the Spanish, having learned to use their own guns against them.

Valdivia's first report to his king, sent five long years after he set off to conquer the southernmost territories, is a pitiful record of misfortunes and pleas for help, and he ends his letter with the pathetic wish that at least those who come after him will be able to enjoy the fruits of his enterprise and the extravagant claim that it is a highly desirable prize. "There is nowhere better in the world," he insisted, where the winters only last four months and the sunshine never fails; the pastures and agricultural opportunities are excellent; and the air is pure. All this is true to this day, though it is not what the Spanish conquerors were looking for.

Meanwhile, Inéz de Suárez was humiliated by her lover, who did not hesitate to disown her in return for having his status as the first governor of Chile confirmed in a court case in Lima, where he was forced to answer his enemies' trumped-up charges, including that he was openly living in sin. "They sleep in one bed and they eat in one dish," claimed the writ against him, which did not go down well with his Catholic patrons. He was a married man, after all, even if he had left his wife in Spain long ago. But he was forced to remember her and bring her to Chile, and Inéz was married off to his most trusted captain, Rodrigo de Quiroga.

But despite his personal and public sacrifices, Pedro de Valdivia never got to sit on his laurels. The battles with Indigenous armies were constant, especially in southern Chile, the heartland of Mapuche territory, and he was killed in 1553, after being the only Spaniard to survive the Battle of Tucapel. Reports of how he died differ. Some say his heart was cut from his chest while he was still alive, to be eaten by his conquerors; others say he was forced to drink molten gold; but these are all apocryphal tales, because there were no European witnesses to record his end. Between two thousand and five thousand Indian slaves fighting for him also died, but nothing is known about them beyond that statistic. As for his wife, Marina Ortiz de Gaete, she arrived from Spain a year after her husband was killed.

History does not record if Valdivia's widow ever met his famous mistress, though it is hard to believe she did not, given the very limited society they lived in. The two women must have been a terrific subject for gossip, but the advantage belonged to Inéz in the end, because Valdivia's favorite captain went on to become governor of Chile not once but twice, and Inéz lived out her long life enjoying the highest status early colonial society had to offer. Marina, meanwhile, got to live a lonely widow's life on her husband's provincial estate in southern Chile for over three decades, before she died aged seventy-nine. Both women used their substantial wealth to sponsor what they considered to be good works, and Inéz is even credited with converting thousands of Indians to Christianity, the height of achievement at a time when the Catholic Church claimed God's blessing for the "Conquest of the Indies." Her method is said to have been extremely persuasive, for those who refused to enter the church for baptism had their heads removed to participate in the ceremony without their bodies.

2

Trails of Discovery

When I was a young child, my grandparents had a wonderful Christmas tradition that required us all to stay away from the sitting room until the first carols could be heard. Only then were we allowed to creep quietly through the door and into a festive wonderland bathed in the soft light of dozens of candles on a pine-scented Christmas tree. Tantalizing presents lay beneath the sparkling decorations and that sensation of thrill and anticipation is as close as I can come to describe how it feels to be in nature in Chile. The beauty is mesmerizing, and the hidden treasures fill you with an unquenchable desire. Always, you know there will be something to discover.

The magic of our new country caught us as soon as we escaped the capital to explore its environs, an early trip taking us to the seaside town of Pichilemu, just four hours southwest of Santiago. The town itself is nothing to write home about, but a broad sweep of sandy beach leads to a headland famous with surfers from all over the world, and its sandy tracks were our destination for a place to stay. We found somewhere tucked just on the other side of the sand dune wall hiding the final curve of the beach, and my young sons, aged eight and ten, were soon hunting for trophies among the tidal rock pools of a massive bulk jutting into the sea: Punta de Lobos. The sea lions and whales that once fed off the bounty in the freezing

Figure 1. Lanín volcano straddling the borders of Argentina and Chile.

Humboldt Current are very rare now, but the ocean still threw up a million shells and brittle body parts for my boys to find, the most thrilling a starfish, and their bounty quickly filled the entire surface of our kitchen table. The variety of shapes and colors was thrilling, but so was the sheer quantity.

A viewpoint perched on top of the jagged cliffs looked out to sea where the bronze light of sunset made huge waves sparkle in bottle-green splendor. The black-suited surfers paddling out far below made you think of seals, except they looked tiny and vulnerable against the razor sharp rocks facing their ride. It takes great skill to avoid being smashed to pieces, which is part of the attraction. The waves are as awesome as the danger and many have failed the

Figure 2. A classic Chilean cowboy. Notice the huge spurs and wood stirrup.

test over the years. A tragic memorial of white crosses studs the rock face, each with a name and dates to recall a life cut short.

It was spring when we first traveled to Pichilemu, so the roadsides were lined with honey-gold California poppies. Pastures framed by poplar and eucalyptus trees undulated toward a patchwork horizon, where snow-capped volcanos rose above a gauzy powder-blue landscape to the east. Looking west, on the other hand, a hard metallic light reflected off the Pacific Ocean beyond many acres of pine plantations, and the road became a roller coaster before escaping into the open vastness of the coast. The route from Chile's central valley was a lovely introduction to the country's famous agricultural countryside, taking us past the vineyards of the Casablanca Valley and into an ancient farmland, where lonely plank homesteads urged us to stop for their fresh baskets of strawberries and homemade honey.

At Punta de Lobos, the thrill was not only on the beach and in the ocean but also in scouring the sandy cliffs for a close look at the surprising variety of flowering cacti and succulents; these were not plants that had ever sparked my interest until now, but I had never seen their spectacularly delicate and beautiful flowers. Clumps of prickly mounds sprouted graceful necks with icing-pink petals; furry stumps were topped by flaming scarlet blossoms, while rubbery cups sprouted slim wisps of microscopic orange flowers. But the most thrilling sight of all burst out of the sides of towering cactus columns, where hand-sized flowers faced the sea like so many ballerina tutus (*Echinopsis chiloensis*). The concentric circles of their delicate white petals hid a deep throat of yellow-tipped pollen threads, where insects had to burrow far to reach the sweet spot. Individual flowers burst from the end of a sleek erection protruding among lethal spikes, and the most amazing feature of all was that each one only lasted twenty-four hours before shriveling into an ugly droop.[1]

Blink and you miss your moment with cacti, even if it is the right time of year, and there are several other spectacular plant species in Chile where timing and location are vital. The British botanical painter Marianne North knew this very well and tried hard to time her visit in 1884 so she could paint the magnificent flowering stalk of the Puya (*Puya berteroana*), a glamorous cousin of the pineapple plant. It rises out of a prickly base like a huge feather duster made of either a thousand china-blue or lemon-yellow flowers and humming birds love it. But the plant she wanted to see more than any other was the famous monkey puzzle tree or Araucaria (*Araucaria araucana*), which was brought to grace exotic parks in England in the late eighteenth century. Except, like so many travelers before and after her, she was told it was impossible, because the forests of

Figure 3. Puya flower.

southern Chile were difficult to reach—as they still are today—and she might not even find what she was looking for, because logging of native forest had already wiped out huge swathes, even in her day. "They said I must sleep out, be eaten by pumas, or carried off by Indians, a noble race which had never yet been conquered by the white man," she recorded in her journal. "But as usual I found when I got nearer the spot that all difficulties vanished." She came home with over thirty beautiful oil paintings, which were the last to be added to her life's work and which you can see to this day in the Marianne North Gallery at Kew Gardens in London.

The city of La Serena, five hours north of Santiago, lies in a very different world of semidesert; it is also the gateway to the mystical

Elqui Valley in the Andes Mountains, where the past and the future shake hands across millennia and humans are reminded just how insignificant they really are. Astronomers from all over the world study the universe through a window of the Earth's clearest skies here, and their observatories dot the barren mountains like so many oversized mushrooms. Of course the historic inhabitants of this region didn't need telescopes to develop the cosmovision that governed their lives, but the thrill today is to rediscover their ancient wisdom alongside the awe-inspiring technology of modern telescopes that let you see meteor showers and planets close up.

Traveling inland from La Serena, you very quickly appreciate how fundamental water is to life. The contrast between the verdant valley floor and the crumpled parchment hills above is striking. Nothing but the famous San Pedro cacti and other hardy plants survive on crumbly ochre outcrops high above, yet the juicy green fields either side of the Elqui River throb with agricultural activity while sunbaked villages hide under giant willow trees. The grapes grown here are some of the largest and juiciest I have ever seen, and they are not just for eating, either. Chile's national drink is also made here, and no social gathering can begin without the famous pisco sour cocktail made with limes, pisco brandy, egg white, and sugar mixed with mountains of ice. Visiting the local distilleries is as popular as a trip to the observatories and there are plenty of tour companies that combine the two for that extra special sensation of taste and vision. But even if you can only afford camping under the stars and buying a bottle in the local supermarket, looking up into a night sky without light pollution feels like sitting in your very own space rocket, because all you can see is a black vastness speckled with a million stars and constellations, purer and brighter than anything you have ever seen.

If we hadn't needed to find a decent school for our sons, I would have happily settled in the little town of Vicuña on the Elqui River. The cobblestone streets and brightly painted adobe houses reminded me of our beloved Antigua Guatemala, except this was better, because there were far fewer tourists and the torpid atmosphere was entrancing: a place to dream and let your creativity take off. No wonder this valley produced the country's first Nobel Prize winner in literature. By this I mean not the more famous Pablo Neruda but the poet Gabriela Mistral, who taught in a local school before escaping to become a glamorous diplomat and whose life was marred by the loss of those she loved, most importantly of her adopted son, who committed suicide at seventeen and left a hole in her heart not even poetry could fill.

Chile is all about extremes, including extreme sports, and one of the most exhilarating experiences of my first year in Chile was to climb the Villarrica volcano, eight hours south of Santiago on the Pan-American Highway. The little town of Pucón at the heart of the Chilean equivalent to Swiss lakes and mountains made it an easy challenge, made even more pleasant by plenty of other climbers with whom to share the adrenaline rush and the sociable hostels.

Climbing the volcano alone is far too dangerous, and I endured my struggle with altitude and a compulsory pack loaded with crampons and ice picks in the company of at least fifteen others. But it didn't matter. Each of us was quickly enclosed in our solitary challenge of one step at a time up the steep cone of Chile's most active volcano. It was like climbing a five-thousand-step staircase with weights on your back and legs, and as we reached the ice and snowline, I tried hard not to think about the swift icepick maneuver we were supposed to perform the instant any one of us slipped. Neither my mind nor my muscles were feeling agile approaching the summit at almost three thousand meters above sea level, and my imagination shriveled into a dumbfounded blank at the thought of the poison gas or pyroclastic lava flows that could descend on us at any moment. But all the agony and sweat was forgotten the minute we reached the edge of the volcano's gaping crater and were treated to an immense vista of the Andean mountain chain punctuated by its centurions of deadly snow-capped cones and the glittering mirrors of myriad lakes on the plain below.

For those who could stomach the sulfurous fumes, there was also the view of heaving lava in the cauldron deep inside the core of the mountain, and my lungs seized up at the poison air and fearful power I saw below. How many tourists had been cooked in that fiery broil? I wondered, and quickly retreated to a safer perch and fresher air. Later, I discovered our compulsory pack should have included gas masks, but *no importa* (never mind), as they like to say in a land where health and safety is never more than optional. We made it, and the thrills were not over yet, because the traditional descent is via an ice chute carved into the snow and ice that deposits climbers at the bottom of the snowline by the seat of their pants.

Pride forced me to follow my companions and I flew down the mountain in timid exhilaration. Truth be told, it wasn't nearly as scary as it looked, because the afternoon sun had turned ice to slush and I even found myself using my hands to get up more speed. Next day, we took advantage of another gift the living mountain has to offer and bathed in a staircase of exquisite hot pools carved into the side of the volcano. Gazing at a cobalt sky through the steam and giant ferns rising above bubbling water, it was easy to have faith that all would be well, and I hugged my slippery loved ones in deep gratitude.

The thrill of getting the best of danger is one of the most addictive sensations of travel in Chile, yet there are few travel books about the country, perhaps because it is still very far away and challenging to reach—and that's just getting to the capital city. Interestingly, almost every travel book published about Chile in the past two hundred years was written by a woman. A notable exception is former hostages John McCarthy and Brian Keenan's *Between Extremes*, and that tells you all you need to know about the kind of person who ends up in this serrated country.

Easily my favorite book written by the select outsiders who

Figure 4. On the summit of Villarrica volcano.

have traveled this way is by Rosie Swale, who felt the overwhelming need to ride horses through the Atacama Desert, all the way *Back to Cape Horn*, embarking on an odyssey that was supposed to take four months but ended up taking over a year. The misery the conquistadors must have suffered in the Atacama Desert is powerfully evoked when she writes, "There is nothing green here, not even a cactus. No birds, no animals, no insects even. Nothing except mineral which horses can't eat and bleached bones." Still, after arriving in the lush forests of Patagonia, she wrote, "Maybe it was because it was so rare, or maybe it was just the wonderful intoxicating smell of the sun's gentle warmth on the wet forest, but somehow the sunshine seemed of a different quality to that found elsewhere in the world." I second that. Whether it is the freezing blues of Patagonia or the glowing lava skies of central Chile, the changing light casts a spell on you every day. I especially love the autumn sunsets, when the distant light over the Pacific Ocean turns from a gentle gold to sharp burned orange, and gun-metal clouds punctuate a fading azure canvas, each lined not with silver but coal-fire red reflecting off a huge crimson sun disappearing over the horizon. It is a spectacle I never get tired of.

"Look at the sky!" I have cried to my sons a million times, and even if they are bored of their mother's repetitive calls, they have never yet failed to come see for themselves, because they know very well it might just be the most amazing sunset they have ever seen.

3

The Poison Chalice

Women in History

The history of both men and women in Chile is often one of thwarted ambition and enforced endurance, except that in the case of women, it has almost always arisen from a lack of power and choice, even when they were high-born. The perfect example of this fate is embodied by Javiera Carrera (1781–1862), popularly known as the Madre de la Patria (mother of the nation) because she designed the independent republic's first flag. In fact, she is nothing of the sort. More precisely, she is one of the most tragic martyrs of Chilean independence and a victim of her brothers' pride and ambition.

Her status as the daughter of one of Chile's richest families should have set her on a path of relative ease: to serve as a vessel to secure both wealth and bloodline with a good marriage and to entertain colonial high society with her skills in music, dancing, and polite conversation. While a formal education was not available to her, she soaked up the sophisticated debates of her father's government circle and developed intellectual skills that meant she was at ease around high-level political decision-making from a young age; so much so, that her father made her his unofficial personal secretary. Nevertheless, she was married off to a wealthy merchant family at fifteen.

But her destiny as an elite matriarch and hostess was already over by the time she was nineteen, when her husband was killed on the dangerous overland route across the Andes to Buenos Aires (1,412 kilometers by paved road today). His horse panicked on a narrow mountain ridge, high above the Colorado River, sending both to a messy death in the depths below. The trek is dangerous to this day and modern horse trekkers who follow in Carrera's path are obliged to sign release forms before they can set off. "There are moments when I am gripped by cold fear as the path narrows and I glance to my left or right and realize that there is nothing there, just a void extending maybe 500 feet to the swirling river below," wrote John McCarthy of his trip along this path two centuries later.

Javiera's trouble was quickly solved, however, when within a year she married a Spanish lawyer two decades her senior, who had come to work with her father in the colonial government. She bore five children in less than a decade, and all the while she was at the heart of political debate and diplomacy—a skill she was shortly going to need more than any other, for the death of her mother meant she had three hot-headed younger brothers to take under her wing.

Juan José, José Miguel, and Luís Carrera were twenty-four, twenty-one, and fifteen respectively when their mother died and Javiera became their guiding light and maternal haven. She was only twenty-five herself but already far more sophisticated than her elite brothers, who had by then enjoyed every privilege money could buy, including a military education. According to Vicuña Mackenna, Chile's most renowned nineteenth-century historian, she was the brains in the family, and "managed" her brothers with her superior intellect. Unfortunately, they often behaved like entitled hooligans. The oldest, Juan José, was apparently more brawn than brains and preferred country life on the Carrera estate outside Santiago. José Miguel, meanwhile, had to be shipped off to Peru to keep the peace after he killed one of the family's agricultural workers; and Luís, aged fifteen, was simply known as "Javiera's boy." But, despite his murderous tendencies, José Miguel seemed to be the most promising candidate for a leading role in Chile's government, so he was sent to join the Spanish army, where he not only distinguished himself in battles against Napoleon but was also exposed to the revolutionary ideas of American independence.

José Miguel returned to Chile strongly in favor of the colony's emancipation, which must have been a horror to his royalist father, and it was Javiera's job to keep the peace. Yet she quickly became the power behind the campaign in favor of home rule mounted by her brothers and was at the heart of the action when José Miguel instigated a coup in 1811 that made him the country's first president. (Note that independence from Spain was not officially recognized until 1818, when Chile formally became a republic). His brothers were given supporting roles as military commanders and Javiera famously sewed the first flag of the new nation state. More importantly, she influenced the content of Chile's first constitution, which granted upper-class women the right to an education for the first time and abolished slavery.[1] In truth, this was a small concession, given the tiny numbers of people involved in both cases, but it was moral progress at least. She also encouraged her brother to import a printing press, which soon led to the country's first newspaper. Just how loyal she was to her brothers is underlined by the fact that her own husband was sacked from his government job for refusing to renounce the supremacy of the Spanish Crown, and neither she nor her brothers helped him to get reinstated.

True to his military background, José Miguel resigned from his own government as soon as there was a war to fight against Spanish imperial forces sent to crush the Chilean separatists and, from then onward, the history of the Carrera family became identified not only with Chile's Wars of Independence (1810–1826) but also with the tragedy of division and betrayal that characterizes so much of the history of Latin America.

Indeed, Javiera found herself at a terrible crossroads in 1814, when the Chilean patriots were defeated at the Battle of Rancagua and her brothers were forced into exile in Argentina.[2] On the one hand, she was the mother of seven children between the ages of seven and eighteen and married to a staunch Spanish royalist who never changed sides. On the other, she was the intellectual backbone of her brothers' revolutionary movement. They needed her diplomatic skills more than ever in the treacherous environment of their Argentine exile, where they were extremely unwelcome for being stubborn Chilean patriots who refused to support the dream of a United States of Latin America, following the North American model. Powerful forces were ranged against Javiera's brothers and she knew she had no choice but to follow them to Buenos Aires if they were to have any chance of surviving the shark-infested waters of political intrigue.

Her husband was horrified, but in a tragic surviving letter she tells him she cannot escape her birthright as a Carrera and must follow where destiny dictates (*la necesidad a que me obliga el destino*).[3] The personal cost of her decision was going to be more terrible than she could ever have imagined and required extraordinary courage, beginning with her horseback journey over the Andes along the very same route on which her first husband had died. How dreadful it must have been to follow in his path, full of the heavy thoughts of a fugitive, and see the cleft where he was dashed to pieces at the very moment she was exposed to the same danger.

As for her children, she took her youngest son, Pedro, who was seven at the time, with her into exile, while the four others from her second marriage were well provided for by her husband and her own extended family. Inevitably, her firstborn son and daughter from her teenage marriage fared less comfortably, and there is a sad report of her eighteen-year-old daughter being left without even a bed to sleep on in one of Santiago's freezing convents. But in that she fared no worse than her mother in Buenos Aires.

Javiera's effort to ensure her brothers' safety was probably doomed from the start, sabotaged by their impulsive natures and the powerful political alliances she could never hope to influence. Within months, for example, Luís was incarcerated for killing an important friend of the Argentine government in a duel, which meant his siblings were also targeted for punitive action. Javiera could do very little when all three brothers became fugitives once more, and her suffering in Buenos Aires and later in Montevideo was pitiful, according to surviving letters to her husband, who never gave up on her. Not only was she desperate for money but she was also very weak as a result of her long journey to Buenos Aires and missed her children desperately.

"Remember me most tenderly to my Pio, Santos, and Ignacio," she wrote of her sons back in Santiago, who were thirteen, eleven, and eight years old. She added, "and my poor Domitila [aged twelve], who makes me sigh so much." Little did she know she was not going to see them again for another ten years, by which time they had grown up without her.

Meanwhile, as her youngest and oldest brothers went into hiding and plotted a clandestine return to Chile, José Miguel escaped to North America and used his contacts there to drum up five ships loaded with men and arms to continue the fight against his rival liberators on the one hand and the royalist army on the other. But his plan was thwarted as soon as his fleet arrived in Buenos Aires, where it was confiscated by the Argentine government, which supported his opponents, and he was lucky to escape with his life to Montevideo.

Javiera did her best to help Juan José and Luís in their secret campaign to take their fight back to Chile, but they were betrayed on the return journey to Santiago and handed over to their enemies in the city of Mendoza. Nothing could save them after that, and they were executed on the main square, where they reportedly faced the bullets arm in arm, without blindfolds, on April 8, 1818. When the news reached their sister, who was incarcerated in a convent in Buenos Aires, it almost killed her too.

After four years in exile, during which she had often had to subsist on starvation rations, Javiera's health and spirit were in ruins, and she would not have survived without the support of her American protector, the mercenary David Jewett, who helped her escape to her brother Miguel in Montevideo, hidden on a Brazilian ship.[4] But her brother's incurable habit of acting without thought for the consequences meant he alienated both his supporters and his enemies, which, according to Mackenna, turned him from the author of his destiny into a pawn in other people's plans. Perhaps he was also blinded by an understandable desire to avenge his brothers and the cruel treatment of his father, who was brought back to Santiago from his island exile only to be held hostage by José Miguel's arch rival for power, Bernardo O'Higgins, who forced the old man to pay not only for the cost of José Miguel's American fleet impounded in Buenos Aires but also for the expenses incurred during the show trial and execution of his sons in Mendoza. He died a broken man the following year.

"Don't trust anyone," Javiera had advised her brother, but of course he failed to take her advice and blazed a trail of death and destruction across Argentina, intent on regaining power in Chile. Incredibly, like his brothers, he was betrayed near the city of Mendoza and put on trial by those who were delighted to get rid of the Carreras, once and for all. The execution took place on September 4, 1821, on the very same square where his brothers had died three years earlier. According to witnesses, he died just as bravely, shouting "*¡Muero por la libertad de América!*" (I die for America's freedom!).

Alone in Montevideo, Javiera fell into a deep depression. Her years of sacrifice had been for nothing, and her adored father and brothers were all dead. Further salt in her wounds came from the fact that José Miguel's bitter rival, Bernardo O'Higgins, was now the "Supreme Director," and it was an open secret that he could have saved her brother from the kangaroo court that was used to eliminate him. To think that O'Higgins was reaping all the glory as the founding father of the Chilean state was sickening indeed, because he would never have had a chance without the early promotions he was granted in José Miguel's own army. His greatest talent was nothing more than switching sides at the crucial moment and being in the right place at the right time. Even his role as the "Supreme Director of Chile" was a fluke, because the position was initially offered to the Argentinean general José de San Martín as reward for winning the battle that sealed Chile's independence once and for all, but San Martín preferred to keep up the fight for an independent Latin America elsewhere.

Returning to Chile as long as O'Higgins was in power was out of the question, and so Javiera was left to grieve alone in Montevideo, while her husband struggled in Santiago and Jewett left to pursue his naval career in Brazil. The loneliness and sorrow of her final years in exile must have been terrible, but at least she did not have to wait too long before O'Higgins was deposed in 1823, which enabled her to return to Santiago and start campaigning for the repatriation of her brothers' bodies.

Javiera's loyal husband died shortly after the end of her ten-year exile, and her only consolation was that the application for the return of her family's estate was successful. She could go home at last. Four years later, the campaign for the return of her brothers' bodies was also successful, and they were reburied with full military honors in Santiago's cathedral. Their Chilean funeral was her final public appearance before she retired to El Monte, outside the capital, where she lived a secluded life for another four decades.

"You could accuse her of having loved too much, but never of being selfish, which is the opposite of love," wrote the historian Mackenna glibly, upon her death in 1862.

Today, there isn't a town in Chile without a Carrera or O'Higgins Street, but the most important monument to Javiera is the botanical park she spent thirty-nine years working on after her return from exile. The native araucaria trees and flowering magnolia she planted almost two centuries ago are her finest legacy, and though her descendants no longer own the property, citizens from all over the world can enjoy her work at the lovely Viña Doña Javiera.

4
The Limache Valley

People often ask me how we ended up in San Francisco de Limache (pronounced *lee-matchy*). Guidebooks do not feature this small country town in central Chile, except perhaps to mention it as the end of the line for the metro train from coastal Valparaíso. Darwin spent the night here, but that's hardly a claim to fame. Today, there are few jobs, unless you are a tomato farmer; or obvious attractions, unless you like strolling around a leafy plaza to watch a tiny world go by; and the cultural attractions are very limited indeed. There is no theater, cinema, or concert hall, and yet the quality of life is so wonderful, Chileans have been coming here for generations.

The great draw is the lovely Mediterranean microclimate framed by the coastal mountains running parallel to the Andes, something the wealthy appreciated long ago, when they built their huge summer estates here. Almost all of those are gone now, destroyed by the combined effects of earthquakes, the dispersal of inherited fortunes, and the agricultural land policies of President Allende in the early 1970s. They have been replaced by a small town of middle-class people looking for a healthier lifestyle, not too far from the economic hubs of the capital and the coast. Downtown Santiago is within commuting distance and the coastal cities of Viña del Mar and Valparaíso are less than an hour away.

Figure 5. Limache Plaza.

My sons disparagingly refer to these people as "aristohippies," because many of them don't appear to need a job or are successful self-employed people. Yet most of our friends come from their circle and I appreciate the delightful choices for yoga, dance, and meditation that have appeared because of them, and especially the privately funded cultural center. Artisan beer and cheese and organic vegetables now invigorate local produce, and an increasing number of lively craft markets have become a regular feature in recent years. Music and dancing often brighten the central pergola of Limache's main square, especially during the long summer. And finally, perhaps most wonderful of all, is the feeling of community. A friendly conversation is always a possibility as you go about your business here, especially if you have children, and that is the key: This is a great place for young families.

The valley can be astonishingly cosmopolitan, too, though you would never know unless you lived here. Musicians, artists, philosophers, writers, and eco-warriors have made their home in the valley in recent decades, especially since the first Waldorf School was founded in 1999. The changes they have brought began slowly, of course, and there was still very little of the above when we arrived in 2006, so it was not unusual for people to say "Why Limache? There's nothing there." In fact, our decision to live here *was* somewhat bizarre at the time, because it was founded on nothing more than chance and a view. We did not know about the famous climate or the Waldorf School community, and I thank my lucky stars to this day that we chanced to live here.

All we knew was that we did not want to live in the polluted capital, so our first months in Chile were taken up with exploratory trips north and south and to the coast. It was during our trip to the port of Valparaíso that we found ourselves heading about forty kilometers inland. The great city was a heady mix of bohemia and filth that would have been fun without children, but after sharing our picnic with many derelicts in one of the city parks, we were glad to escape on the metro train. Why not see where it takes us, we thought, and that is how we ended up at the end of the line in Limache. According to our map we were at the beginning of a valley enclosed by the coastal mountains of La Campana National Park, so we decided to hop on a bus to the little resort of Olmué, and in the twenty minutes it took us to get there, a nice woman had already given us a recommendation for somewhere to stay. Half a dozen cabins set among lemon trees around a central swimming pool made a wonderful setting, but even better was the terrific view of the russet-domed mountain glowing above a sunset valley (*campana* means bell), where the Indigenous Picunche once mined gold and quartz. Relaxing with a pisco sour, it was easy to decide this was our spot.

By the time the year was up, we had found a little wood cabin to rent on a dirt road near the main square of Olmué (the accent means you pronounce the name like a matador's *olé* at the end, rather than making it sound like something a cow would utter), and it was a relief to exchange the gray pall of concrete Santiago for a village surrounded by groves of hawthorn and towering native trees, like the fragrant Boldo (*Peumus boldus*), whose cut wood smells like cinnamon, and the mighty Peumo (*Cryptocarya alba*), which often shades urban parks here. Best of all, from our porch we could see the mountain once climbed by Charles Darwin. Apparently, he passed this way during his second voyage on HMS *Beagle* in 1834 and famously remarked you could see both the Andes and the Pacific Ocean from the mountain's summit.[1]

All we needed now was a school, but what had seemed so promising during my research trip turned out to be much less so on closer inspection. At the handful of schools I visited—even as far afield as Viña del Mar on the coast—I was appalled by the grim neglected buildings and lack of facilities. Libraries and science labs were unheard of luxuries outside the most exclusive private schools, and even modern school books were a novelty, with most predating the 1970s. Worse, each classroom seemed to have a minimum of forty children in it, and I knew my young sons would sink without trace in an alien world full of foreign words they could not understand. What had we done? Our plan, all along, had been to integrate into ordinary Chilean life, rather than hide in a cocoon of expatriate privilege and private international schools, but the inescapable fear that we were damaging our children's prospects pressed hard on my conscience.

"Why don't you have a look at the local Waldorf School," someone said.

A Rudolf Steiner school? Here, in the Limache Valley of Chile? I had no idea, but the minute we crossed the threshold of the ancient gates into what was once the summer residence of the Chilean ambassador to France, I was sold. A magical nineteenth-century walled garden of flowering vines and herb beds opened up along a grid of dirt tracks, where grapes and kiwi grew on trellises above our heads and ducks quacked noisily beside their pond. A resident working horse used to plough the fields lived in the furthest enclosure climbing up the side of the valley, along with a couple of cows and a goat. There were geese, which stiffened their gaze accusingly if you so much as dared to touch their fence, and a flutter of unthreatening chickens, and even less intimidating rabbits, who shyly loped to greet a child's stroking hand.[2]

It was almost too good to be true, but it was so. A visionary Waldorf teacher from Santiago, who also happened to be the partner of the most recent incumbent of the Ramos Estate, had persuaded him to donate the land to create Chile's first Rudolf Steiner School outside the capital city. Conveniently, the owner was a professional architect, and very proud of his master plan for an auditorium, an anthroposophical health center, craft workshops, music rooms, and lovely sunlit classrooms built using only wood.

With Jorge responsible for the school buildings, Angelika was able to focus on what she knew best, initially starting the school with just one pupil. Word soon got around, though, and a steady trickle of families started to arrive from Santiago, and even from abroad. Luckily for my boys, we stumbled on this haven just in time; today, newcomers have to join a waiting list already full with hundreds of others. Half a dozen additional Waldorf nurseries have been founded to serve the flood of young families in search of a more meaningful and healthier life, and the days when all parents knew each other by name are a nostalgic memory.

When we arrived, however, there was a long way to go. The property was still being salvaged after having been abandoned from 1968 to 1988, during which time every stick of the lovely furniture brought back from the World Exhibition in Paris in 1889 had either been stolen or used for firewood by those who squatted the land, while the Ramos family exiled themselves back to France. By the time Jorge succeeded in reclaiming what was once his grandparents' home, the *casa patronal* had been vandalized and burned and every other construction on the property was broken, including the two large swimming pools, once lined by marble statues. Virtually nothing but dirt and rubble remained: gone were the lemon and almond trees, apple and peach groves, as well as the iconic vineyards; and gone, too, were the dozens of servants and workers whose families had once lived here for generations. To his credit, Jorge employed several of the squatters to help restore what they themselves had destroyed, wisely combining self-interest with a social conscience. It was a profoundly significant step I only appreciated much later, when I realized the dates his family left Chile suggest they fled Salvador Allende's socialist dream, not the military dictatorship that followed the coup in 1973.[3]

We quickly discovered that becoming part of the local Waldorf community meant hard labor planting trees and painting walls, as well as constant fund-raising for essential educational items, such as expensive beeswax crayons and musical instruments. But it was fun, and there is no doubt in my mind we would not have found such a welcome anywhere else in the country at the time. Of course the tensions arising from gentrification have also become a reality in recent decades, yet it is mostly the (Chilean) newcomers who are trying to save this lovely valley from the environmental problems it faces.

Historically, San Francisco de Limache's main claim to fame is that it was Chile's first garden city, designed in an elegant grid of country estates along a huge boulevard leading off the railway station built in 1856. The line was designed to be an important commercial connection between the port of Valparaíso and the capital of Santiago, and the original route did not include a detour up the Limache River. But a major bribe ensured an elegant loop via the new real estate, and the original town on the other side of the river has felt somewhat hard done by ever since. It is a resentment that continues even to this day, and the locals will tell you Limache Viejo is *más pueblo* than its fancy twin across the river, which can mean "more common and authentic" or more "impoverished and ugly," depending on your point of view.

In fact, both sides are pretty scruffy these days, the result of almost total destruction after the massive earthquake of 1906 and a complete absence of town planning. The cracked pavements are fatal to any pedestrian not paying attention and, except for the magnificent boulevard lined by mighty plane trees, there is very little to recall Limache's nineteenth-century glory days. Most of the lovely mansions and their gardens have been replaced by a hodgepodge of residential housing, and the cleverly designed canals that once watered immaculate orchards have been left to collapse.

So it was all the more thrilling when I spotted a "for sale" sign for an acre of land just three blocks from the school that not only retained its historic 1897 house but also the flowering arbors and fruit trees.

"Don't buy that, Mummy," said my ten-year-old. "It looks like a shack."

And it was true that nothing hinted at the gorgeous home hidden beyond a mighty wrought iron gate. With its gray sheets of corrugated iron covering adobe walls and tall grilled windows, the property looked like a stranded ship by the side of the road. But stepping past the romantic tangle of mauve wisteria and purple bougainvillea hung over the entrance was like arriving at the nearby school all over again. A secret garden lay beyond a long bough of grapevines, and the house revealed itself as a mighty gallery with four-meter-high ceilings and beautiful tall windows looking toward the afternoon sun. A second floor opened out onto a roof terrace with stupendous views across the valley and toward the distant coast, and I knew from the very first moment that I had found the most beautiful home I could ever have imagined.

My heart beat faster with every overgrown nook I discovered on

Figure 6. My beloved Quinta.

the property outside. There were avocados, oranges, and lemons; apricots and plums; apples and pears; pomegranates and strange local fruit I had never heard of, like *nispero* and *cherimoya.* Best of all was the fig arbor, complete with hammocks.

"It's far too big," said my mother, who happened to be visiting, and of course she was right.

Yet she must have fallen under its spell herself, because it was she who enabled me to buy this dream. Incredibly, there was no competition from others at the time, because most Chileans would much rather have a brand-new home with double-glazed windows and a designer kitchen than a historic house requiring constant maintenance and loving care. But for me the magic has never faded, even while the dream has cost me more than I could ever have imagined. Visitors are always entranced, and the most frequent comment is "Wow. You are so lucky to live here!" But my favorite response was by an American couple, who informed me I live in the Garden of Eden.

5

Riches from the Sea

Chile's cuisine tends to be oversalted and heavy on meat. A standard dish is vegetable soup with a generous lump of greasy chicken or beef called *cazuela*, and another favorite is a corn-based pie known as *pastel de choclo*. Cooked with loving attention in a domestic setting, these dishes can be wonderful, full of the delicious aromas of coriander and a hint of lemon, but in your average eating house or *comedor*, they are nothing more than belly fillers. The heaviest weapon against hunger, however, is the *completo*, which can range from the size of your average hotdog to an arm's length of indigestion loaded with mayonnaise, mashed avocado, ketchup, and mustard, along with a generous portion of deep-fried potatoes. Desserts are as sweet as main courses are salty and often contain a sticky caramel paste that can strip the enamel right off your teeth.

No wonder over 70 percent of the Chilean population is overweight or obese, according to the country's own health surveys, which is almost double the rate for the United States.[1] Equally shocking is to discover that only 15 percent of the adult population eats fruit or vegetables every day, though British adults are not faring much better, considering UK government health surveys put their national figure at 28 percent. Poverty and overpricing by the supermarket chains is as much to blame as a lack of nutritional education and, certainly in Chile, a healthy diet is something most people simply cannot afford, because they no longer live in the countryside where they could grow their own food.

Yet there are wonderful weekly agricultural markets in every town up and down the country, where you can buy freshly harvested fruit and vegetables, as well as almost anything else you could desire, from homemade sauces to cheese, and plastic spoons to shoelaces. I love the chaos of sights and sounds and the good-natured maneuvering to get at the best stands; and I adore the aromas of freshly cut produce and the humorous marketing calls of stand holders, some of whom have made their slogans into regular art forms of urban music and poetry. For years there was an egg-stall man in Limache, for example, who serenaded all his customers with his own original verses, eliciting smiles of admiration and loyalty in equal measure.

A unique culinary pleasure in Chile, though, is the huge variety of seafood provided by its eternal coastal waters, and exploring the possibilities of the daily catch at one of the country's fish markets is an unforgettable experience of sights and smells that is not all pleasant but definitely an invitation to be brave and try something you have never eaten before in your life. Some things I have not learned to like to this day, like the disgustingly slimy tongues that come out of sea urchins, but a plate full of grilled razor clams bathed in a parmesan sauce is divine, and a handful of tender scallops in white wine sauce is heavenly, too. But those are just morsels to whet your appetite. The main dishes are provided by hearty steaks of conger eel, sea bass, or swordfish; or the more delicate textures of bream and hake; or morsels of all of the above in a delicious seafood stew called *paila marina*. Yellowfin tuna fish from distant Easter Island is a gorgeous treat, and so are the coastal lobsters and arctic crabs, especially the giant king crab known as *centolla*, whose meat you order by the kilo. But if the pungent smell of the markets is too much, an excellent way to enjoy the fruits of the Pacific Ocean is to head for the adjacent fish restaurants or, even better, find a seaside town or village and let the ocean breeze fill your nostrils instead, in places like Quintay, Papudo, or Neruda's old haunt at Isla Negra—and that's just in central Chile. There are many other well-known seafood resorts up and down the country, not least on the island of Chiloé, in the south.

Discovering the coastal fishing villages of Chile was definitely a highlight for us when we first arrived, which gave us not only some mouthwatering meals but also unforgettable sights, such as the fishing boats at Horcón being pulled ashore by muscular working horses, and others lifted on and off the sea by cranes at Portales outside Valparaíso. An additional treat at Portales was the grunting crowd of sea lions that heave their mighty bodies onto shore near where the fish-gutting happens. They have to stand their ground against a hoard of stray dogs, which can lead to terrifying encounters of bared teeth, but the agility of the dogs usually saves them from serious injury. People come from far and wide to buy at the fish market there, and the row of beachside restaurants are a major tourist attraction. But the most exciting day of all to be at Portales is June 29, when the fishermen honor their patron Saint Peter by turning their boats into colorful floats. Competition for the most inventive figurehead is intense and can involve anything from brightly painted papier-mâché to intricate creations of wood and copper.

To see the hundreds of fishing and sailing vessels festooned by a kaleidoscope of flags and flower garlands set off for their watery procession across the huge bay of Valparaíso is thrilling, but even better is to find a captain who will take you onboard and let you toot the horn and wave at the thousands of onlookers lining the beaches and promenades between Portales and Membrillo, its twin to the southeast. The end of June is winter in Chile, so there can be a bitterly cold wind blowing during the crossing, but nobody minds. Bodies are packed tightly on the open boats and everyone looks forward to the banquet of fried fish and alcohol that awaits and to the

Figure 7. Historic Santiago market hall.

spontaneous dancing that will accompany the traditional troupes that make up the final entertainment of the day.

Bizarrely, those dances are called *bailes chinos*, though they have nothing to do with Chinese culture and are rooted in pre-Columbian traditions, when the Quechua word for maidservant was "china." The costumes and masks worn by the dancers are as elaborate as the boat decorations and have often been handed down from one generation to the next, and the musical instruments comprising traditional Andean drums, flutes, and bells are also often handmade heirlooms. In fact, to be a member of one of the

brotherhoods that make up these ritual dance troupes is a huge honor and involves rehearsals and practice all year round.[2]

The adventure of discovering all the different kinds of seafood to eat quickly became part of our new life in Chile, so it was no surprise when my son Sascha chose a meal of king crab over a new bicycle for his eleventh birthday (the price was the same!), and therefore we headed to the most famous place to eat this dish outside Tierra del Fuego, which is at the central market in Santiago. Even the location was grand, as the market is housed in a magnificent nineteenth-century wrought iron building reminiscent of the great European exhibition halls and railway stations of that era. A luminous dome of glass and iron covers the heady sights and sounds of the market stalls, and virtually the entire atrium is lined by restaurants serving every dish you could possibly make from the produce on sale.

The menu in our chosen spot was intimidatingly long, but thankfully our only choice was how much centolla we were going to try. We went for two kilos and soon a trolley arrived with a giant mound of spikey crustacean parts. Thankfully, it was part of the service to watch the waitress wield what looked like giant nutcrackers and we tucked in to perfect white crab meat that was so much nicer and more delicate than your average seaside dish back in Europe. I don't even like crab, but this was nothing like the stinky sandwiches I remembered from childhood summers in England and was much more like lobster. All it needed was a drizzle of butter and lemon. Afterward, I staggered into the sunshine with my stomach full and my wallet empty, but it was without a doubt one of the most exciting lunches Sascha or I had ever had.

The one fish we made sure not to eat in Chile was salmon, however, because although it is famous and the second-most important Chilean export after mining products, I was shocked to hear early on that the country's salmon farms use over forty times the amount of chemicals, such as antibiotics and antiparasitic medications, that are permitted in Norway, the world's leading producer. How wrong I was! The true figure, according to Greenpeace and Chilean media, is five hundred times the Norway standard, which beggars belief until you discover that salmon exports are worth about $5 billion to the Chilean economy and companies will do almost anything to cash in on that bounty.

The worst of it is that over sixty companies that have set up in Chile's waters are Norwegian-owned, according to the *Los Angeles Times*, attracted by the high returns and lax environmental protection, though the Chilean offices of Greenpeace and Oceana, along with local investigative journalists, are doing their best to expose them. One such multinational that got caught out as recently as

Figure 8. Birthday spider crab lunch.

2019 is the company Nova Austral, which was found to have kept double accounts for the mortality levels at its salmon farms, which matters, because the government obliges farms to reduce their fish stocks if they experience a level of mortality beyond the official maximum, meaning less profits. So Nova Austral hid the fact that thirty million of their salmon had died over a certain period and even sold their fish at a premium, because it is marketed as "antibiotic free salmon," which increases sale prices by up to 30 percent. It is truly a scandal of massive proportions, yet this same company is doing its best to expand into pristine Patagonian waters in the

Beagle Channel so it can market its products to gourmet customers in North America and Europe as coming from the purest seas in the world.

The environmental danger is huge, not least because the Atlantic salmon used by the industry is not a native species to the Chilean Pacific Coast, and whenever the fish escape from their floating cages, as they often do during storms and whenever seals attack those tempting free dinner installations, the survivors become predators of native fish species. Considering there are now over one thousand salmon farms operating in the country's southern seas, the problem is not rare and can sometimes involve hundreds of thousands of escaped salmon in one incident. For example, a few years ago, over 900,000 fish escaped from a Norwegian salmon farm near the city of Puerto Montt, of which only 250,000 were recaptured, according to a 2018 *Bloomberg* report dramatically titled "The Great Salmon Escape." But there are other grave environmental issues as well that result from the seabed contaminated with fish excrement and uneaten food pellets, which has massively increased nutrients for algae and other microorganisms, thereby unbalancing fragile coastal ecosystems.

Yet, despite the known risks to Chile's unique marine environments, the Department of Fisheries has issued no less than 416 salmon farming concessions in officially protected coastal areas, of which an astonishing 317 alone are in the remote Las Guaitecas Forestry Reserve, located about level with Puerto Aisén, in the countless fjords and islands of Patagonia. It is tempting to think officials are relying on the idea of "out of sight out of mind" to get away with this scandal, but in fact they are doing nothing wrong according to Chilean law, because fish farming is only illegal in national parks and at natural monuments. Anything called a reserve or protected area is therefore permissible territory, unless there is a management plan that clearly states its mission is to protect biodiversity and someone has made a formal fuss about it. But Las Guaitecas, for example, was founded as long ago as 1938, long before such documents were part of the process of setting up protected areas, and of Chile's twenty-eight marine areas with some kind of protection status, only five currently have a management plan.[3]

The danger posed by the salmon farming industry in Chile is a matter not just of physical environments but also of human survival and entire ways of life, which was most dramatically exposed during a deadly algal bloom that hit the island of Chiloé in 2016. The news was full of images of distraught *chilote* fishermen and their families surrounded on the beaches by dead fish, seals, and maritime birds, a red slimy tide stretching as far as the eye could see. It was truly a horrible sight, made so much more disgusting by the fact that it was an entirely avoidable disaster facilitated by the Chilean government when it authorized local salmon producers to dump five thousand tons of dead fish at sea. Their decomposing bodies could have filled about fourteen Olympic-sized swimming pools, but instead of dispersing into the vast Pacific Ocean, local currents washed them toward land, where they acted as a massive fertilizer that turned naturally occurring algae into a toxic "red tide" of devastating proportions that made whatever sea creatures survived unfit for human consumption.

To the companies involved that loss represented $800 million in lost exports, but for the 150,000 people on the island of Chiloé who depend on collecting shellfish and fishing, it was the destruction of their livelihoods for that year and possibly the next, with very little chance of compensation from the government. No wonder the people of Chile's most southerly region around the Magellan Straits are fighting tooth and nail to stop the *salmoneras*, as they are known, establishing themselves there. But it is already happening, and only much stricter government regulations can stop it; and in the meantime, local fishing communities are already struggling to catch enough fish to eat, let alone sell.

Meanwhile, all individuals can do is stop buying commercial

salmon, which is hardly a great sacrifice, considering how expensive it is; and it is heartening to know that more and more conscientious chefs around the world are taking salmon off their menus. As the owner of a well-known restaurant on Tierra del Fuego commented a few years ago, refusing to sell salmon is an act of self-preservation for the ocean environment he depends on for his livelihood, as well as a mark of respect for all marine life, including the blue whales, penguins, and dolphins tourists spend a fortune to see on their trip of a lifetime. The photos don't look nearly as good when your perfect shot is interrupted by the floating pens of industrial fish farms, yet that is exactly what will soon happen, if the four current applications for such facilities at Cape Horn succeed.

6

The Flowering Desert

The Norte Chico

There is something almost psychedelic about seeing flowers in the Atacama Desert. The disconnect between your brain and your vision just doesn't make sense. You know this is one of the driest places on earth, yet cornflower blue petals carpet the dry escarpments as far as the eye can see. Across the barren plains, a delicate net curtain of pink or yellow seems to have been thrown over the land. The artist Christo, who once wrapped entire islands, could not have done better; and yet this is natural. Still your brain argues with you: How can this be? But then you get down on the ground, close up, and see green pokers topped with a bright red or yellow triumvirate of amaryllis-type flowers, which are the lovely Añañuca (*Myostemma advena*). If the stems and the flowers are more delicate, they might be the lily-like purple Macaya (*Placea amoena*); or if they are very short with a spray of star-shaped white blossoms, they are Estrella de Traub (*Traubia modesta*). But my favorites are the fuchsia "guanaco feet," or Patas de Guanaco (*Cistanthe cachinalensis*), whose lovely faces display a crown of gold-tipped stamens. They are the ones responsible for the dramatic pink carpets you see alongside the Pan-American Highway, if you are lucky enough to pass by during the right season.

Where normally you are kicking dust on barren ground, you find yourself tiptoeing like a ballerina to avoid stepping on the precious life that has emerged from the seemingly dead ground. It isn't

Figure 9. Flowers in the Atacama Desert.

always the flowers themselves that are notable, either. Sometimes it is the beautiful leaf patterns of the ground-level succulents that stop you in your tracks: a mound of intricate star shapes or a mosaic of intricately joined segments that might have inspired the builders of Cuzco with their asymmetrical surfaces. The cacti proliferate in extraordinary shapes too, from the photogenic towering pillars to densely packed prickly cushions. One of the most stunning varieties is the sea-urchin Copiapoa cactus, whose bulbous mounds sport vicious spikes. A false step near one of those and you will be very sorry.

The magical nature of experiencing the flowering desert is also enhanced by the thrilling knowledge you are witnessing something that might only happen once or twice in any decade, so to have made it to the right place at the right time is an exquisite gift. If you can share it with friends and sleep under a star-filled canopy, your trip is complete; and if there can also be a bottle of Chilean red wine and the sound of the Pacific Ocean pounding the shore nearby, you know you've touched perfection.

Not to experience the flowering desert if you live in Chile is to feel there is something missing in your relationship with the country, so I was very excited when an exceptionally rainy winter gave us a reason to plan that road trip we had so often dreamed of. Luckily, three of us were free to drop everything and urgent planning was soon in top gear. A pickup truck to deal with the unmade sand and gravel roads was fundamental, but we also needed provisions, maps, and up-to-date information on the ground to ensure correct timing. A two-thousand-kilometer drive is not something you want to embark on for nothing, so when the news arrived that the desert was indeed in flower, we set off for the seven-hour drive north to the town of Vallenar, where we treated ourselves to guesthouse beds before the more rustic days ahead.

The journey north reminded me that while the Atacama Desert is famously the driest place on earth, the reality on the ground is by no means homogeneous, because this huge chunk of northern Chile is actually divided into two very different ecosystems. The one we were going to explore only encompassed the compact semi-arid region known as the Norte Chico, roughly marked by a 660-kilometer stretch between the town of La Ligua and the desert city of Copiapó.

The truly dismal landscape that blurs over one thousand extra kilometers into the horizon, as far as the border with Peru, is the Norte Grande, another world entirely. That is where you find a place so dry, scientists use it for their preparatory research for explorations of Mars; it is a wasteland that has endured for as much as two hundred million years and makes the Sahara Desert look like

Figure 10. Diaguita pottery.

a youthful sprinkling of sand full of life. Yet there *is* life to be found, even in the northern Atacama, especially on the remote high altitude plateaus near the mountain border with Bolivia, where salt lakes teem with pink flamingos and thousands of duck species and llamas and guanacos roam the treeless waste. The legendary event known as the "flowering desert" is therefore somewhat inaccurately described, but it sounds good in the tourist brochures.

Our route crossed several transversal river valleys that cut a swathe of green across the balding landscape, and was punctuated by towns that are only the most recent incarnation of human habitation going back millennia. In fact, the reason I wanted to stop over in Vallenar was because I wanted to make a detour east, up the valley of the Huasco River, where my favorite pre-Columbian pottery comes from. I love it for the astonishing variety of geometric patterns that decorate duck-shaped pitchers and beautiful serving bowls. The clever repetition of black stripes and zigzags or rectangles creates beautiful and inventive decorations on a warm terracotta base I enjoy very much, and I wanted to see the land of the people who devised this art.

In truth, the Diaguita culture does not exist anymore, as its people were long since acculturated by their Inca conquerors before the Spanish arrived and then forced to assimilate into colonial society when their ancestral lands were divided up. By the early nineteenth century, they had even forgotten their own language; and yet their rural traditions of pottery and weaving, storytelling, and shamanic healing have survived to this day, simply by virtue of the remote nature of the upper reaches of the Huasco Valley. Even now, the traveler has no reason to head up into the tight creases of the Andes Mountains here. The unpaved road beyond Alto del Carmen does not go anywhere (unless you are a miner), and there is nowhere to stay. But to me it was worth the hours of bumpy driving just to see the picturesque canyon where ancient geology exposes many hues of ochre, red, and copper and gut-wrenching precipices provide fabulous views of the valley. There was a man-made reward too, in the shape of the oddest church spire I have ever seen: a wood cabin with a pointy hat perched on beams supported by two pillars, not on top of the nave but in front of it, like a raised sentry box over the entrance. If we had had enough time to make the right contacts, we might even have been able to visit the local potters and weavers who still subsist up here, but that was going to have to be another trip. For now, I contented myself with having got this far and tried not to show my friends how worried I was because the petrol gauge was on red. But it was downhill all the way back to Vallenar, and I was glad to be able to laugh it off and make sure we were safely tanked up the next day, when we headed off-road into the desert.

Our destination was a campsite in the Llanos de Challe National Park facing the Pacific Ocean, and after many flower-hunting stops, we were thrilled to find a spot for our tent embraced by weather-beaten sandstone to shelter from the wind. The beach was right in front of us, and it felt good to breathe in the moist air after our dusty explorations. Firewood brought all the way from central Chile added a warm glow to the orange sunset, and we soon fell under its meditative spell. Tomorrow, we would explore the red carpets on either side of tracks leading inland, to see yet more flowers, and maybe even spot the most coveted of all, the endangered Lion Claw (*Bomarea ovallei*), with its tightly packed brush of red or orange trumpets.

The unmade road above sandstone cliffs dropping into the ocean provided a dramatic baseline for tentative steps into the hinterland and the hours slipped by quickly. Treasure hunting in the desert is addictive, even if it is only for flowers, and we compared finds like excited children. But we tore ourselves away at last, to head forty kilometers inland once more, where the Pan-American Highway led us to our final destination outside the port of Caldera, famous for marking the end of the country's first railway line, built to serve the copper, gold, and silver mines beyond the city of Copiapó, eighty kilometers inland. The mineral riches of the desert are the bedrock of Chile's economy to this day, but we were looking for a very different reward in the shape of one of the country's most famous beaches, named Bahía Inglesa for a notorious seventeenth-century English pirate who sacked Spanish ports and haunted the seas all the way up to Panama.[1]

And so we found the photogenic arc of white sand and aquamarine sea curved around a large bay and, best of all, the resort was out of season. The Humboldt Current ensures that most of Chile's coastline is washed by freezing waters, so spring is no time to be heading to the beach for swimming. In fact, I find it too cold for anything more than a quick splash, even at the height of summer. Yet this beach is packed every summer, not least with millions of Argentineans, who come flooding over the Andes each year whenever they are not trapped by their perennial economic disasters.

Our host was a dead ringer for the errant chemist in *Breaking Bad*, which added an extra frisson to our journey, especially since

Figure 11. Our host at Bahía Inglesa.

we were the only guests and his property had that forlorn atmosphere of the New Mexican desert. How did this man earn his living during the long empty season, we wondered, and I really hoped he was lying when he told us he worked as an electrician in Caldera. The mining towns of northern Chile are famously drug infested, after all, still populated by men who lead harsh solitary lives that need quick fixes of pleasure to endure the monotony.

Next morning, we steeled ourselves to make the long eight-hundred-kilometer drive home in one go, and set off early. We all needed to get back to reality in Santiago and Limache, but the desert gave me one last flash of its hidden treasures in the shape of a flock of olive green parrots. I had no idea such birds existed in Chile, for the dramatic electric blue wing feathers and splash of red on a yellow breast that caught my eye were spectacles I associated with the jungle, not this arid land. But they could be nothing else, unmistakable for being so large, their bodies easily the height of a table lamp. Once more, my mind and my vision could not compute, but I was delighted anyway. Back home, the mystery deepened, because I discovered this endangered Burrowing Parakeet is an extremely rare species found in Chilean Patagonia and, to this day, I cannot explain what it was doing by the side of a noisy highway in the desert. Perhaps they were visiting from Argentina on the other side of the Andes, where they are more common.

About an hour into our drive south, we passed a nondescript turnoff for what was once Chile's richest silver mine, though today no hint lets the traveler know what happened there in the past. Blink and you miss it, like so much in the desert. But, once upon a time, Chañarillo drew thousands of men to a heap of obscure mounds in the desert, whose perilous shafts famously yielded over two hundred tons of silver in just one year (1855) and enabled Miguel Gallo Vergara to not only found one of the wealthiest dynasties the country has ever known but even to finance a new political party.[2]

Today, however, nothing but abandoned rubble remains. The historic station is just a sand-blasted mound in the pockmarked landscape, and not even the graves in the cemetery have survived the oblivion of an incessant wind. Nothing recalls the thousands of men who scraped and heaved in the dirt here, and while the Gallo-Goyenechea family went on to leave their mark all over Chile, funding infrastructure from roads to railways and building themselves the gorgeous Cousiño Palace in Santiago, the memorial to the illiterate mule driver who handed them their wealth amounts to a statue in Copiapó and a forgotten ghost town next to the former mine: Pueblo Juan Godoy.

And the person who first knew of the fabulous silver seam in the ground is not remembered at all, namely Juan Godoy's Indigenous mother, Flora Normilla, who shared her knowledge as sacred inheritance with her son, before she died in 1832. Tragically, she advised him to trust only Miguel Gallo, the mining patron she had often met on his scouting rounds in the desert. She must have believed his stature would help her son, but instead he persuaded Juan and his brother to part with their rights very soon after their joint registration. The sum he offered his naïve partner was a small fortune, giving him the chance to build a house and acquire a sudden glut of previously unknown relatives. But, predictably, he lost both the home and the family within one short decade and died penniless in 1842, having blown not even 1 percent of the overall profits that were made from the silver found at Chañarillo during the four short decades of its heyday. Of course even that fraction was a great deal more than his fellow miners enjoyed, who were lucky if they could improve on their meager salaries by inserting grease-covered lumps of stolen ore into their anuses. The practice was so common it even acquired a name, becoming popularly known as *la cangalla,* which gave rise not only to a thriving black market but also a lucrative sideline for a notorious local doctor, who surgically removed contraband that refused to be expelled naturally in return for keeping this back passage booty.[3]

Chilean mining continues to be controversial to this day, and yet another unequal struggle over resources is being played out in the very valley where our journey began; for the modern Diaguita descendants are fighting to protect their natural heritage as I write. In fact, the campaign to stop the transnational open-pit gold mine known as Pascua Lama has been one of Chile and Argentina's bitterest environmental struggles in recent decades. At stake are the profits from mining what is believed to be around 450 tons of gold straddling the Andean border at 4,500 meters, versus the geographical and socioeconomic costs to two nations, and one tiny group of people in particular.[4] What matters more is far from decided, but current global economic and political instability might just make that irrelevant, and the most recent court case in 2020 forced the project to shut down.

7
2010 Earthquake

The rumble started under the bed. No, it was under the house. Then the ancient wood frame began to creak and large pieces of plaster started coming off the ceiling (one narrowly missed my son's head as he instinctively moved from his pillow); walls began to crack, ceiling lamps swung violently from side to side, and a terrified screaming could be heard outside.

"Get out of the house," I shouted, but the boys were way ahead of us as we stumbled naked into the darkness of the night.

Outside, the concrete-bound iron pillars that frame our grape arbor were swaying like giant windshield wipers. The dogs barked hysterically at our feet, unable to comprehend the heaving earth and the terrible creaking noise coming from our house, as every single window and door dislocated from its frame.

We clung to each other in speechless fright, clutching our bedsheets under a starry summer sky, feeling very vulnerable indeed. A million car and house alarms rang in our ears as we tried to comprehend the unreality of the earth moving beneath our feet and the horrible noise coming from our home. It was all so shocking, especially at 3:45 a.m., when each of us had been fast asleep in our beds, possibly the safest and coziest hour in any human life lucky enough to be surrounded by warmth and the company of loved ones.

Speech returned in repetitive questions. "Did you hear the

ground?" we kept asking each other. Fire engines and police sirens wailed all over town as we debated what to do. The house had not fallen down and spending the rest of the night outside did not appeal. Incredibly, our lodger on the second floor had not appeared, but when we called to her, she confirmed all was well upstairs. A tentative walk around the house by candlelight revealed dramatic changes, but nothing that could not wait till daylight. There were no broken pipes or ripped wires; no fire, thank goodness, and so we shook the dust off our sheets and crept back into bed, as if our flimsy covers could somehow block out what had just happened and make it a bad dream we would wake up from in the morning. But violent aftershocks kept us on tenterhooks and our flight instincts remained tuned to their highest frequency. There was no sleep to be had. Instead we fell into the wordless respite of mental shock, bodies rigid and eyes tightly shut.

When we reconvened, later in the morning, we explored the house and garden like dazed shipwreck survivors. The walls of our bedrooms had been transformed into a mosaic of cracked and broken plaster revealing the original straw and mud adobe walls and the bright orange cladding of electricity wires, added much later. Amazingly, not a single window was broken. Instead, the windows had simply snapped open without breaking. I cannot remember if we had water, but I know there was no electricity or cell phone connectivity, and we sat in the car to listen to the radio, where the true scale of what had occurred in the night was already being reported in grim statistics. Bizarrely, the early-morning rubbish truck passed down the street outside, a feature of our normality that already seemed to belong to a different life.

One of the most shocking immediate facts we already knew was how long this earthquake had lasted: ninety eternal seconds, almost two minutes. Apparently, the epicenter was in central Chile, about 450 kilometers south of Limache, and the record-breaking magnitude of this mega seismic event was already being confirmed:

8.5 on the Richter Scale and 8.8 on the more current Moment Magnitude Scale (Mw), which not only made it the country's worst earthquake in the last fifty years but also put it in the top ten for the entire planet for the past century.[1] The energy released by the Nazca Plate flipping up the South American Plate was the equivalent of a mind-boggling eight hundred thousand bombs like the one dropped on Hiroshima, and almost Chile's entire central coast was given a violent shove during the eternal competition for space that is the movement of the earth's crust.

The Sunday newspapers the next day (the earthquake happened predawn, on Saturday, February 27, 2010) were full of dramatic photos and stories of miraculous survival and tragic fatalities. Already, there were 214 confirmed deaths and an estimated two million people who had been made homeless overnight, and we thanked our lucky stars not to be among them. The majority of buildings that had collapsed were nineteenth-century houses like ours, and the historic centers of Santiago, Valparaíso, and dozens of central Chilean towns had been reduced to rubble. The worst affected was a town called Talca, where almost no buildings remained standing along its high street. But in nearby Chillán the collapsed buildings also brought an unexpected opportunity for 269 prisoners, who suddenly found themselves looking at freedom when a prison wall collapsed. According to the papers, only sixty had been recaptured by the following day, which was hardly surprising, given the level of damage to roads and bridges and more pressing emergencies to deal with.

Neighbors gathered on our street outside, and I found myself in conversation with people who had passed me wordlessly until that morning.

¿Todo bien? was the most common refrain: Everything OK?

The disaster somehow bridged the cultural gap that had kept us apart during our early years, Chilean reticence and my own foreign awkwardness suddenly erased by the simple fact of our common humanity, our common fear, and our common need to share our relief that we were alive and well. It was one of the few gifts of the terrible event we were all living through and, from that day on, my neighbors greeted me with a friendly smile and a brief exchange about our loved ones. Henceforth, I was no longer just the mysterious foreigner who had bought the big house on their street but a mother and wife with a name. Offers of food and help were now part of our interactions, which felt good, even if they were just formula conversations. It was a step in the right direction and, as the years passed, I even joined the local neighborhood association and became an accepted member of the community—a stranger always, but a known unknown.

The ribbon of the Pan-American Highway was snapped and broken in many places up and down the country, and even air transport was difficult, with cracked runways and air traffic control reduced to radio messages. But army and media helicopter crews were soon revealing the awful destruction up and down the country, especially in the south-central region of Chile, near its second-biggest city of Concepción, just sixty kilometers from the epicenter of the earthquake. One of the most shocking images was of a brand-new fifteen-story tower painted in bold white and orange that had simply snapped in two, like a pile of child's building blocks. A hundred people, who had just moved in to their pristine apartments, were missing under the collapsed slabs of concrete and twisted steel, and it was heartrending to read of the father waiting patiently for his son, who had just bought his first home, inside the rubble. How could this have happened in a country with strict seismic-resistant building regulations? Only now was the catastrophic decision to allow construction companies to self-regulate revealed. Compliance with building standards is no longer a local authority matter in Chile.

But the most heartrending scandal of this terrible disaster was the failed tsunami warning, which would eventually be held responsible for 178 additional lives lost. One hundred seventy-eight people who might have survived that terrifying night, if they had been given the vital fifteen minutes to run for their lives, between 3:34 a.m., when the earthquake erupted, and the four giant waves that hit Chile's central coastline between 3:49 and 6:40 a.m.

Incredibly, the Chilean Navy did not confirm a tsunami had actually happened until eight hours after the event, while the National Chilean Office for Emergencies failed to issue a mainland alert, because the official chain of command had to come from the navy first.[2] In fact, an investigation, years later, revealed the navy had, indeed, issued a tsunami alert at 3:51 a.m., but due to the collapse of telecommunications, only eight early warning stations up and down the country received it. Another fatal misinterpretation of early data also led officials to hugely underestimate the danger, because of an erroneous belief that if the epicenter of an earthquake is inland, it cannot cause a tsunami wave at sea. But subsequent research revealed the epicenter was, in fact, under the sea, very close to the coastline, and a five-meter-high wave swept into the port of Talcahuano and toward the nation's second city, ten minutes after the earthquake hit, depositing huge boats on its streets and drowning at least thirty-two people in their homes. Despite this, the regional governor put out a radio message at 5:20 a.m., advising the population there was no tsunami alert, and though many thousands refused to descend the hills and return to their homes, some had faith in what was an official announcement and died in the third and fourth waves that hit the coast at 6:00 a.m. and forty minutes later.[3]

The waves destroyed our beloved Pichilemu's entire seafront, annihilating holiday cottages and homes along its gorgeous beach in one terrifying surge, while a dozen fishing villages along the coast were flattened like so many matchstick houses, leaving survivors hanging in trees and wading through cold wet slime to search for loved ones. The picturesque fishing port of Constitución was inundated, with the worst tragedy occurring on the island campsite full of young families enjoying the last of the summer holidays at the mouth of the Maule River. The people knew they were in danger as soon as the earthquake happened, but there was no boat to take them to the riverbank. One of the fathers jumped in the river and swam ashore as fast as his arms could move him, but the local naval station refused to lend him their lifeboat and he could only watch as his wife and children and many others were swept upriver and then crushed and battered among floating debris by a much fiercer third wave (one of his daughters survived).

There was horror on land as well, as desperate and angry people began to roam their ruined streets. Looters were soon carrying off whatever they could find in the city of Concepción; they also set fire to supermarkets and other symbols of the consumer society they felt excluded by.

"What are those assholes saying," one young man reportedly said. "The people we are robbing actually steal from us every day!"[4]

Armed neighborhood vigilantes defied the government curfew to remain outside their ruined homes, in an attempt to keep whatever furniture and white goods they had left, but the army forced them to leave.

It made me even more grateful to be safe in our own cracked home in our little town inland, away from the chaos of nearby Valparaíso and Viña del Mar, where the scenes were almost as ugly as further south. But there was much to think about as reconstruction got under way. The earthquake had revealed some ugly gaps in Chile's society that had nothing to do with nature and everything to do with people. The country's tidy front room, where it had shown off its modernity and wealth to the world, had suddenly collapsed to reveal the ugly poverty in the back of the house, where *empleadas* (maids) work for starvation wages.

It had not taken us long to discover the shiny veneer of Chile's free market success story was a lie for the vast majority of the population, starting with our failure to find a decent state school for our sons. Going to the supermarket was also a shock we still found astonishing, where the bill for a week's supply was the same as in Europe, despite incomes in Chile certainly not being on the same level. About three quarters of the population earn less than six hundred dollars a month to this day, even in middle-class professions like school teaching or office work. Economic survival is a matter of scrimping and dodging in the unofficial cash economy, and getting into debt up to your eyeballs is normal. Every shop that accepts debit cards will always ask if you want to pay by installments and if you do not have a bank account or access to official credit, you go to the Colombian hairdressers who double as money lenders. Limache has around a dozen such places, and it took me a while to figure out how they made a living, because you rarely see actual hairdressing customers.

The stress of making a life in Chile is crushing, and it was very worrying to be told that if we had been psychiatrists, we could have done a roaring trade, because mental health services are one of the fastest growing sectors in Chile. The 2010 earthquake must have been a terrific boost too, because now there were huge numbers of people suffering from post-traumatic stress disorder as well. More than ever before, in the period since democracy had returned there was an urgent awareness among many people that the price for economic success in Chile was too high and the rewards too unevenly spread. Most people's existence, including our own, was precarious, and all those shiny new office buildings and shopping malls and TV satellite dishes did not represent a decent quality of life or happiness. Instead they inspired an inescapable level of unfulfilled desire and resentment that was surely going to lead to more political violence one day, even while ordinary people's resilience and humor was never absent.

"I'm an honest man as long as I'm not in need," my gardener Silvio informed me once.

It was an uncomfortable context, however, because part of our motivation for making a new life in Chile was certainly to escape the rigid class system and philistine consumer society of Britain. We had definitely not been looking to join the ranks of the privileged.

Yet that is exactly where we found ourselves, and our naïvety was embarrassing, if only to us. We tried hard to overcome the cultural and economic gulf by treating everyone with respect, no matter who they were. But treading the line between grateful humility and not getting ripped off was a challenge, especially when it came to finding builders to replaster our lovely house after the earthquake. It took a year before I found someone who came with a trusted recommendation and was also available, but at least it was the summer season once more, and stacking our belongings outside among the fruit trees was no hardship.

8

Sundays with Don Guido

To be wrapped in the arms of Guido was repulsive and joyful in equal measure.

"Natascha! *¡Que bueno verte!*" he would invariably cry on seeing me, and I would try hard not to hesitate, willing my senses to rise above the sickly aroma of neglected old man and my heart to respond to his sincere embrace.

It was a challenge in finding common humanity that got harder over the years, as he fell ever more into decrepitude and the distressing physical problems associated with diabetes and a lack of teeth that made sharing a meal with him yet another exercise in mind over matter, especially when his favorite egg sandwiches invariably failed to stay in his mouth or remained stuck to his stubbly chin and whatever crumpled shirt he was wearing. But these were just details that did not matter compared to the intense pleasure he bestowed on his audience every Sunday, when my dear friends Howard and Caroline turned their sitting room into a public concert hall and opened their doors to anyone who wished to join them for an old-fashioned salon of piano music and afternoon tea. And what a treat it always was, for Guido was musical inspiration personified. No one who experienced him play could ever forget him, and I am sure that if he had lived in a worldlier place, he would have been a renowned concert pianist instead of a retired librarian whose wife and daughters had abandoned him long ago. But he was our private treasure, and to be allowed to share that lovely bond of music and simple fellowship was a very special gift. The sincere welcome of our hosts was also a lesson in compassion that will stay with me forever.

The changing gallery of visitors at Howard and Caroline's was another attraction, because you never knew who might turn up in addition to the central core, which was already endlessly fascinating. There was Bill from Minnesota, a Christian do-gooder who would have been easy to laugh at, if it hadn't been for his tragically unhappy marriage to an Iranian woman, who exuded judgmental disapproval to all and sundry but saved her deepest disgust for "poor old Bill," as he was generally referred to. He used to walk around the town just to get away from his angry wife, yet they had only been married a short decade, so their aversion to each other seemed out of proportion, until he confided to me that it was based on a bottomless pit of self-inflicted disappointment. They had made the terrible mistake of getting married on a whim, after meeting at a Bahá'í convention in Argentina. She was a divorced exile, he was a divorced lost soul, and their common faith seemed a bond worth sharing; except getting married on the basis of an idea alone did not make for a happy relationship, and they quickly discovered they had absolutely nothing in common.

Another regular was a handsome poet, who miraculously survived being a revolutionary during the horrors of the Chilean dictatorship and never failed to eat his fill without either contributing or clearing the table afterward. But he could find an opinion on every topic, a solution to every problem without lifting a finger, and listening to him pontificate was an exercise in diplomacy I only endured because hearing Guido play, as soon as possible, was much more important than giving that man a piece of my mind. But his bad manners upset me, especially because I knew he came from a wealthy family that enabled him to live in their empty seven-

Figure 12. Guido playing for Caroline.

bedroom mansion down the road, where his greatest challenge was feeding the birds and keeping the weeds down.

Yet, in the decade of Sundays we shared, the astonishing generosity and good will of our hosts never wavered, except once, when an impoverished grand dame from Santiago informed them their Christmas turkey was not up to scratch. That hurt, and a crestfallen silence fell over the beautiful table complete with firecrackers and paper hats for everyone. But even then, nothing was said, and the lady did us the favor of dying of rancor before she could spoil any more free dinners.

"What shall I play?" Guido would ask, and it didn't matter if it was Chilean folk music, Beethoven, Bach, or Chopin: he could summon a vast repertoire from memory, finding his connection in a moment of hushed silence, before launching his horny fingers onto the keys and liberating a musical drama that left us agape in wonder.

How he did it was a mystery, even to him. For the maestro was not only playing from memory but actually inventing the piece as he went along, using famous motifs and recognizable musical phrases to create an entirely original, never to be repeated, improvisation.

"It just comes from God," he would say, always humble, with a shrug of the shoulders.

He also had a gorgeous tenor singing voice and could serenade us in Spanish, Italian, and German. He even had a few English songs up his sleeve he performed phonetically, without any idea of what he was saying; but my favorite selections from his singing repertoire were the compositions by his Chilean compatriot Violeta Parra, whose "Gracias a la vida" never failed to bring tears to my eyes, and to Guido's as well. In fact, he was a very emotional performer, who was sometimes so overcome he would have to stop and sob quietly over the keys. It was always a deeply moving and painful moment, because we all knew he was remembering his beloved mother, or some other part of his former life, before illness and misfortune had reduced him to the stumbling ruin he was now. But a kind pat on the back from Caroline usually helped him to return to the present, and he would play on, reviving with every bar of music that miraculously sprang from his fingertips. Our applause was even more heartfelt on those occasions, acknowledged by a grave nod over the shoulder and, if we were lucky, another spectacular encore of inspired invention.

Guido's Sunday recitals were the core event, but they were not the only highlight of our Sundays. For Howard and Caroline were equally brilliant individuals, whose intellectual rigor and hands-on Christian faith had led to a lifelong commitment to social justice and political activism, and their gatherings invariably included serious political and philosophical discussions with visiting scholars and activists from as far afield as South Africa, but mostly from across Latin America. To sit in on their discourse was a masterclass in philosophy and politics and it was thrilling to be among people who were actively trying to find solutions to Chile's dysfunctional democracy. Often as not, one of Howard's new papers would be read for discussion, presented in bilingual Spanish and English to include all guests, and invariably I came away with my ears ringing to the sounds of Don Guido, and my mind buzzing with Howard's latest thesis. The only thing missing at their teetotal salon was a great glass of wine, but it made mine back home taste all the sweeter, a perfect end to another unforgettable Sunday.

Working for social justice in Chile is like pissing in the wind of history, but some people never give up, and Howard and Caroline are among them. In fact, they were the first gringos to settle in the Limache Valley, as long ago as the 1960s, when they came to be part of Allende's socialist dream of a fairer society. Caroline once told me they would have liked to go to Cuba but, as American citizens, it was easier to come to Chile. The CIA-backed military coup in 1973 forced them to leave, but retirement from teaching posts at the Quaker Earlham College in 2004 enabled them to return and the work to be done remained as urgent as ever. Only the COVID-19 pandemic stopped Howard from keeping to his busy schedule of international teaching engagements in Argentina and South Africa, alongside his commitments at the University of Chile and several think tanks, and his undiminished perseverance is astounding.[1]

Howard and Caroline are living examples of Mahatma Gandhi's exhortation to "be the change you want to see in the world," which they carry out on many levels, both intellectual and practical, on an international scale and locally. Yet, what always troubles me is the seemingly eternal gap between good intentions and reality, and I am utterly baffled how they find the heart to carry on regardless, especially Howard, who stubbornly keeps coming up with new ideas and projects, whether anyone cares or not, at an age when

Figure 13. Howard and Caroline.

most people would be happy to just water the roses. But as long as he breathes, he will be coming up with new ideas, and if only a fraction bear fruit, it will have been no less productive than your average spawning in nature. In his own words, "The bottom line is ethical: meeting needs is what community means. That is what solidarity means. It is what a care ethic means."

Guido was Caroline's project and it was touching to witness the deep bond between them, born of their mutual passion for music. She had the piano, he had the art, and the exchange brought joy to all of us. Over time, he became more like a member of the family, and it seemed only natural to help him with his many needs, whether it was medical treatment or transport, cash or food. There was an unworldly innocence about him that made it very necessary too, because he was always getting himself into scrapes with unscrupulous people, especially his lodgers, who often took advantage of him. At some point, it seemed easier to buy his crumbling house before the bank or others could take it from him—his wife had already emptied it of all the furniture long ago—and thus he was assured of at least some security in his final years.

The Guido project was a success, or so it seemed, until it was suddenly pulverized by a horrible row that went beyond the ability of either party to transcend. Sundays were never the same again, and it wasn't long before the weekend salon faded away into a wistful memory.

"What on earth happened?" I asked Caroline, sometime later, and it turned out to be yet another version of Chilean mistrust pitched against a foreigner's good intentions.

Even after all those years, the deep well of resentment between the haves and have-nots in Chile had bubbled up, just when it made the least sense; for the issue at hand had been to oblige Guido's lodgers to sign formal rental agreements, which would make it easier to evict them for nonpayment. But what had seemed like a straightforward practical solution to one side suddenly felt like a paternalistic imposition to the other, and Guido had roused himself into such a fury of indignation there was no going back without losing face—especially with his Chilean friends and relations, who had never stopped querying what the gringos were up to, not least since they had bought his house.

"You think they are trying to help you?"

"Don't you realize they are going to make a huge profit when you are gone?"

And so the seed of bad faith was watered by the drip, drip, drip of envy that no amount of loving care could neutralize. Put another way, the shame and sense of impotence caused by Guido's poverty and dependence was made intolerable by his benefactors' failure to acknowledge his need for agency and self-respect. Without meaning to, my friends had robbed him of his dignity and turned him into a performing monkey for their Sunday gatherings. Yet the tragedy for Caroline was that she really did love Guido and was sincerely in awe of his musical gift. The material benefits were nothing more than tokens of her high esteem and a simple desire to help because she could. But the inequality between them was fatal to their relationship, and it was inexpressibly sad when the call came to say Guido had fallen into a diabetic coma, six months later. The only consolation was that limited friendly relations had been reestablished, and even though Guido never played the piano at Caroline's house again, he did manage to express his profound affection for the woman who had brought as much light into his life as he had to hers.

"I hope you don't forget me," Caroline always used to say, during their farewells in happier days.

It was a catchphrase that stuck and she repeated it during what was to be their last encounter.

"I could never forget you," he replied. "Not in this life, or the next."

Guido's final alms was a suit for his corpse, because not a single item of clean clothing could be found to dress him for the traditional Catholic wake at his local church, and so he was given the dignity he never had in life to lie in his coffin like a napping bank manager, his face set in a severe pose that gave no hint of his suffering, nor of his scintillating character and joyful musicianship. Chopin's "Heroic Polonaise" in A flat major, Opus 53, rang out on the church speakers as we filed outside after the funeral ceremony, and we all knew we would never be able to listen to that piece again without thinking of the extraordinary piano man of Limache.

9
Rapa Nui (Easter Island)

Bringing the love of my life and the father of my sons to Chile did not solve his depression. It just prolonged his agonizing departure from our lives and made my path a hundred times lonelier, as I found myself responsible for two young boys in a culture that abandons women without a man to their fate. The hardest time of all was Christmas, which just wasn't the same without Daddy, and so I decided from 2009 onward that we would have an adventure instead. Chile's Easter Island, or Rapa Nui to the locals, seemed a great way to start that new tradition in our lives, and so we flew off to the most isolated island on the planet, a speck in the Pacific Ocean, 1,850 kilometers (1,150 miles) from the nearest landfall in any direction and 3,512 kilometers (2,182 miles) from continental Chile.

We knew nothing of this obscure place, other than that it was famous for its isolation and its mysterious statues, and we came to the island with the happy ignorance of tourists ready to be entertained. But we did not get off to a good start, because our tropical garden campsite in the island's only town turned out to be a rain-soaked patch among construction rubble at the back of someone's half-built house. It was unwelcoming in the extreme and the indifferent owners could barely be bothered to show us where the bathroom was, much less help find a decent spot to camp among the knee-high dripping weeds outside. The boys quickly abandoned me to explore the municipal beach down by the dock and take delight in a giant turtle cruising the fishing boats for scraps, while I was left to make sense of our dismal accommodation on my own.

Christmas dinner was a limp fish cooked over an improvised grill of brick and wire, but it did not matter, because by that time I had found a fabulous alternative campground to move to the next day (Mihinoa, just outside Hanga Roa town), complete with a kitchen and a friendly atmosphere, not to mention a dramatic cliff-top view over the breezy ocean. The magical sites of the island had also begun to reveal themselves, despite our astonishingly negligent hosts, and our first adventure was to the ancient Orongo ceremonial site perched on the rim of one of Rapa Nui's three extinct volcanoes. Finding ourselves whipped by gusty winds on a three-hundred-meter-high precipice between the ocean and Rano Kau's watery crater was utterly exhilarating, while climbing hundreds of meters up from the deadly rocks below seemed impossible. But that is exactly what brave youths did for generations, when the Birdman Cult demanded they swim out to the nearby islets to bring back the first egg laid by the thousands of sooty terns that once nested there. Many no doubt died, either in the shark-infested water, smashed against the rocky shore by the incessant waves, or from losing their grip as they climbed the slippery cliffs with their bare hands and feet. Hard to believe anyone actually succeeded, but they did, right up until Christian missionaries banned the practice in the 1860s.

My sons were not interested in history lessons, obviously, but they enjoyed riding horses into the central uplands, where treeless meadows made for panoramic views and the gentle slope for a picnic among munching horses was also the perfect viewpoint for appreciating just how tiny an island we found ourselves on: a triangle whose dimensions are no more than twenty-four by sixteen by twelve kilometers. We could easily see the ocean in every direction and it was astonishing to me to think a complex Polynesian culture

Figure 14. Rémi on Easter Island, Christmas 2009.

of several thousand people had once lived here. The lack of trees and the seemingly barren land give no hint of the millions of palm trees that originally covered the island, and there are no obvious signs of human habitation either, except for the hundreds of three-meter-high stone giants with their backs to the sea that have been puzzling Europeans ever since they first set eyes on them on Easter Sunday, just three centuries ago. In fact, these artifacts were all toppled and broken when the Dutch seafarers originally passed by in 1722 and have only been restored in recent times; their history remains unclear to this day. The island's unique engraved script on rare wooden tablets is another secret no one has been able to crack entirely, though modern craftsmen do a roaring trade in exquisite reproductions carved onto driftwood or expensive imported off-cuts.

Figure 15. The mighty Moai of Easter Island.

The most dramatic platforms of Moai statues are near the seashore, where their magnificently haughty gaze takes no notice of the tiny humans under their bellies, but the best place to marvel at the sheer creative imagination and skill of the ancient islanders is the mountain quarry at Rano Raraku, where outsized stone heads litter the landscape in a chaotic jumble, as if some giant's cart had overturned on its way to market. The black volcanic stones are covered in velvet patches of gray and green lichen that add an interesting patina to their rough surfaces, and some also have intriguing carvings on them, including the image of a European galleon that obviously made a big impression when it was sighted. Unfortunately, the greatest mark outsiders left on Rapa Nui is the almost complete extinction of the native population over an astonishingly short period of time, so that the several thousand people who were estimated to be present by the first Dutch arrivals had dwindled to just 111 islanders by 1877, and of those only thirty-six were original inhabitants of Rapanui.

The island's genocide was not intentional, however, despite about half the population being kidnapped by slavers, who sold their captives to work themselves to death in Peruvian gold and silver mines. Most simply died of imported diseases, beginning with syphilis brought by North American sailors in 1811, smallpox carried back by the handful of survivors from Peru, and leprosy that came from Tahiti. The tragedy of this human destruction is also why it has been almost impossible to decipher the mysteries of Rapa Nui's past, because the guardians of knowledge and tradition had all died by the time foreigners arrived who were interested in honoring and recording the island's history and culture. Instead, it has been extrapolated from oral histories and songs and research throughout Oceania's island community, which especially applies to its language and boat-building traditions but has not helped much to decipher the intricate pictographic script panels that survived the zealous burning by French missionaries.

But the sad fact is that Rapa Nui's Golden Age was over before any European voyagers arrived, and even though we do not know what happened in detail, existing records show that much of the population may have died during intertribal warfare, about forty years before the Dutch anchored offshore; and there were no trees left by around 1850, probably as a result of seed-eating Polynesian rats imported from other islands and deforestation by humans. Some authors have even argued that Rapa Nui is one of the world's prime examples of human-induced ecocide and societal collapse, due to an environment that could no longer provide a sustainable living.

This theory has been seriously questioned, however, because modern science has been able to demonstrate that the Pacific region, and Rapa Nui in particular, suffered a severe, century-long drought between 1450 and 1550, which could have precipitated the ecological and demographic collapse on the island. Thus, by the time European contact occurred, the surviving Rapanui were already struggling to survive and the epidemic of old-world diseases was simply the death knell in a much longer process of decline. But the difficulty in proving any of these theories lies in Rapa Nui's volcanic nature, which provides very little opportunity for the kind of scientific soil excavations that would yield definitive answers.[1]

Much has been written about the enigmas that make Easter Island or Rapa Nui so endlessly fascinating, but, for me, the biggest question is why the island officially belongs to Chile. After all, it is thousands of kilometers from continental South America, and despite Thor Heyerdahl's famous *Kon-Tiki* voyage to prove that migration was possible from the east, modern DNA testing has made it clear that Rapa Nui forms the southeastern tip of the Polynesian cultural triangle, with Hawaii and New Zealand making up the other two points, and that the island was settled by aboriginal people who traveled from Taiwan and eastern Asia along the Micronesian and Polynesian corridor of islands and ocean routes, reaching Rapa Nui about twelve hundred years ago. So while it may just be a speck in the Pacific Ocean, it is a Polynesian speck and not an American one.

Yet the Republic of Chile annexed Easter Island in 1888, even though it took no further interest in the island and promptly rented it out to the British Williamson-Balfour Company until 1953, which used it as the company's private sheep station and kept the remaining islanders imprisoned in an enclosure that is now the island's capital of Hanga Roa. It is yet another grim story of Indigenous people being marginalized in their own country for the profit of more powerful outsiders; and so the thirty-six Rapanui and their descendants spent several generations as prisoners and indentured laborers, prohibited from setting foot outside their walled enclosure without permission from the commercial tenants of the island, and denied even the basic right to speak their own language and educate their children in anything other than the Christian doctrine. The only exception to this imprisonment came when a substantial number of Rapanui were taken to work on Tahitian plantations belonging to the French Catholic Church, which resulted in yet another unintended side effect; namely, the many family ties between the two islands.

Incredibly, the Rapanui were not allowed to leave their island prison until the 1950s, because they were seen as a risk for spreading smallpox and leprosy; and despite being subjects of the Chilean state, they were not granted citizenship or entitled to Chilean passports until as late as 1966. Most contentiously of all, to this day, the Chilean state owns over 70 percent of the island and continues to prevent its Indigenous population from living off its ancestral lands, due to the fact that most of the island is now officially a national park. All peaceful attempts at protest, such as occupations, have been met with extreme violence by the authorities and negotiations are mired by intransigence on the part of the Chilean government and divisions among the Rapanui. Some want self-government and the right to pursue autonomous Polynesian social and political relationships, while others prefer to continue benefiting from Chilean citizenship and access to mainland opportunities, as well as individual land titles that give them access to private investment profits, over ancient communal traditions. Meanwhile, the Chilean government found a way to evade the issue in 2017, when it granted the association representing the descendants of the official Rapanui families a fifty-year concession to manage and profit from the UNESCO World Heritage site that is Rapa Nui National Park.[2]

No wonder our welcome was less than hearty. Partial freedom to earn a tourist dollar has not undone the wounds of the recent past, and some are obviously less good at putting on a show than others. In fact, there was an uncomfortable undercurrent on several occasions during our stay on Rapa Nui that we could only understand in retrospect, and I, for one, found the manufactured tropical idyll of the island's trinket shops and tourist venues bogus and depressing. Most of the lovely shells for sale were not even from Rapa Nui but imports from Tahiti. On the other hand, the local Rapanui family that owns and manages the Mihinoa Campsite could not have been more friendly and helpful, and I especially enjoyed the irony that we were enjoying a five-star location without paying the five-star prices of the foreign luxury hotel next door. But the culture clash all around us was striking, not least when a giant cruise ship docked offshore to unload the next batch of big spenders in private zodiac boats.

I discovered the colonial link to Chile is not as absurd as it first seems, however, when set in its nineteenth-century context, and that background also goes a long way to explaining why the Chilean government has never shown any sign of giving up control of the island, even to this day. Just like the British in relation to the Falkland Islands (Las Malvinas) and the United States in relation to Hawaii, keeping jurisdiction over Easter Island or Rapa Nui is a matter of national pride for the Republic of Chile, as well as a strategic and economic decision, even if it is increasingly difficult to justify according to the values of self-determination that have gained currency in the twenty-first century and are also enshrined in the 2009 United Nations Declaration on Indigenous People.

When Chile annexed the island in 1888, it was part of a global maritime strategy on the part of a newly empowered imperial nation. Formal independence from Spain had been won by 1818, the Mapuche Nation had been "pacified," and the country had recently doubled its territory by winning the War of the Pacific with Peru and Bolivia. The republican future looked bright, and despite having a tiny population compared to other Latin American nations, Chile controlled 13 percent of the southern continent's trade and enjoyed its highest level of GDP. Of course it needed foreign possessions and the obvious place to look was the Pacific, where the Chilean

Navy and merchant ships were developing vital maritime trade routes to Asia, and especially to China, which is Chile's main trading partner today. Conveniently, these ambitions did not clash with French hegemony in Polynesia, much less with the French Catholic Church, and after the archbishop of Tahiti made the administrative decision that distant Easter Island (four thousand kilometers away) should be managed by the missions based in Chile, there was no resistance when that country's navy turned up to claim the island. Soon, there were Chilean consulates all around the Pacific Rim, from Sydney to Shanghai, and Chile's status as the "Britain of South America" was complete.

Tragically for the people of Rapa Nui, Chilean annexation coincided with the global decline of imperial nations, which is why they quickly found themselves abandoned by their absentee landlord, who first left them at the mercy of a foreign business enterprise and then to the management of the Chilean Navy. Today, at least, the island has been declared a "special territory," which will ensure a certain amount of autonomy for administrative decisions, and it is fully plugged in to mobile phone and Internet services, as well as banking and all other state structures, such as education, policing, and health care. On the flipside, however, continental Chileans who came to live on the island to take advantage of the tourism boom that began with the weekly flight service established between Santiago and Rapa Nui in 1970 now make up 60 percent of the population, which is yet another source of conflict over the very limited resources and efforts to keep the Rapanui language alive in the education system.

Yet, even with all the tragedy and current strife, there is much to celebrate on Rapa Nui, and the most exciting aspect of that is the resurgence of its Polynesian pride and identity that has resulted from renewed connections with the wider Pacific island community of Oceania. It is not an entity that is taught in any Western geography class, which is entirely based on a Eurocentric map of the world, but ignorance of the facts does not make them go away, and Pacific Islanders have been reasserting their ancient community in ways that are thrillingly at odds with traditional Western concepts of dependency for island nations in the "middle of nowhere." Turns out that nowhere is a known world of Pacific Ocean cultures, whose links go back thousands of years, beginning with the prehistoric Asian seafarers who set off to found kingdoms and cultures that were traditionally connected by an intricate network of known maritime routes.

The existence of what modern academics have called the "cognitive map" of Polynesia, for example, was most clearly proved for Rapa Nui islanders when the first voyaging canoe to be built in six hundred years successfully reached them from Hawaii, in 1999. Much like a double-hulled catamaran, this vessel was an authentic revival not only of ancient boat-building techniques but also of navigational knowledge that was almost completely lost and could only be shared because one of the last surviving Pacific navigators agreed to pass on his priceless wayfaring skills that depend on a lifetime of learning the star compass, the physical nature of the sea and sky, and the seasonal habits of the wind. His name was Mau Piailug, and he ought to be celebrated as one of the finest sea captains who ever lived, not least because he proved the islands of the world's greatest ocean were not populated as a result of accidental shipwrecks and chance; rather, they were explored and settled using historic maritime highways. Remote Rapa Nui was the last island to be settled, but that does not invalidate its place in the Polynesian diaspora, and those who dream of self-determination are doing nothing less than fighting for their birthright.[3]

10

Mummies in the Desert

The Norte Grande

The challenge of Chile's astonishing distances is irresistible to travelers, and while most don't have the time to explore any other way than by using airplanes, we decided a school holiday was the perfect moment to drive just over three thousand kilometers (1,864 miles) roundtrip to Chile's most famous desert oasis, known as San Pedro de Atacama. A mistake, all things considered, because the overland route there and back, which is about the same as driving from Mexico City to Chicago, has got to be one of the most exhaustingly dreary experiences you could inflict on yourself. It is not improved by breaks at any of the towns en route either, especially once you have passed the semidesert beyond the city of Copiapó and entered the true dead zone of the Atacama Desert.

I struggle to understand how anyone ever thought it was a good idea to come this way on foot and on horseback in the sixteenth century; not even the fabulous wealth of the nitrate, gold, and copper mines discovered later seems like a good enough reason to spend your life scrabbling in the choking dust, especially since the majority of people who worked themselves into early graves did not take home the loot. That went to the wealthy investors who paid others to risk their lives for them, and so it is to this day; and while miners are some of the highest paid workers in Chile, they also suffer great hardships and rarely get compensation after life-changing accidents. The fate of the famous thirty-three who were trapped underground for sixty-nine days in 2010 are a case in point: Over a decade after their rescue and temporary fame, they have yet to receive compensation from either the mining company or the government, and none benefited financially from the Hollywood movie or the books written about them, because they were collectively persuaded to sign away their rights.

It took us two long days to reach San Pedro, as everyone calls it, by which time our hostel had given our room to someone else and we had nowhere to stay. It was not a good start, especially not with two very bored and frustrated young boys, but we made up for it the next day with a trip to the famous Valley of the Moon, where they got to surf down giant sand dunes. The name says it all, and the landscape is indeed an otherworldly place of wind-blasted sandstone and awe-inspiring desolation. Yet when the baking canyons glow red and orange during sunset, a transitory light bathes everything in magical beauty and you almost forget how desperately inhospitable this landscape is. There are plenty of other interesting things to do based in San Pedro, but if I ever go there again, it will definitely be by airplane.

The strangest thing for us, coming from an obscure town in central Chile where we never heard a foreign word, was to find ourselves surrounded by people speaking English, French, and German. For San Pedro is a "gringo town," whose existence depends 100 percent on tourism, and if it was not for the near one hundred thousand visitors every year, this tiny hamlet would be nothing more than a dusty outpost, like all the others hidden in the barren landscape. Instead, you can find the height of luxury in designer hotels and friendly international chefs touting their menus on the sandy high street, as well beautiful bars and hostels in restored adobe houses with lovely "Indigenous" decorations imported from nearby Bolivia. It is a proper picture-book version of a desert resort and no one cares if the weavings and crafts on sale are not authentic and ridiculously overpriced, though it must be shocking for backpackers coming from Peru and Bolivia.

San Pedro de Atacama is, in fact, a carefully edited version of desert life, because almost all the original Aymara and Quechua inhabitants of this land were "Chilenized" over a hundred years ago, after they suddenly found themselves highly marginalized citizens of the Republic of Chile, as a result of the War of the Pacific (1879–1883). That was when Peru had to give up a huge swathe of its southern territory and Bolivia's navy was banished to Lake Titicaca (because it lost the land giving access to the sea), while Chile secured its wealth to this day from the Atacama Desert's mines. Ironically, it is modern conceptions of sustainable tourism and multiculturalism as a good thing that has revived Indigenous communities in northern Chile, and there are more and more tour companies in San Pedro that genuinely try to support local producers of art and culture.

But there are uncomfortable issues nevertheless, especially in Arica on the coast, where the country's most famous Andean carnival was established in 2001. On the one hand, it is a celebration of all things Aymara and Quechua, but, on the other, local Indigenous people have accused the organizers of falsifying the festival by importing dances and traditions that have nothing to do with their own local heritage. In other words, it is yet another Bolivian import packaged as a highly lucrative Chilean tourist attraction.

The city of Arica, close to the border with Peru, is another 695 kilometers (432 miles) from San Pedro, so we did not go on our first desert trip. But we did fly there from Santiago a few years later. I persuaded the boys it was a good idea, because along with discovering some famous desert sights, we could also catch a bus to the city of Iquique, which has one of South America's largest skate parks on its mighty beach; but the deal was almost off as soon as we arrived, because the semiderelict and boarded up streets we found ourselves cruising on the way to our surf hostel were truly dismal.

Arica has the feeling of an abandoned ship, not least because the duty free port of Iquique, about three hundred kilometers south, has sucked most economic life out of this dead-end border town, and unless you are a surfer or smuggler, there is really no good reason to come here. (Hence the annual carnival to bring in some money.) But it does make a good starting point for renting a car and heading out into some remote corners of the Atacama highland desert known as the Altiplano, where a vast silence is only broken by the croaky cries of pink flamingos and migrant birds at the salt lakes that hug the Bolivian border. Lago Chungará, 190 kilometers inland from the coast, is the easiest to reach, because it is on the main route to Bolivia's capital of La Paz, and the village of Putre is a classic Atacameño outpost, where the tightness in your skull really lets you feel its thirty-five hundred meters of altitude. Perhaps this is what San Pedro was like before modern tourism arrived, but that is not to make a value judgement, and we were glad to know we would never be eating rubbery alpaca stew again. I know scientists, naturalists, and mining engineers find much to be fascinated by in the desert. I even know a British museum curator who had an Atacama fly species named after him, but I have to admit it does very little for me. I need green and water.

Back on the coast, we followed the Azapa River inland to the only other place that is a "must see" in this part of the world, which is the archaeological museum at San Miguel, where a selection of the world's oldest mummified humans is kept. Egypt's mummies are the most famous, because they are the remains of aristocrats from a mighty kingdom and came with fabulous riches hidden in pyramids. But Chile is home to the oldest human effigies, by several thousand years, and the most amazing thing about them is that the technology evolved to create them was developed by a sedentary tribe that left few other traces, because they had neither stone nor metal tools and produced neither pottery nor weavings.

The coastal communities of the Chinchorros (9000 BC–3500 BC) that endured between the modern-day ports of Arica and Iquique were inhabited by humble fishermen who used cactus thorns and shells as hooks and made simple harpoons to kill seals, while their wives and children gathered seaweed and shellfish and used the rib bones of sea lions to pry mollusks off rocks. Their only source of drinking water came from the handful of rivers that reach the sea across the desert, and there is very little evidence they ventured inland for the first five thousand years of their existence. In fact, despite their having an obvious reason for not traveling away from their main food sources, it seems climate change was an issue even then, because scientists have identified a two-thousand-year period of "extreme aridity" that only improved after 3000 BC, when the archaeological record shows they began to have contact with highland people and added camelids, potatoes, and quinoa to their diet.

For some reason that is still not entirely clear, these simple communities began mummifying their babies and even fetuses seven thousand years ago, only including adults in the practice substantially later. The question of why this complex rite was first applied to children has been puzzled over by generations of modern archaeologists, but the most current theory is that it was the result of a serious problem with miscarriages and infant death as a result of the high arsenic level in the drinking water, which is a hundred times higher than the maximum deemed acceptable by the World Health Organization. In fact, it is a problem to this day, and scientists have recorded excessive levels of arsenic in the Atacama Desert region that cannot solely be blamed on industrial mining, because it is a naturally occurring phenomenon in the region and women still suffer significantly higher rates of miscarriage and infant mortality than elsewhere in Chile. So the theory is that mummification of children and babies was a response to collective grief and a way to keep the dead close.

The original phase of mummification developed by the Chinchorro people lasted about two thousand years, until 4800 BC, and is characterized by the Black Mummies, so-called because of the black manganese pigment used to paint the bodies. The process involved in creating theses effigies has been studied closely and seems gruesome to the modern reader, who is generally far removed from the realities of death. But for the Chinchorro, it was a way to remain close to their loved ones, and the activity of cleaning the bones, repositioning the skeleton, and creating a new body is believed to have been a ritual community act of healing. The first step was to bury the human remains in swampy wetland by the mouth of the river for speedy decomposition to take place. Then, about a week later, the body was dug up and the bones were thoroughly cleaned of all remaining body tissues and dried in the sun before being realigned in the anatomically correct position. This was followed by the addition of a wooden pole to fix the skull in place, and other sticks and poles were used to give the whole skeleton rigidity, before it was wrapped in reeds and embedded in sufficient clay to create a new body that was then covered in a combination of human and seal skin and included a sculpted face with open eyes and mouth, as well as a wig of human hair. Archaeologists believe this painted black figure was then presented to the clan in a ritual ceremony intended to reintegrate the lost member into the community. Afterward, bodies were laid to rest near dwellings and positioned on their backs so they could "see" the ocean and everyday life.

The tradition of keeping the dead in society is deeply ingrained in many cultures throughout the Americas and has endured to this day, in the form of celebrations for the Day of the Dead in November. The most famous celebrations of reunion are in Mexico, but keeping deceased loved ones visible and part of society in the shape of effigies is fundamental to Andean cosmology as well. In fact, the Christian burial practices imposed by European missionaries were considered an abomination, because they denied Indigenous people the possibility of feeding and clothing their dead, leaving them to starve alone in the ground.

The so-called Red Mummies created from 4800 to 4000 BC were processed very differently, using a series of incisions into the dead body to remove organs and muscle tissues, drying out cavities with hot ash before inserting sticks and poles under the skin, and filling out the body with soil, feathers, and hair. The sun-dried body was then painted red with local oxide, though the faces were still painted black and left with their teeth in place and given a wig of long hair.

But no matter how fascinating the history, the pathetic broken fragments of human remains we found at the museum did very little to inspire us, and the baby and child mummies were just sad moldy relics, to be honest. Seeing them out of context in glass boxes probably did not help, and the museum felt as old and neglected as its famous exhibits. In fact, I discovered later the mummies were literally molding as a combined result of inadequate storage conditions and recent changes in climate that have brought the coastal fog much closer inland, thereby reviving dormant bacteria on the mummies that have been turning their surfaces into a black ooze. The dramatic deterioration of the world's oldest mummies alerted scientists around the world and was even reported in 2015 in the *Harvard Gazette* as "The Case of the Rotting Mummies," shaming the local authorities into investing much-needed money to build a new, climate-controlled exhibition center. It seems they were successful, because the Chinchorro mummies were given UNESCO World Heritage status in 2021, but I doubt I can ever persuade my sons to return for another visit.

11

Silence

The Undigested Past

"Did you hear they found human remains at the derelict tomato factory?" my son Rémi asked, after coming home from skateboarding.

"How do you know that?"

"It was on the local radio," he replied.

He was fourteen at the time, and not generally interested in news reports, but this gruesome story had caught his attention, especially because all his friends were talking about it on the plaza. Frustratingly, he had no precise details to tell me, so I made a point of buying all the local papers the next day. But there was nothing. Not a single word anywhere.

The wife of the owner of the radio station taught at our school, so I purposefully found her to ask what was up with that story, but, to my surprise, she became very brusque, and even slightly angry, and insisted she knew nothing. When I phoned the radio station, I again received a firm brush-off, as if they didn't know what I was talking about, which was odd, because this well-known family is severely critical of Chile's so-called democracy. The radio station is at the heart of political debates in the valley and it is no secret the current owner has ambitions to become the mayor of Limache. Archibaldo Arellano is the proud torch bearer of his father, Hugo's, socialist legacy; Hugo was a renowned local personality who not only founded what is today known as Radio Latina but was also a personal friend of Salvador Allende and an active promoter of his agrarian reform policies that were key to Allende's successful presidential election in 1970. The price he paid for that support was the bombing of his radio station by Pinochet's henchmen, arrest, torture, and exile. In fact, that bomb on his radio antenna was the first to be dropped during the military coup, prior to the attacks on the capital city.[1]

But the mysterious report evaporated into an awkward silence and I could find no one willing to enlighten me, which was unsettling, because it was 2013, and supposedly we were a long way past the era of clandestine graves and extrajudicial activities. Worse, the old tomato factory is just four blocks from my home, and it was horrible to think that something sinister had happened so close to where we lived.

"Do you think it is possible that human remains were found at the old factory?" I asked Silvio, our gardener and source of all things local.

"Oh, sure. Probably, they were thrown down the well there," he said, without batting an eyelid. "Everyone knows it was a torture center after the coup. The neighbors could even hear the screaming," he mused, leaning on his hoe.

"How dreadful," I replied, and asked, "Do you know whose remains they might be?" Silvio just shrugged his shoulders. Over the years, he had explained to me many times that General Pinochet saved the country from those crazy communists who just brought chaos and food shortages.

"Chileans need a firm hand," he used to say. "They don't understand democracy."

"But wasn't the price of Pinochet's law and order too high?" I asked, but Silvio insisted that he was sure the roundup of people was necessary and, who knows, perhaps they deserved it.

"We all felt much safer after Pinochet took power," Silvio insisted. "Maybe his guys made a few mistakes, but mostly they did a good job."

It was a view I had heard several times over the years, part of the mental fabric of life here, and what I found most surprising was the way it cut across all classes, so it was never a good idea to bring up the subject without a reasonable sense of someone's stand on the matter first.

Chileans would rather choke than tell you what they are thinking at the best of times, which makes difficult conversations all the harder, no matter what the topic.

"Sharing your opinion could get you killed in the 1970s and '80s," my friend Flavia observed, when I asked her about her people's renowned reticence.

"Old habits die hard," she said, and of course those who denounced people to the secret police, tortured them, or disposed of their bodies are even less inclined to discuss something as grave as crimes against humanity, especially if they were never charged or imprisoned for their crimes, as most perpetrators in Chile were not. But the silence is ugly and haunts not only victims and perpetrators but also anyone else who comes to live among them. Because they are everywhere, in all walks of life, and you can never be completely sure whose pain or guilt you might inadvertently expose with a careless comment. You learn to say nothing, unless you know each other really well, and even then you might come to regret opening a can of worms that can quickly be the end of your relationship. The depth of this cultural trait is defined perfectly by Isabel Allende in her most famous novel, *The House of the Spirits*, when she describes her character Clara as not believing in giving problems a name, in case they become real and can no longer be ignored.

There are ongoing valiant attempts to shine light on Chile's dark past, however, and one of the most moving places you can go to learn about the reality of what happened during and after 1973 is the Memory Museum, or Museo de la Memoria, in Santiago, built and sponsored by the government of Michelle Bachelet in 2010, who was herself a torture victim and daughter of an air force general who died as a result of his incarceration by Pinochet's men for refusing to support the coup (he was denied his heart medication). The exhibition spaces and presentations are superbly well done and provide an excellent balance between factual reportage and personal testimonies, though some are very hard to take, such as the metal bedframe used for administering electric shocks alongside audio recordings of victims describing what it was like.

A visit to this museum is an intense combination of the visceral and intellectual that lays claim to all your senses and faculties at once, especially the huge cinematic screen where you can relive in black and white the bombing of the presidential palace and hear the tragic final speech Salvador Allende made via the Chilean Communist Party's official radio station, Radio Magallanes.

"I am certain that the seed we have planted in the good conscience of thousands and thousands of Chileans will not be destroyed," he says, during his short six-minute speech. "Workers of my country, I have faith in Chile and its destiny. Other men will overcome this dark and bitter moment when treason seeks to prevail . . . but sooner, rather than later, the great avenues will open again and free men will walk to build a better society. These are my last words," he says, before the recording ends with the sound of gunfire.

Today we know he chose to commit suicide rather than renounce his office, dying of a self-inflicted gunshot within hours of his final address to the nation.

A striking photographic installation at the entrance of the museum records the memorials to victims of human rights abuses that have been erected up and down the length of Chile, though I looked in vain for the location of the one for Limache, because there isn't one. I found this disturbing, years before I knew about the tomato factory, because I had learned early on that of the eighty-nine recorded cases of disappeared individuals in our region, the only one that has been solved to date relates to the manager of the local beer factory in Limache, another derelict eyesore on our urban landscape that is impossible to overlook.

Not only is the former Compañía de Cervecerías Unidas—universally known as the CCU—physically the largest building in town but it was also the heart and soul of many generations of Limachinos' social and economic life, until it was closed in 1993. The factory had its own brass band, football team, and worker's village comprising over 250 dwellings, where the families of former CCU workers live to this day. The closure of the factory left a huge gap in the life of many hundreds of local people, who still have fond memories of an era when Limache hosted the country's most important annual beer festival. It is therefore impossible not to have heard of Jaime Aldoney, because there are simply too many people who remember that he was arrested a day after the coup and never seen again. And yet there is no obvious public memorial for the victims of the dictatorship in the Limache Valley.[2]

For years I thought this might have something to do with the fact that the valley was a favorite recreational place of Augusto Pinochet himself, who loved having lunch at Rancho Carolina, which exists to this day, and who even owned a country estate here (the Quinta Croce in Limache Viejo, today an ugly housing project).[3] Because this is an agricultural valley, society here is also deeply conservative, and my gardener's views are certainly also representative of political convictions that are still mirrored by many of today's landowning and business elites. The voters of Limache have only ever elected right-wing mayors, so there is very little enthusiasm among the powers that be to put up memorials that tarnish the memory of someone they consider a hero.

Despite my best efforts, I was unable to establish if human remains really were found at the place that was once the Parma canning factory. None of its workers or other residents are recorded as missing, so if prisoners were thrown down the well there, they were not local people. The undisputed facts I discovered instead are terrible enough, recorded in great detail in the court investigations that took place between 2006 and 2011.

"Don't hand yourself in," Oscar Farías's good friend, the local head of police, insisted, on September 11, 1973. Apparently, they had many arguments about it that night, but thirty-three-year-old Oscar was certain their friendship and common membership in the local Masonic Lodge meant he was completely safe. They had grown up together, after all, and he was loved and admired throughout the community, not only for being a popular primary school teacher but also for being a highly effective political organizer for the Chilean Socialist Party. He had been the obvious candidate when the nomination came up for the job of government representative (*interventor*) to manage the newly nationalized canning factory after Allende's election. The workers knew and trusted him, and the respect was mutual. He could find no reason not to have faith in his good standing.

So Oscar Farías voluntarily followed the order to hand himself in at the local police station the following day, and when the command came to remove him for interrogation to the naval airbase at the nearby town of El Belloto, his childhood friend, Captain Hugo Cáceres, took personal charge of driving him there, a decision he would come to regret for the rest of his life.

According to official witness Pedro Arellano, what followed after Oscar's transfer to the naval airbase was a horrific three-day period of mental and physical torture that included being exposed to Russian roulette, having a gun held to his chest and head in mock executions, and having cigarettes stubbed out on his flesh.

"I've got that guy well sorted," Navy Captain Pedro Arancibia told Mr. Arellano during his own torture. "I am softening him up and he is spilling the beans, just like Jaime [Aldoney] and your father [the founder of Radio Latina]."

It seems the new authorities were convinced the workers at the factory had been hoarding arms and they wanted to know where they were. It was a popular myth around Limache as well, because piano man Guido told me he remembered their own family friend in the local police telling him the workers had guns they were going to use to shoot his mother.

Meanwhile, Oscar's wife, Emilia Marcone, was going the rounds of the navy airbase in El Belloto, the navy headquarters in Valparaíso, and even the naval sanatorium on the road between Limache and Olmué, without success. No one was willing to tell her where her husband was being held, not even another childhood friend at the sanatorium, who testified that Mrs. Farías's appearance had made him feel very uncomfortable. It was coming up to Chile's National Independence Day, so there were many navy personnel waiting to celebrate, and Oscar had, in fact, been taken to be tortured on the *Maipo*, a vessel in the bay of Valparaíso. Afterward, he was flown back to the Parma factory by helicopter, to be paraded in front of the terrified workers detained there.

For days, their manager's hooded body was brought before them, savagely beaten, and then locked in a tool shed, where they could hear him screaming in pain. The only thing that could end Oscar's suffering would be a confession regarding the arms cache, they were told. But since there was none, no one could help him, and so the workers were forced to witness the mutilation and destruction of their beloved manager, who was also repeatedly submerged in the factory effluent pool and in the cooling pond for machinery. Apparently, he was tied to a rope attached to a helicopter and dragged to the liquid tanks for repeated dipping, where the noise of the helicopter blades drowned out his cries.

Back at the naval base in El Belloto, Oscar was recognized by other prisoners, as well as by friends who were navy officials there, one of whom testified he was shocked at the severity of Oscar's injuries, which included dislocated hands and feet. By this time, he was in such agony he was begging to be put out of his misery, but all the other prisoners could do was carry him into the sunshine during a moment of respite.

After the Independence Day celebrations on September 18, Oscar endured two more days of torture at the factory, before his lifeless body was put in a sack on the back of a pickup truck on September 20 and taken to Valparaíso. According to an anonymous court witness, Captain Arancibia ordered his sergeant to stop the truck en route to Valparaíso and to shoot the prisoner's body, so they could officially claim he had been killed while trying to escape custody. But the sergeant refused, and so did his colleague, until their boss got out of the truck and did the deed himself.

Without the formal witness statements of the court investigation carried out over thirty years later, it would be impossible to record these events, not least because the navy hospital reception papers for cadavers received between September 17 and 24, 1973, were incinerated. Oscar's sister Mirta only found out that her brother had been transferred to the morgue at the Van Buren public hospital in Valparaíso because yet another childhood friend at the navy sanatorium in Olmué took pity on her and told her where to look. When she identified the body, she found he had bullet wounds in his forehead and chest, as well as shown obvious signs of torture, and she knew without a shadow of a doubt he could not possibly have been shot while trying to escape, which was confirmed by another court witnesses who stated Oscar could no longer walk when he saw him in El Belloto, even before being taken back to the factory.

The radio report about human remains being found at the old tomato factory in Limache may well have been made in error. But that at least one person died a horrible death there is true. He lived just a short walk from my house, and his name was Oscar, husband of Emilia and father of Karina. Their civil claim for compensation against the naval captains charged was denied, due to the national statute of limitation for crimes committed over thirty years ago. But in acknowledgement that agents of the Chilean state failed to respect internationally accepted norms on human rights, and of the suffering endured by his family, Emilia and Karina were awarded 100 million Chilean pesos each, the price of a substantial house in Limache at the time.

12

Gracias a la vida

Isabel Allende's novel *The House of the Spirits* is undoubtedly one of the best introductions to Chilean culture you can find. The magnificent roller coaster of stories describing the lives of several generations in the middle of the twentieth century gives you almost everything you need to know about life here, with one glaring exception, and that is the heritage of the Indigenous people, in particular of the Mapuche, who are a significant cultural reality in Chile. Critics of Allende's work would no doubt tell you the absence of native Indians in her novel reflects the racism of her white and mestizo upper class, which is simply blind to the existence of such people, but that is unfair. After all, you cannot write what you do not know, and political correctness is rarely the source of a great read.

Instead, what you will find is a hundred pearls of Chilean cultural truth woven into a tapestry of irresistible human drama and plenty of gritty reality that is unfortunately all too real to this day; in particular the suffocating patriarchy and violence against women. But one of my favorite quotes from Allende's work comes from her memoir dedicated to her daughter Paula, a perfect example of the author's sly wit and creative wisdom: "What actually happened isn't what matters, only the resulting scars and distinguishing marks."

There are those who say scars and damage and woe are the most distinguishing features of Chilean creative art, especially of the music. Almost every song seems to be a lament of some kind and the whiney tone can really get on your nerves. There is none of the steamy passion of the Caribbean here, no sexy Colombian salsa, no sensual Brazilian samba. Instead you have the coy *cueca,* which is the embodiment of repressed desire and dutiful propriety and so boring it has to be dressed up in sickly melodrama and oversized hats for the men. In fact, Chile's national dance is inspired by the jaunty mating ritual of chickens, which is embarrassing by any measure; but what is worse, according to Chilean historian Rodolfo Follegati, is that it reflects a sanitized old-style Chilean society, where people knew their place and doffed caps to their superiors.[1] No wonder then, that it has been confined to clubs and schools, whose students compete up and down the land, especially on Chilean Independence Day, while otherwise popular Chilean dance culture has been overtaken by the huge global phenomenon from Puerto Rico that is reggaeton, which goes to the other extreme by being mind-numbingly penetrative in beat and content and is often extremely misogynistic. Yet its offensiveness is also part of its power and attraction, because it has brought the brutal reality of life for most people in Latin America right out into the open. There is nothing coy or repressed about it, and nothing humble or submissive either; in this it resembles its cousin rap, of which one of the best Chilean artists is Andi Ferrer Millanao, better known as Portavoz. His 2012 hit about inequality, "El otro Chile," spoke to millions and still does.

But Chile did not need to wait for reggaeton or rap to have a fearless artist who spoke truth to power. The visual artist and classic troubadour Violeta Parra was born a century ago in 1917 and ought to be much better known than her Nobel prize-winning compatriots Gabriela Mistral and Pablo Neruda, but she paid the price of independent-minded female artists throughout history, whose free spirit was a challenge to the status quo and whose passion was often mistaken for aggression. She also refused to play the game of polite society and of the male establishment and was therefore sidelined and patronized by the guardians of national culture, even while she was loved by her compatriots the length and breadth of her country for giving the harsh reality and injustice of their lives a voice. A famous early song, for example, was called "The Marriage of Blacks" (Casamiento de negros), in which a newlywed coalminer's wife soon dies of an unexplained illness local cures cannot save her from. One of her rousing late songs begins with the words, "Look how the presidents smile, as they make promises to the innocent" (*Miren cómo sonríen los presidentes cuando le hacen promesas al inocente*); and a song that has sadly become an anthem for current times, even though it was composed over fifty years ago, is titled "Arauco tiene una pena" (Arauco Is Grieving). The song laments the centuries-old injustice perpetrated on the Indigenous Mapuche of the Araucanía Region and reminds the listener that the modern Chilean state continues to perpetuate it by failing to hear their grievances today.

But Violeta Parra was far from being merely a critic of injustice. What makes her beloved by those who have grown up with her music is the universality of her songs, which cover every aspect of the human experience, from love and loss to birth and death, and the deep joy of nature's cycles, sometimes all in the same beautiful tune. They do so most famously in "La jardinera" (The Gardener), which begins with the evocative line "I will cultivate the earth to forget you . . ." Her most famous song of all, however, is the heartbreaking "Gracias a la vida," composed in 1966, a year before she committed suicide, just short of her fiftieth birthday. It is the sum of her lyrical and musical art, an expression of gratitude for everything a human life encompasses that has rarely been matched by anyone else and is no doubt the reason why it is also one of the most covered Latin American songs in history, first brought to an international audience by the North American folksinger Joan Baez in 1974.

The power of Violeta Parra was an elemental force, undimmed by the constraints of an authoritarian and stultifying education and forged on the streets, where she played guitar and sang for money or food to help her widowed mother feed eight children, from the age of twelve onward. The tough exterior she developed was inevitable, but it meant her vehement rejection of injustice and human frailty was often mistaken for violence itself. The novelist Patricia Cerda has children calling her "Violenta" in her bio-fiction. But she literally needed her fighting spirit to survive, and the power of her art is that her songs combine the unique everyday of Chilean culture with the beauty of profound and revolutionary art that speaks to the universal heart. She was as powerful as the wind or a root upending concrete: impossible to ignore and not always convenient, but an enduring force, nevertheless.

Being a live performer was a way of life for Violeta that naturally evolved into composing her own original songs based on her experience of traveling up and down the country singing at local festivals and in circuses, in mining communities, and even in brothels. By the time she was in her forties, she was so well-known she got a slot on Chilean national radio and brought traditional folklore to an even wider audience, going well beyond the guitar-based dance songs of central Chile to include music characterized by Indigenous drums and flutes from the high Andes and Spanish waltzes from the island of Chiloé. She was rewarded with the prize for best Chilean folklore artist in 1955 as a result, and soon she was also being invited to represent her country at international music events from Poland to Paris.

It was the height of the Cold War, and her protest songs resonated just as much with the coal miners of Eastern Europe as with leftist intellectuals in France. Violeta Parra therefore paved the way for what became the socialist movement known as Chilean New Song, which turned the political protest song into a recognized tool for change in her country and made stars (and targets) of her children Isabel and Angel Parra, but also of Victor Jara, Quilapayún, and Inti Illimani in the 1960s and '70s. Many of their songs are national anthems in Chile, sung with the same vibrancy and commitment to social justice that is still so profoundly lacking here.

Without a doubt the finest torchbearer of Violeta's musical art today is the beautiful Pascuala Ilabaca, who is not only a stunningly original performer but also a composer and musical researcher in her own right. But she is not alone; there are plenty of young musicians in Chile who deserve international attention, not least Nano Stern, whose voice speaks to the soul and whose commitment to human rights burns just as passionately as Violeta's. One of his most recent compositions, titled "Regalé mis ojos" (I Gave My Eyes) is a case in point: It is a fund-raising song in support of Gustavo Gatica, the twenty-two-year-old student who was blinded by police pellets during the Chilean uprising that began in October 2019. It is a song worthy of Cat Stevens's finest, with a political message that is loud and clear.

What is far less well-known about Violeta Parra is that she was also an extraordinary visual artist, whose fighting spirit was equally well expressed in unique embroidered tapestries, papier-mâché artworks and sculptures, and paintings. It was a self-taught art with roots in traditional Chilean craftwork, such as the famous embroidered cloths known as *arpilleras*, but what looked like primitive art to establishment figures actually had profound revolutionary depth that was recognized abroad, if not in Chile.

Thus she became the first Latin American artist to be honored with her own show at the Louvre in Paris, no less, where twenty-six paintings, eighteen tapestries, and fifteen sculptures filled two galleries in April 1964. As the Franco-Spanish writer Fanchita González has commented, "She had the gift of simplicity, but that doesn't mean she was simple." Or, as her son Angel phrased it, she was like a shiny black quartz: brilliant and unmistakably authentic.

Her most highly regarded tapestry is titled *Contra la guerra* (Against War) and is easily as moving and profound as Picasso's *Guernica*. Made in 1962, at the height of the Cuban missile crisis, when the world was on the brink of World War Three, it is as universally relevant today as it ever was and a brilliant example of Violeta Parra's unique combination of artistic inspiration and commitment to peace and justice. It is also simply beautiful, and it is shocking to think that this wonderful artwork languished in exile, along with many members of the Parra family, after the military coup in 1973 and was never considered worthy of inclusion in Chile's national museums. Instead, it had to wait for the privately funded Violeta Parra Museum to be opened in Santiago, as recently as 2015.[2]

After her return from Paris in 1965, and true to her commitment to ordinary people, Violeta decided to found a national university of folklore in a giant circus tent erected on land given to her by the mayor of Santiago's La Reina district. The idea was to create an inclusive space where anyone could feel welcome, not only to hear Violeta and invited artists sing but also to see her visual art, and even to learn how to create for themselves. Daytime courses were complemented by musical shows in the evening, and of course there was also wine and food. But, unfortunately, it was impossible to reach the tent by public transport and even though the mayor of La Reina was a fan, his municipal colleagues and the official arts administrators of the capital failed to support her project, so progress was hamstrung by a lack of funds, mainstream indifference, and Violeta's own inability to play the establishment game. Audiences of ten or less were not unusual and, by the summer of 1967, she had to face the fact that her project was a failure, even though the next generation of folklore artists, such as Victor Jara, Patricio Manns, and her own children Isabel and Angel were ever more popular in their own right.

The humiliation was terrible, but what made it unbearable was the enforced solitude, because Violeta Parra was all about sharing and connecting with people to inspire them to make the world a better place and to never accept second best. In a French documentary she was once asked, if she could only choose one of her art forms to work with, which would it be? To this she replied she would simply stay among the people, because they were her only inspiration. She could not give up on that. But without her audience and without the love of her life, who had chosen a different destiny in Bolivia, she must have lost faith and shot herself. Her goodbye note to her brother Nicanor stated simply, "I am not committing suicide for love, but because of the overflowing pride of the mediocre."

But the heart of the matter is contained in another sentence: "I wanted to give, but I didn't find anyone to receive."[3]

Compromise was not in her nature, and when the renowned Chilean philosopher and transcriber of Violeta Parra's music Gastón Soublette was asked what he thought she would do if she could see the state of Chile today, he replied, "She would not tolerate it, she would kill herself all over again."[4]

13

Señora Gilda

Poverty in Person

The first time I answered the bell to Gilda I assumed it was a prank, because there was no one visible when I came to the gate. But then an elderly lady shuffled into view, and thus began a relationship that grew by barely discernible increments into tender affection, over a period of ten years.

"*Buen día*," she said.

"*Buen día*," I replied into the awkward silence.

"*¿Cómo le va?*" How are you doing?

The ritual phrases proper to beginning a conversation with strangers evolved slowly, but I knew better than to rush. Getting straight to the point just isn't how conversations work in Chile. It is important to set a cordial tone and adhere to the proper greetings, followed by general conversation on neutral topics, such as health or the weather, and only then is it polite to say what's on your mind, even if it is just buying a bus ticket. But if the business is to request a favor, this phase can stretch to almost intolerable lengths for the sensibilities of a European or North American, and I have learned the best way to cut it short is a friendly "*¿En que le puedo ayudar?*" What can I do for you?[1]

"*Es que me da mucha vergüenza*"—it makes me ashamed—she said.

But, at last, she explained through tears that she was forced to go begging because her monthly pension of one hundred dollars did not leave her enough to buy food after paying the rent for her room, which was seventy-four dollars, much less to buy medicines or pay any other bills.

I could hardly believe my ears, but the shocking truth is that even as recently as 2019, the average monthly pension for women in Chile stood at $98, while men received an average of $305; and this in the context of a national minimum wage set at $363 for that year, which cannot sustain a single person, let alone a family. Even more shocking is that according to research by the Chilean journalist Alejandra Matus, Chile's private administrators of the compulsory national pension funds established during Pinochet's dictatorship only use a third of their capital to pay out pensions; the rest is used for investments to their own corporate benefit. Thus every formally employed or self-employed Chilean is obliged to cede 10 percent of his or her income to enrich the handful of companies that administer the national pension (with the exception of the wealthy, because a cap on contributions beyond a certain income means they can use the majority of their income as they wish). Equally appalling is that the current pension administrators could easily afford to lift 80 percent of retired Chileans out of poverty by doubling their miserable pensions and still have plenty left over to play the stock market, but successive Chilean governments since the return of democracy have failed to address this scandal.[2]

"I only eat every other day," Gilda said proudly, as if that were an acceptable solution.

But the threat of eviction was not something she could counter and that was the reason she was ringing my bell to ask for help that first day.

"I just need another ten dollars," she informed me, because she had already gathered almost enough to pay the landlady.

"May God bless you," she said, quickly folding the bill into her pocket. "Sorry to bother you."

I assured her she was not bothering me at all and we said our good-byes. But her visit left me feeling very uneasy. I struggled to pay the bills with ten times her income, and even though my living conditions were obviously very different, it still made no sense to me that anyone should be trying to survive at her level, especially since her pension was supposed to cover the costs of her retirement after a lifetime of work and contributions in one of the most highly developed countries in Latin America. I simply could not believe it, but my Chilean friends confirmed it was so and that elder poverty is a huge problem, especially among women, who receive so much less than men. It reminded me of a distressing encounter in Peru—a much poorer country—where my Andean hosts kept their grandmother in a shed at the bottom of the garden.

"She doesn't know how to die," they told me, matter-of-factly.

The shock of my first encounter with Señora Gilda was profound, though it was a long time before we knew each other's names, because her visits were very rare. She must have had a carefully designed schedule to ensure she never made anyone feel she was depending on them, so a few years passed before our conversation progressed to personal information. I discovered the story of her life by irregular installments that were so thinly spread I often needed reminding of where we had left off. Sometimes a whole year passed before she reappeared.

"Remember me?" she would ask with a shy smile, by which time it was our custom for her to come and rest on my terrace, where she accepted a cup of tea or a bowl of soup with a dignified nod.

The cruelty of her landlady was a recurring topic, though not because Gilda brought it up. Rather, it was me who worried the topic like an old bone, trying to fathom how a defenseless old woman could be treated with such a lack of charity and compassion. But she just shrugged her shoulders and looked forward to the day when a death in her neighborhood would allow her to move up the waiting list for free housing. Social services were aware of her case, she informed me, but there were simply too many people in need. I discovered this was true throughout the country; in the southern town of Los Angeles, for example, there were so many abandoned elders in the local hospital that the director had made an official statement via the local radio to implore people to come and get them, because they were blocking urgently needed beds.

There were many things I struggled to understand about Gilda, not least that she had two grown-up children who I assumed could have been helping her, but who did not even know their mother was living in such dire straits.

"Why don't you ask them for help?" I said, but she always shook her head with a sad smile.

"They have their own problems," she informed me, and I never did get to the bottom of what had come between her and her son and daughter.

But the problem is not unusual, and the private charity known as the National Commission for the Protection of Old Age (Conapran) claims there are ten abandoned old people for every child in Chile. It is a shocking statement, but even a small town like Limache has a few well-known elderly street dwellers begging at traffic lights. When we first moved here, there was a one-legged man who used to walk up and down the nearby highway all day long, rain or shine, and I often wondered about him. Finally, I asked the neighbors if they knew his story and was shocked to be told he actually owned a house, but had been thrown out by his own relations.

Family is supposed to be sacred in traditionally Catholic Latin America. Yet it seems modern life and poverty have broken those ties in countless irrecoverable ways, and abandoned children are not unusual, either. For example, I was dismayed to discover that most of the little ones at the local orphanage in Limache were not orphans but rather children whose parents simply could not afford to keep them. A lucky few got weekend visits, as if they were merely at boarding school, but most never saw their families at all and simply graduated to the juvenile home on reaching twelve. The girls' home is right next door to the local prison, which always struck me as a horrible indication of their likely source of husbands.

Señora Gilda's husband, if there ever had been one, never came up in our conversations, but she was proud to tell me she had not always been poor. Once upon a time, she had owned her own house and a business in the coastal city of Viña del Mar and enjoyed a good income making ready meals for the local factory workers.

"My situation now is my own fault," she told me, without a shred of self-pity. "I should have made better plans for my old age," she said.

But her plans had not included getting breast cancer and having to sell her house to pay her hospital bills, which also meant she lost the kitchen where she produced the meals for her customers. Before she even had time to fathom it, she found herself homeless, with no one to take care of her, and no resources to start again.

"A flat has become available for me," she was proud to tell me on one of her visits.

"How wonderful!" I replied. "Where is it going to be?"

The location was not great: a nasty bit of urban sprawl near the industrial shopping center of a nearby town. But there were good public transport connections and a pharmacy within walking distance, so Gilda was happy. Her only challenge was to find furnishings and implements for her new home and I was delighted to be able to give her surplus pots and pans and an old kettle. I insisted she should come back soon for towels and bedding and if she had let me, I would have gladly driven her home with a truck load of goods, but she flatly refused. Her shame was her hardest burden, and I was not allowed to see her world.

One day, she turned up during the winter rains wearing nothing but an overcoat and slippers. Tears followed the creases on her face as she told me drug addicts had climbed in through her window and stolen everything, even her shoes.

"They took my radio," she said sadly, her only company for passing the long hours alone.

Houses in Chile almost always have metal grilles over their windows, but Gilda explained her little apartment was along an open walkway and none of the small bathroom windows next to the front doors were secured.

"They must come and put metal over your window," we agreed.

But, in the meantime, she needed a mattress to sleep on, and she also needed paint, because the robbers had vandalized her walls with obscene graffiti and horrible images. Did I have any old tins, she wanted to know, as I struggled to imagine how she would manage to do the work herself, but she insisted a neighbor was going to help her.

I found some old socks and walking boots that miraculously fit over her bunioned feet and she allowed me to tie the shoelaces for her.

"How old are you, Gilda?" I asked, as I kneeled by her stick-thin legs.

"What do you think?" she replied coyly.

"Seventy?"

"Eighty-two," she said, smiling.

Over a year passed before she rang my bell once more, and I tried not to think the worst.

"Hello!" I said, embracing her in a hug.

"Did you think I had died?" she asked brightly.

I admitted as much, and it could well have been so, as she explained.

"A car ran me over as I crossed the street last year, and I was in the hospital for many months," she explained. "I broke my leg in the fall and they had to insert a metal pin."

Recovery had been long and painful, but because she was now classed as indigent, the hospital doctors had refused to discharge her until she was strong enough to walk unaided with a crutch.

"They made me eat every day and gave me pills for my heart," she reported.

"But what about the person who ran you over?" I asked. "Did he get caught?"

"No. He didn't even stop," she said. "But I was very lucky, because someone called an ambulance and I received much kindness."

Figure 16. Señora Gilda.

Her tale was shocking to me, but she just shrugged her shoulders, the way she always did.

"I am grateful to God for my life every day," she insisted.

"That accident was a test from him and I am very happy I passed," she said. "Look at me! I am fit and well, I can walk, and soon I will be given a new home without steps to reach it."

Her lack of bitterness was astonishing to me, but according to her own values she was a proud survivor and grateful for every small kindness that came her way.

"You have always been so good to me," she said. "God will repay you," she insisted, and it was my turn to be embarrassed and ashamed.

I would have liked to give her so much more, not least to assuage my unease at my own good fortune and every moment of self-pity I had ever indulged in. But where I saw injustice and misfortune, she saw God's will. Where I found reason to be angry and resentful, she found reason to be grateful for every human mercy shown, and I had to accept her placid gratitude was not only a valid approach but even healthy, because it gave her the peace and strength to carry on, however slowly, knowing without a doubt that all would be well in the great scheme of things.

"Will you let me take your photo?" I asked.

I knew it would be the only memento of this remarkable woman I would ever have. She agreed reluctantly, flattered that I cared, and I am so happy she did, because I never saw her again.[3]

14

In the Land of the Monkey Puzzle Tree

When Chileans talk about "the south" they are not usually talking about the roughly two-thousand-kilometer length of territory that extends between the town of Puerto Montt and Tierra del Fuego. They are talking about the mythical land of the monkey puzzle tree that once made up the home of the Mapuche Nation. It is the sacred earth that officially begins south of Chile's second largest river, the Bio-Bio, just over 550 kilometers south of Santiago, where the Spanish conquistadors and Indigenous warriors fought and killed each other over hundreds of years, where treaties were signed and broken, and where European immigrants were given huge swathes of land in the nineteenth century, in return for clearing it for agriculture and settlement, which was, in the end, the most effective way of destroying the native people's hold on their ancestral heartland.

It is a mesmerizingly beautiful region of Chile, where countless rivers spill from the Andes Mountains in glittering threads and foaming waterfalls that often create gorgeous bottle-green pools lined by weeping willows and pebbly beaches on their way to the Pacific Ocean itself, which is lined by eternal sweeps of sandy beaches and lovely rocky outcrops crowded by thousands of colonies of maritime birds.

Between the mountains and the sea lies the undulating central valley that was once covered in dense forests and which, from Villarrica onward, is now a picture-book landscape taken straight out of a Germanic dream. Bucolic lakes and pastures dotted with small towns and villages hum with cattle ranching and agriculture, and many of the original wooden homes built in the style of their Bavarian founders survive to this day. Some famous examples are in the village of Frutillar, built on the banks of the most awesome lake in the area, Lago Llanquihue (860 square kilometers), easily a match for Lake Geneva (580 square kilometers) and with even finer views, if you like your snow-capped mountains alive with volcanic plumes. Truly, it is a land worth dying for, and many have.

But its most emblematic symbol is the famous *Araucaria araucana,* otherwise known as the monkey puzzle tree. Europeans have known it as an exotic feature in their botanical parks, ever since it was first identified and imported in the eighteenth century. But to the Pehuenche, the mountain-dwelling Mapuche, it is a fundamental and sacred part of their lives, providing an important source of food with its seeds that can be roasted like chestnuts.

To see a mountainside of Araucaria trees towering above lichen rocks and gnarly shrubs is one of the most extraordinary sights anywhere in the world, for not only are you looking at a living fossil that can live up to a thousand years but its shape is utterly unique. The candelabra of branches, set up to forty meters above the ground, make beautiful silhouettes against the sky; up close, its prehistoric heritage is made real in its asymmetric armor of bark plates and tightly packed leaves that look like the layered segments of a spikey dinosaur tail.

No wonder it is the national tree of Chile and was declared a national monument in 1990, making it illegal to fell a monkey puzzle tree or even to alter its immediate environment. It was high time to do so too, because 50 percent of this unique species had already been destroyed by uncontrolled logging for construction, due to its perfectly straight trunk. Today, the Araucaria is officially endangered, not only because of human encroachment but also due to climate change that has made the trees vulnerable to fungal diseases as a result of the extended drought in Chile, which has also caused extreme risk from lightning strikes. One such tragic event was the mega fire at the Malleco National Park, where thousands of hectares of Araucaria trees were incinerated in 2015. Due to the extremely slow-growing nature of the tree, it will take hundreds of years for the forest to recover and, in the meantime, the local ecosystem has been devastated and no one goes to Malleco anymore.

But deep in the high Bio-Bio Region, up against the remote mountain border with Argentina, traditional life still goes on, despite the many threats, and it is a great privilege to stay with the local people there to witness the harvesting of the famous pine nuts the locals call *piñones*. The native Choroy parakeets love them too, and their noisy bright green flocks are a good indication of where to search the ground for a generous sprinkling of pine nuts, though failing that, a skillfully thrown set of ropes tied to stone weights is used to fix onto a cone-bearing branch and give it a sturdy jiggle to release a shower of shiny brown lozenges. A riskier alternative, and a skill that has almost died out, is to tie a rope around the tree and a human waist and use a combination of body weight and leg power to lever oneself up the knobby trunk to the terrifying height of the tree's crown. Perched up there, a man can shake all the branches containing sun-ripe cones and empty them onto the distant ground; but one false move, and a broken bone or worse is almost guaranteed, with no chance of modern medicine to help or rescue. The rewards are as great as the danger, however, and a good harvest of pine nuts can provide the foundation of a nutritious diet all year round. In fact, this gluten-free, high energy food has become very fashionable in the high-end restaurants of Santiago, thereby causing yet another environmental threat due to overharvesting of what is now marketed as a gourmet delicacy. Back in the surviving Pehuenche communities, it is simply the foundation of their lives, stored in sacks underground or at the chilled bottom of wells, or oven-baked and peeled to be sundried for turning into flour.

The beauty and abundance of this land of eternal rivers evokes a deeply visceral response in human beings, whether they have Indigenous blood or simply spend their summer holidays there. Nature feels very close and also stirs sentiments that make it seem completely obvious there is a connection between the sparkling rivers below and the Milky Way above, between the sun and the moon, and that we as humans have a duty to respect these elemental and spiritual relationships or perish.

But the Vale of Tears that is Chile's south has been massively compounded by globalization and the huge power of transnational companies to oblige the government to cede control over its own economic and natural resources for the profit of mostly foreign investors. Not that Chile's military dictatorship between 1973 and 1990 needed much persuading. The regime's economic policy was shaped by a firm belief in the privatization of the entities responsible for exploiting Chile's natural resources, and thus the former state department of the National Electric Enterprise was sold off in 1988, with catastrophic social and environmental consequences that are only fully appreciated today, as the impact of deforestation and pollution has translated into seemingly irrevocable damage.

One of the most crass examples of this includes the hydroelectric power stations on the upper Bio-Bio River, which the University of Chile's Energy Research Program condemned as designed to produce electricity "far in excess of what Chile needs in the foreseeable future, and at an unacceptable high social and environmental cost" as early as 1996, while the Chilean government's own National Commission for Indigenous Development judged the proposed Ralco Dam to be illegal, according to the 1993 Indigenous Law Number 19253. The law prohibits the sale, rent, or alienation of Indigenous land. Nevertheless, the project was funded by the World Bank and other institutions, and the Ralco Dam alone resulted in thirty-four hundred hectares of highland river valley being flooded, a site that was once the ancestral home and final resting place for ninety-one families living around the villages of Quepuca-Ralco and Ralco-Lepoy. It also sealed the fate of twenty-seven species of mammals, ten species of amphibians, nine species of reptiles, and eight species of fish. They perished from a combination of the flooding and the illegal logging and concomitant erosion and pollution that resulted from the newly built access roads to areas that were once inaccessible to motorized vehicles. Meanwhile, on the Bay of Arauco at the mouth of the river, which is one of Chile's most important maritime fishing grounds, the lack of nutrients because river sediment is now blocked from reaching the sea has greatly reduced the natural breeding cycles of significant commercial species.

For those who live along those new access roads, the incessant noise of huge industrial-sized trucks thundering past their homes day and night has also drastically diminished their quality of life, both physically and mentally, reminding them every day that they are redundant in this new environment that no longer allows for a pastoral life. In fact, one of the most heartbreaking studies on the region has found that "suicide by hanging from trees was the primary cause of death in 2008 in the Pehuenche district."[1]

Of course the five hundred to one thousand people displaced by the hydroelectric dams were offered both monetary compensation and resettlement elsewhere. But, aside from the nasty fact that those who refused to be deported from their own land were threatened with forced relocation without compensation, this policy completely ignored the cultural context of the Pehuenche's identification with the earth they were born on, which cannot simply be exchanged for somewhere else that holds no historical or spiritual meaning. There were practical issues too, for the alternative lands they were offered tended to be covered in snow for most of the year, making them unsuitable for any kind of crop planting or animal husbandry.

The magnificently fierce environmental campaigner Nicolasa Quintremán succinctly summed up the heart of the issue for her

Perhuenche community when she said, "*¡Nadie vende su madre y su padre!*" (Nobody sells their mother and father). She and her sister Berta almost single-handedly stopped the multinationals in their tracks for nearly ten years, before the Ralco Dam was finally built in 2004. Tragically, Nicolasa was found floating face down in that dam on Christmas Eve in 2013, just a few weeks after her seventy-fourth birthday. We shall never know if she slipped or jumped, or was pushed, but we can be pretty sure she knew where she was going.[2]

Meanwhile, a different tragedy has been playing out over the past forty years in the highlands of the Nahualbuta Range and adjacent coastal regions, where most of the Chilean native forest has been replaced by huge commercial pine plantations that stretch as far as the eye can see in every direction. In fact, according to the documentary *Plantar Pobreza, el negocio forestal en Chile* (Planting Poverty, the Forestry Business in Chile) produced by ResumenTV in 2014, 67 percent of the original forest between the Maule and Itata regions of southern Chile was already destroyed by 1990.

Here too, away from the gaze of most foreign tourists, the local population has been cruelly impoverished by the government's subsidy of massive transnational forestry operations, such as the Arauco Company founded in 1979, that produce wood products for export and look great in Chile's development plans, even while the reality is a devastating monoculture that has not only acidified the soil and sucked the water tables dry but also made life almost impossible for other living beings, including humans who once farmed there. Most of the employment now available is low-paying manual labor that is often not only offered through insecure temporary contracts but also dangerous due to the nature of industrial wood processing. Amputated fingers and even limbs are not uncommon.

The extreme drought of recent years has also caused a massive fire hazard, and powerful winds fan across the land at terrifying speed, burning not just the tinder-dry plantations but also any village that has the bad luck to be in the way. One such place was Santa Olga, a short distance inland from the fishing port of Constitución. I was shocked to see its remains when I visited a dear friend nearby, a year after one of Chile's most devastating fires ever, which resulted in the loss of eleven lives and the destruction of two hundred thousand hectares of land. Where once there had been a logging village comprising a thousand homes, there were empty lots characterized by rubble and heat-warped roof panels of corrugated iron. Solitary new chipboard houses stood forlorn in the stumpy blackened landscape, and the isolated attempts at color in the form of plastic flowers and Christmas garlands were unspeakably sad.

The biggest worry, a year on, my friend Tati told me, was not so much waiting for the government subsidies to rebuild the village but how people were going to earn a living in the future, given there were no trees left to process. Apparently, a local wit suggested creating a "forest fire trail" to attract disaster tourists, who enjoy visiting sites of natural or manmade devastation.

Another friend, who had happy memories of exploring the coast between the city of Concepción and the fishing port of Puerto Saavedra, was shocked by what he found twenty years later, when he wanted to share his love of the land with his young family. Instead of charming villages and beautiful countryside, he found the locals living in extreme poverty; and where once there had been rustic guest houses and interesting traditional customs to share, there were ugly industrial settlements, depressingly impoverished villages, and very few attractive places to stay.

The ruined natural landscape was shocking enough, but what made my friend really sad was to see how the people he met seemed to have lost their spirit. Very few were interested in sharing a friendly conversation with an outsider. This was deeply disappointing for me as well, because I, too, had wanted to travel in that same area in the footsteps of the nineteenth-century British painter Marianne

North, to see the beautiful landscapes she painted in what is now Nahuelbuta National Park.

"If you go very early in the morning, you will probably be safe enough," a friend from Concepción advised, but that was hardly reassuring.

For an additional problem now is not only the environmental devastation but also the violent battle being waged between a variety of armed Mapuche environmentalists and self-appointed freedom fighters and entire battalions of police and army. Atrocities have been committed on both sides, and the situation between the town of Ercilla and the city of Temuco is very tense indeed. Road blocks and burning lorries along the Pan-American Highway are not unusual there, and the level of violence appears to be escalating.

"This is no time for you to be heading south," I was firmly told by worried friends in Santiago.

¡No te metas a las patas de los caballos! (Don't get in the way of horses' feet), as they say in Chile.

15

The Open Wound of the Araucanía

In 2018 the young farm laborer Camilo Catrillanca was hunted down and shot by a police battalion (including helicopters, armored vehicles, and sharp-shooting foot soldiers) because he was under suspicion of having stolen a pickup truck, but that was not his crime. In 2016 the young woman Lorenza Cayuhan was chained to her hospital bed and forced to undergo the most intimate physical examinations related to her late pregnancy in the company of male police guards, and later endured an emergency caesarian with her legs chained to the bed, because she was a prisoner completing her five-year sentence for stealing a chainsaw and other items, but that was not the reason for her humiliation. Just as there was no reason that makes sense to anyone with a shred of humanity for the seventy-four-year-old Nicolasa Quintremán to end up face down in the dam she fought so hard to prevent in 2013.

But these three individuals, and so many other Indigenous Mapuche who are currently incarcerated or have mysteriously committed suicide, do have one thing in common. They are or were all community leaders, or their close family relations, whom authorities wanted to neutralize. The word is so incompatible with the concept of democracy that it smacks of paranoid conspiracy theory, but unfortunately Chilean investigative reporters have discovered that it is an accurate description of the secret policy revealed as "Operation Hurricane," which comes complete with photographic identification of targets, including Camilo Catrillanca.[1] This is important to know, because it places what happened, and continues to happen, within the larger backdrop of the violence and crimes against humanity that are being carried out by the national army and police force in Chile's southern regions of Araucanía, Los Ríos, and Los Lagos, which correspond to the historic Mapuche territory between the Bio-Bio River and the city of Puerto Montt. It is an ongoing situation that is not only damaging the country's international reputation and economy but has also poisoned local society there, pitching mestizos against Indians, landowners against laborers and the landless, entire local communities against their transnational industrial neighbors, and anyone trying to make a tourist dollar against anyone who is destroying the peace and private property.

It is tempting to say the Mapuche are simply yet another Indigenous people on the wrong side of colonial history; that they just need to get over it and move on. But the injustices of the past are brutal and live in the blood of people trying to make a life today, as the violent conflicts in places as diverse as Palestine and Myanmar show. Finding peaceful solutions is virtually impossible, not least because the four pillars of peace are, in fact, justice.

The victors and the vanquished can never be friends, especially not if property and economic resources are at stake, but what makes peace especially unlikely in the Chilean case is that it is not a simple matter of conquest, because the Mapuche Nation never was defeated by the colonial army. Instead, the Spanish Crown was forced to recognize their borders in legally binding treaties—sixty-six no less—and the subsequent Independent Republic of Chile signed another twenty-eight, although they tried hard to persuade the Mapuche leadership to join the dream of a unified Chilean state. But the Mapuche, who were and had always been independent, had no interest in becoming Chileans in the new republic.

Thus the Mapuche became "enemies of the state," whose insistence on autonomous rule was incompatible with the new republic's vision, and a final military solution was found in what the republican Chilean government euphemistically called "The Pacification" of the Araucanía, which they successfully carried out between 1861 and 1883. In fact, it was a war of extermination fueled by a virulent racism and included such famously horrible policies as offering a bounty for every pair of Indian hands or ears delivered. (This was also applied to the tribes on Tierra del Fuego, who are mostly extinct now.)

Afterward, huge tracts of land were offered free to European immigrant farmers, in return for developing and settling the land. But the historian Carlos Contreras Painemal has made the electrifying argument that this entire process was illegal according to international law recognized at the time, as well as according to Chile's own constitution approved in 1833, because the government never officially declared war. Therefore, all territory taken was an illegitimate act and the modern Chilean state extends beyond the Bio-Bio River in fact only, but not by right. The urgent demand to go back to the negotiating table is therefore totally legitimate, even now, but that is not something the current Chilean government is even remotely willing to consider.

Instead, it prefers to frame the Mapuche activists as "terrorists" and condemn them under stringent antiterrorism laws that carry prison sentences far in excess of the civil code applied in all other criminal cases. This is at the root of the open wound that is the Araucanía, and it shames us all. The violent overkill of the authorities in the form of militarizing the area affected by the Mapuche conflict, as well as the criminalization of anyone who objects, even peacefully, is truly shocking, as well as profoundly at odds with Chile's election to the United Nations Human Rights Council, as recently as 2022.

It is not just interfering foreigners and internationally respected organizations, such as Amnesty International, who are saying this, either. Plenty of ordinary Chilean citizens, who have nothing to do with the Mapuche conflict, are just as horrified by the humanitarian crimes being carried out in their name, and even the mainstream press has run articles sharing research showing, for example, that if you are Mapuche, you have a 25 percent higher risk of not getting bail while you await trial, a measure that increased by 40.7 percent between 2007 and 2017. Yet up to 90 percent of the accused are later absolved of the crime they were charged with, by which time they have often spent several years in prison. This is not only an injustice in itself but is also perpetuated in people's lives afterward, as they find it difficult to find employment or otherwise fit back into society.[2]

Perhaps that is why the Mapuche flag has been such a striking presence at every single demonstration since the Chilean uprising that began in October 2019. The fight for social justice includes everyone these days, and people are well aware that not only have the Mapuche been fighting for it longer than anyone else but they also have valuable contributions to make toward finding solutions, if only those in power would listen. But the demands for equal access to health care and education and fair pensions do not fit with Chile's famously neoliberal economic agenda, any more than claims for the restitution of Indigenous land; so while ordinary Chileans have, perhaps for the first time, discovered how much they have in common with their Indigenous neighbors, their chances of success are equally slim, unless there is a fundamental change of heart among the corporate business elite on how the globalized economic system we all live by is managed.

In the meantime, North American sociologist Patricia Richards has brilliantly shown that those in power in Chile prefer to grant "cultural recognition without the economic and political redistribution that would lead to greater equality." In practice, this means plenty of social handouts, empowerment workshops, and subsidized artisan cooperatives that celebrate a multicultural vision of the country, but no structural economic changes that would address the fact that transnational timber companies own three times more land in ancestral Mapuche territory than the original inhabitants, because such changes would threaten valuable exports.

Those who willingly accept the dependent roles offered are

praised and celebrated as *authorized Indians*, in Patricia Richards's words, while those who rebel or insist on self-determination and independent access to resources are labeled *insurrectionary Indians*, who must be dealt with by using the full force of antiterrorism legislation. Chilean protesters caught up in the law since 2019 have often found themselves similarly labeled as terrorists and have suffered very similar human rights abuses. It is a terrifying new world that has its roots in the North American war on terror, in which suspects can be held without charge indefinitely (as at Guantanamo Bay); anonymous witnesses can be used to whom defense counsels have no access; and far longer sentences can be handed out than for the same crime under civil law. In this way, much of what was once ordinary civil dissent in a democratic country has been reconfigured as a criminal act.

The abuse of human rights and the failure to address the impact of climate change in Chile appear to go hand in hand, because both are the result of the country's famously neoliberal economy that puts profit before people or the environment. Many of my friends, both foreign and native, have seriously considered leaving the country because they are so horrified by the way legitimate protest has been crushed, and the shocking speed at which natural resources are being destroyed up and down the country. But where should they go? There is nowhere to hide in our globalized world, so they might as well stay home and work for change in whatever way they can. Certainly the Mapuche have nowhere else to go and know better than anyone that we all just have one earth to live on.

For myself, I have often dreamed of leaving Chile and returning to Europe. But whenever I seriously focus on what I might do once I got "home," a deep wave of wistfulness for South America overwhelms me. I have spent so much time on this continent and invested so much of myself here that my past life has become a distant country I no longer belong to. Like all immigrants, I must find home where the heart is, whether I belong or not, and my little piece of land and the people I love here have taken the best of me.

16

Araña de rincón

The Spider in the Corner

An important reason we chose Chile as the place to make a new life with two young sons was the fact there are no deadly diseases or animals in this country. Except one: the recluse spider (*loxosceles laeta*), known as the "spider in the corner" because it lives in every Chilean home, behind book cases and picture frames, in dark cupboards, and even in the recesses of clothes you never wear. But, in general, this arachnid does not bother humans if left alone and Chileans learn not to worry about it, though it is never wise to have pictures hanging over the bed, not least because they can also fall on your head during the regularly occurring earthquakes.

People are at peace with their spider cohabitants and every child is taught the standard safety procedures of looking carefully before moving old toys in the garage or playing under the bed, and adults know better than to move furniture or wall hangings without using a duster or vacuum cleaner to scare off danger. But one of the hardest things to control is fear when the unexpected happens, and people are more likely to die from the effects of adrenaline on the heart or stupid decisions made in the heat of the moment than of the spider bite itself. For example, when one of my sons picked up an old piece of wood and the dreaded spider ran up his sleeve and bit him on the shoulder, it set off a chain of events that could easily have led to tragedy. It was his left shoulder, nearest to his heart, so I immediately feared the worst, though I tried not to show it.

"Don't worry," I said. "You know the only people likely to die from this spider bite are children under five and old people." (He was twenty-one.)

The local emergency unit at the public hospital kept us waiting for two hours as we became more and more agitated, knowing time was of the essence. But an ambulance arrived with a heart attack victim and others were deemed to be in more urgent need, and so we waited. But the pain on Sascha's shoulder was spreading down his arm and into his chest and the ice pack had melted a long time ago. We decided to try our luck at a health center in Olmué, a twenty-minute drive away, the other end of the valley, but the doctor there refused to treat my son because he had forgotten to bring his identity card. So I jumped back in the car and drove like a mad woman to look for the ID card in Limache, ten kilometers away. The road between the two towns is straight and I was driving at motorway speeds on a country route that regularly includes horse riders and bicycle traffic, but by this time I was in full terror mode, remembering the heartrending story of Kuki Gallman's son dying in her arms after a snake bite in Kenya, and my maternal fear would not let me take my foot off the gas.[1]

Sascha got a shot in his behind and was fine, but recovering our nerves took longer, and I tormented myself with the thought that the most likely fatality that day could have come from my driving. A couple of years later, it was my turn to get bitten, but this time I was not going to give in to fear or waste my time in waiting rooms and decided to use ice packs to stop the poison spreading and stay calm at home. I had not even noticed when the bite happened, which must have been when I put my trousers on, because the site was at the top of my thigh and the first I knew about it was when I felt an itchy, pea-sized lump. There was no pain, and I wasn't even sure it was a recluse spider bite until the next day, when the bite developed a black center, which is a sure sign of venom. By day two, my upper leg was very hot, but since I felt completely well and had no pain, I simply carried on with ice packs at bed time. But the heat and the red discoloration was spreading. By the fourth day, I could have fried an egg on my leg, which had now turned a dark purple color, but still I thought I could wait it out and did not make an appointment to see a doctor until the fifth day, when the darkening purple had spread around most of my upper leg and down to the knee.

"*Esto esta poniéndose feo*," said the friendly Cuban doctor.

That is turning ugly.

"You need to go to hospital," he informed me, "if you want to keep your leg."

"What d'you mean?" I said, treating his comment as macho bravado.

But by the time I returned home with my antibiotic and antihistamine pills, I could no longer ignore the fact that the black and purple patch spreading down my leg at alarming speed was necrosis capable of causing deep-vein thrombosis and even affecting my thighbone, which was beginning to ache, if I was honest. So I asked my younger son, Rémi, to drive me to the accident and emergency unit in a nearby town, where the public hospital had a better reputation than ours. But again we found ourselves waiting for hours and by 11:00 p.m., I decided to give up. The waiting room was packed and, even after three hours, the nurse informed me there were at least seven patients to be tended to before it was going to be my turn. My leg was not a priority case, even then.

The next morning, however, I was feeling decidedly ill and asked Rémi to drive me to a private hospital instead. The waiting room was virtually empty at nine in the morning and I was attended by a nurse and a doctor within five minutes. An echocardiogram was ordered because my heart was hurting and another doctor was called for a second opinion. Still, I was calm; after all, I was not a baby or elderly. But the second doctor took one look at my blackened thigh and informed me I needed to be admitted to the hospital for immediate intravenous treatment.

“Can’t you just give me some pills?” I asked truculently.

“At this stage,” he said, “that would be trying to put out a forest fire with a garden hose.”

“Ah,” I responded glumly.

“If you agree,” he continued businesslike, “I will send over the man from the finance department who will have you sign the payment guarantees, and then the nurses will induct you upstairs.”

It seemed I really was in trouble, though I still could not fathom the seriousness of the situation and was more concerned with the unsightliness of my leg than the thought I might lose it or suffer permanent damage. It was simply too preposterous. I hadn’t even noticed the bite happening, after all.

But my delay in seeking medical help had left me with a very serious problem and the doctors insisted on keeping me on a drip for two days, while I tried to accept their help with good grace and not listen to the proverbial cash till clinking with every additional treatment I received. I knew every swab, needle, and fresh pillowcase was an item going on my bill, not to mention the luxury hotel price for my bed in a shared room and three dismal meals. I would have minded less if I had felt I was getting value for money, but despite the wonderfully friendly nurses and auxiliary staff, I still had to ask for basic items like a towel and soap for the shower, where I had to rinse my neighbor’s blood off the floor before I could use it.

But what if I had been someone who could not afford to pay for this unexpected emergency? The forms I had had to sign committed me not only to paying in full but also to accepting the hospital’s right to sue me at my expense, should I fail to cough up according to their strict timelines. It was a terrifying thought and brought home to me the grim reality experienced by the majority of Chileans, whose national health system entitlement frequently does not amount to the life-saving treatment they need, either because it is not available, if they live far from the capital city, or because they are unable to pay the difference between what the entitlement provides and the additional bills. Indeed, historically, Chilean hospitals were not designed to save people's lives or provide more than basic health care. They were where the poor went to die. (The rich had house doctors and never set foot in hospitals.) This is also why you see so many people with missing teeth, because swift and efficient dental care is usually only covered by private health insurance, which only around 20 percent of Chileans can afford. The average insurance bill for a family of four amounts to the same as most people's monthly income.

Worse, only patients with private healthcare insurance have a chance of surviving long-term or chronic illnesses, and even then the insurance companies find ways to wriggle out of their obligations. Being sent home to die or being trapped in your home for lack of a wheelchair is not unusual at all in Chile, so I was very grateful to be able to pay the $960 my forty-eight hours in the hospital cost me and shuddered to think what the bill might have been had I needed an operation. No wonder there are regular collections and raffles for individuals who cannot afford their medical expenses, but it does not seem right that citizens of a developed country like Chile should have to rely on the lottery of good luck or charity for their health and survival.

Spiders are the stuff of nightmares and fear all over the world, which ecologists have long tried to teach us makes no sense. After all, they provide a useful service by trapping and eating other bugs around the house and their presence outside is a sign of a healthy ecosystem; but in our hygiene-obsessed modern world this is often forgotten and, anyway, most of us would rather not have creepy things nearby. Modern Chileans are no different in this attitude.

Yet in many cultures the spider is also honored in ancient myths and legends, more often than not as a source of wisdom and benevolence, rather than of horror, and so it is among the Indigenous Mapuche, who know the "Old Mother of the House," the spider Llalin Kushe, as the ancestral guardian of all the arts relating to yarn.

She is a feminine power to be loved and honored, which makes profound sense in a culture where knowing how to spin and dye yarn from sheep's wool is fundamental to the traditionally female art of weaving and knitting. The Indigenous poncho, for example, needs to be as delicate and resistant as a spider's web, and just as beautiful. It must be able to withstand the rain and wind, but it must also be convenient to wear and double up as a comfortable bedcover, while the decorative symbols in the weave display not only the artistry of its maker but also her clan's cultural heritage. The best ponchos are therefore priceless heirlooms passed from one generation to the next and worn only on special occasions.

According to the legend that goes with this ancient art, a young virgin was washing clothes in the river one day, when a stranger appeared who ravished her and took her off to live with him in a far-away land. Years went by, until the day he announced he was going on a journey, to the other side of the mountains.

"When I return," he told her, "you must have turned all our wool into yarn."

But the young wife did not know how to spin yarn, because she had been taken from her mother too young, and so she sat by the fireplace and cried.

"Don't cry," said a woman's voice from the fire. "I will find Llalin to help you."

And, sure enough, the old spider came down from her web and told the young woman to observe her.

"You must do as I do," she instructed.

"Watch me," she said.

And from then on, the spider came every evening to work the wool and provide guidance, until the young wife became highly skilled herself and was able to spin all the yarn before her husband returned.

The violence and the survival contained in this legend reflect the reality and needs of traditional life in southern Chile, which is both harrowing and inspirational. Yet there is also tenderness, and one of the loveliest practices born of the spider legend is contained in the initiation rites for Mapuche girls. When they are newborn babies, their hands are traditionally wrapped in webs to transmit the wisdom and art of old mother spider.

It would never have occurred to me to think of spider webs as something benevolent, much less as a substance I would want to have on my skin; but knowing the Mapuche legend of the old spider has helped me feel less repulsed by the countless webs and spiders in my home, and even grateful for a reason to leave them alone and resist the prejudices of modern domestic life. Meanwhile, the dark shadow on my leg faded slowly, over many months, leaving me with just a small red island on my natural skin as a permanent reminder to shake out my trousers.

17

Patagonia

Patagonia is the magic land; a place of profoundly silent nights and days when the invisible power of the wind can knock you over, even wearing a full backpack. The vast scenery of volcanic black mountains flecked with white patches of snow and the occasional gnarly tree recall the giant mastodons and dinosaurs that once roamed here, and it is hard to look where you're going when your eyes are constantly drawn to the monumental horizons. Occasional guanacos (like small llamas) or a lone horseman with his flock of sheep prove smaller life continues, despite the harsh climate that brings everyone to a standstill under a blanket of snow for eight months of the year; but that is impossible to imagine during the lovely seasons of spring and summer, when the mossy plains and rolling hills are covered in wild flowers, the striking red of the Chilean fire tree (*Embothrium coccineum*), and the edible blue berries of the iconic Calafate bush (*Berberis microphylla*). Eat of the berry and you are destined to return, so they say, but you don't need to. Once you have been to Patagonia you can never get it out of your system.

Tourists to Chile often fly straight down to Patagonia from Santiago, without so much as a look elsewhere, which is a mistake. But then the country is so absurdly long, it is impossible to visit every corner, unless you have a lot of time and money. Renting a motor home to explore the famous southern highway known as the

Carretera Austral for a month can easily cost $12,000, for example, and that's without a single tank of expensive petrol for the thousands of kilometers you will need to drive. Consequently, not even Chileans know much beyond the area they live in, and the vast majority have never seen their most famous national park: the Torres del Paine, which is impossible to reach overland from central Chile, unless you cross the Andes to Argentina to find a remote road that will take you back over the mountains once you have reached the Magellan and Antarctic Region, a journey of 2,795 kilometers, which is almost exactly the distance between London and Beirut, and somewhat longer than the route between New York and Mexico City.

It is therefore not surprising that it took five years after our arrival before circumstances allowed me to set off with one of my sons, and what a privilege it was to fly two and a half hours south, to the old sheep station of Puerto Natales on the banks of a beautiful glacial fjord framed by mountains. Our challenge was to hike the legendary five-day W trail, which takes its name from its zigzag route around the famous triumvirate of granite towers often perfectly mirrored in a freezing patch of aquamarine water, to the delight of photographers from around the world.

It was twenty-two years since I had last set off into the Andes with a full backpack, and my fifteen-year-old quickly left me behind, as he strolled without breaking a sweat, where I tried hard not to groan too loudly at the effort of walking uphill with fifteen kilos on my back. But it didn't matter. Both of us were in our own worlds of excitement and anticipation for the days ahead and I was full of gratitude to be back in my favorite environment, and also for the campsite halfway up our route, which meant we could dump all our weight before the final push to the Paine Towers (Torres del Paine), from whence we would simply skip down the mountain gully at dusk.

Giant trees lay upended with their root base exposed in a tangled crown, while others seemed to have been twisted free of their bark like filigree ironwork supporting a green canopy that sighed to a gentle breeze. But the evidence of nature's seasonal violence

Figure 17. The famous Torres del Paine with Sascha.

was all around us in massive rock falls and a wild torrent, and in the magnificent erosion sculptures on boulders the size of apartment blocks.

My son insists to this day that I asked him to carry my day-pack for the last stretch, but that is downright slander. He offered and I accepted, and who wouldn't? But all agony was forgotten as we scrambled over the last massive stone marbles shoring up the crystal water below the famous needles jabbing at the sky. Their gray cliffs were beautifully framed by the cobalt blue above and we quickly took our photos before a scudding cloud could darken the light. What bliss to splash our faces in the freezing lake and lie on our backs to gaze up at the towering view. A lone madman even jumped into the water, but the brain freeze must have been painful, because he was out of there in a flash.

Day two was very different, as we retraced our steps for a while, before following the contours of undulating foothills above a millennial landscape stretching out toward snow-capped mountains beyond several elongated lakes. The milky sky cast a haze over the horizon as we followed a sunbaked track among flame-red bushes and violet lupines. Heather and prickly alpine shrubs alternated with delicate flowers hiding from the wind in the nooks and dells along our path, and it felt good to be taking it easy after the tough hike of the day before. Our campsite for the night was near the pebbly shore of a lake where we gladly soaked our aching feet, and we retired to our sleeping bags in deep contentment.

But the ever-changing weather of Patagonia slapped us to attention the very next morning, when we were forced to decamp in the pouring rain and make an inadequate breakfast on a soggy bench. The damp cold gnawed at our stiff bones as we reluctantly heaved packs onto our backs and wrapped ourselves in plastic ponchos, and we set off in grim silence, which is the only way at times like that, because any conversation is bound to turn into an argument about whose fault it was that this or that got left out in the overnight rain.

Of course we managed to argue anyway, because the trail was hard to find in the increasing fog as we climbed back into the high mountains, and once it began to snow and the weather closed in, we knew we were not going to make it to our destination that day. The famous mountain amphitheater of the high Valle Francés was not going to be revealed to us and, to cap off our frustration, I forgot my camera behind a rock and had to retrace my steps while my son sulked guarding our packs in the gray drizzle.

But day four was a new dawn that changed our dismal campsite into a sun-speckled grove and the bounce returned to our step as we followed a lovely lakeside path and soft leafy tracks through a forest of Lenga beech trees. Birds sang and our spirits flew, much improved by an overpriced lunch at a lakeside refuge, followed by overpriced beer at the hotel and campsite on the shores of Lake Pehoé. Best of all, the hotel had fixed domes on individual platforms for rent, so we treated ourselves to an easy night with the possibility of sun-drying our equipment and sodden clothes. All was forgiven and we laughed at the memory of being strung up to our noses in plastic as we sipped our beers gazing at the jagged massif we had emerged from.

The grassy slope leading down to the waterside sheltered clumps of delicate green and yellow porcelain orchids (*Chloraea magellanica*), and I was astonished to discover such flowers could survive in this frigid land. There was plenty of birdlife too, from stately upland geese grazing on the boggy shore to multicolored ducks and little black grebes ducking their white tufted heads on the astonishingly aquamarine waves of the lake.

Our final treat was a long hike over a rocky pass to Glacier Gray, where we experienced the full force of Patagonian wind that almost had us advancing on our hands and knees with our heads tucked down onto our chests so we could breathe. But what a thrill it was to spot the first ice-blue fragments floating in the dark waters of Lake Gray and then to see the jagged curtain of the glacier itself. A beautiful cabin on the shore provided us with bunk beds that meant we could enjoy this last day unencumbered by camping gear, and it was glorious to be able to relax and enjoy the views without a job to do. It was my son's first experience of Andean hiking and he had loved it.

"We could do something like this every year, if you like," I said.

"No, Mummy," he replied. "You're too old."

Not even a handsome fellow hiker's comment that he had a pretty cool mom to take him on such an adventure convinced him

I was anything other than embarrassing company, but I knew I had planted a seed, and years later he admitted he had had the time of his life.

Seven years later, when my sons were twenty and twenty-two, I invited them for another adventure, this time to follow the southern half of the famous Carretera Austral to the end of the road at the waterborne village of Caleta Tortel. According to my information, it was possible to travel the entire stretch (455 kilometers) from the city of Coyhaique by public transport, which would leave more money for the two designated highlights of kayaking to what is known as the marble cathedral on Chile's biggest lake and traveling via the Baker Canal to the Jorge Montt Glacier that makes up the northern tip of the Southern Patagonian Ice Field.

Coyhaique is "only" 1,693 kilometers south of Santiago, but still it made sense to fly to the nearest airport of Balmaceda before setting off on our journey. Except our trip was almost over before it began, because I had failed to account for the capital's rush hour traffic, which meant we arrived at Santiago airport ten minutes before boarding and it was only by the grace of my best tearful face and no luggage that we were able to jump the queues fast enough to be the last passengers to find our seats that morning. It was another of those moments for silence, and I thanked my lucky stars we were not driving back to Limache instead of spending Christmas in Patagonia.

Coyhaique is the capital of the remote Aysén Region, whose lovely setting in a bowl nestling against a rounded table mountain is tarnished by a shocking brown cloud of pollution that puts it at the top of Latin America's list of most polluted cities. Hard to believe, until you discover that its fifty thousand inhabitants use firewood to heat their homes from April to November and the smoke tends to stay sitting on top of them, due to the cupped position of the town. But on a sunny day in December we sensed little of this deadly problem, and it was easy to thrill at the purple and yellow lupine groves that lined our route into town, and at the grandiose view from the top of the steep street where our hostel sat.

Next morning and with Christmas approaching, we were lucky to get the last three seats on a bus heading south to the village of Puerto Tranquilo, and we settled down for the long, four-hour journey that took in one of the most spectacular routes I have ever seen. The first hour was simply beautiful, winding through the grassy steppes of the Simpson Valley with a broad vista of distant mountains, but when we descended over the edge of an escarpment sweeping down to the foothills of Cerro Castillo (2,318 meters), the endless views of the Cordilleras abutting the Northern Patagonian Ice Field made my heart beat faster and I ached to escape the bus and set off on foot. But this Patagonian journey was all about transport, and the reason we were heading to the village of Tranquilo was to kayak on a tiny section of the mighty Lago Carrera to reach a set of wind-carved rock formations known as the Marble Chapel and Cathedral.

Embraced by the mouths of two small rivers emptying into Lago Carrera, Puerto Tranquilo is an adorable little place of a dozen dirt roads that hardly merits the description of a port. But the Chilean Navy has a station nearby to monitor activity on the water, not least because the eastern portion of the country's largest lake of 978 square kilometers is cut by the border with Argentina, after which it stretches for another 880 square kilometers to become Lago Buenos Aires.

"Are you familiar with using kayaks?" we were asked on the next day's balmy sunny morning.

"Of course," we said, grossly exaggerating our occasional paddle on placid waters.

But the fates overlooked our hubris and granted us an exclusive guide, due to the absence of other customers, and a peaceful lake without the dreaded wind that can whip up fatal waves in a minute; and so just four of us set off to our nearby destination, barely

Figure 18. Instead of Christmas. Kayaking to the marble caverns on Lake Carrera.

a stone's throw from the shoreline, and it was easy to enjoy the views over the lake as our arms got into a steady rhythm, making smooth progress. Soon we were butting against a great head of rock poking out of Carrera's aquamarine water (this is what is known as the chapel), supported by a latticework of smooth marbled arches negotiable on our narrow craft, and it was thrilling to explore the passages and even be able to drift while we found the best angles to photograph this unique natural formation created by thousands of years of wind and water. The cathedral, farther on, was even more fun, as we followed watery passages through marble arches that swept over the water like mighty stone brush strokes of many shades of black, gray, white, and yellow.

As we raced each other back to shore, my heart filled with gratitude as I etched every second onto my memory to recall the joy in future years, when my sons would be gone to their own lives, and also gave a silent bow to a widow's grief and the memory of the visionary environmentalist Doug Tompkins, who had died on this very lake during his last kayaking adventure, almost exactly three years previously, on December 8, 2015. On that day, our guide told us, the weather changed suddenly and the waves were simply too large for anyone to help the seventy-two-year-old back into his kayak, which left no outcome other than a fatal case of hypothermia from the freezing water.

We got a taste of the capricious weather the very next day, when instead of blue skies and glassy waters, the lake turned angry shades of black under rolling clouds, but it didn't matter. We had had our adventure and continued south to Cochrane, the last town before the Baker River cuts its glorious path to the tiny logging village of Caleta Tortel, famous for its stilted walkways built of the local Guaiteca cypress (*Pilgerodendron*) once used to make canoes for the seafaring Chono nomads.

Our luck had held at Lago Carrera, but we all felt the cold breath of death when we flew to what could easily have been our final destination forever, as the madman who collected us in his pickup truck never let the speedometer drop below a hundred kilometers an hour, despite slippery gravel, blind bends, and impossible humps that had us flying at uncontrollable speeds no brakes could have saved us from in the event of an oncoming vehicle or an unwary animal. Obviously there were no working seat belts either, and I spent the entire journey cringing at the thought of us crushed in a pile of twisted metal.

I knew better than to waste words on the man at the steering wheel, but it took all my South American fatalism to remember that if it was our destiny to die that day, there was nothing to be done about it, and if we were going to live, it had already been decided.

Figure 19. At Jorge Montt Glacier on the Southern Patagonian Ice Field.

The worst of it was that we had no chance to properly enjoy the spectacular course of Chile's largest river, nor time to stop and marvel at the beautiful temperate rain forest and the giant leaves of Chilean rhubarb (*Gunnera tinctoria*) that spilled onto the road. Lovely bell-shaped Copihue flowers (*Lapageria rosea*) were just flashes of vermillion in the corner of my eye, as I clutched my seat and willed our suicidal host to slow down.

The next day, when I asked his wife if he always drove like a lunatic, she laughed, and proudly confirmed he was well-known as the fastest man on wheels. Yet we were grateful for his passion for speed the next day, when he whipped us down the salt waters of the Baker Channel courtesy of two giant engines on his boat to reach the mighty Jorge Montt Glacier. Even so, the journey took three hours, and our bodies were stiff with cold and the moist air by the time we scrambled over glistening scree to get close up to

Figure 20. My boys forgive me many things, but not the matching suitcases I got them for our Carretera Austral adventure.

the centuries-old ice crumbling and creaking into the fjord. Again I was grateful, for I wanted my sons to see an example of this frozen phenomenon before climate change eradicates it forever. Just thirty years ago, our journey would have taken half as long, our captain told us. Yet there are still areas of the Southern Patagonian Ice Field that remain unexplored by humankind, one of the few places in the world that may never be known before they disappear.

Happily, a bumbling slow bus was set to take us back to "civilization" and a restaurant for Christmas dinner. But, once more, my planning skills let us down, because public transport ended at Cochrane that day due to the holiday, and we found ourselves joining a desperate handful of other travelers by the side of the road.

Figure 21. You can rent mules to carry your stuff for trekking, though we never did!

"A bit of a lacuna, mother," said my younger son tersely, as we gazed at the silent highway, over three hundred kilometers from our destination.

But the fates and money were on my side, because a man with a van was persuaded to take us to Puerto Tranquilo, and from there we were unbelievably lucky to get the only seats on a tour bus full of day-trippers back to Coyhaique. Journey's end was achieved, though I don't think my sons will ever let me forget the miserable packet of peanuts for Christmas dinner, as not a single restaurant was open by the time we reached the city.

18
The Unluckiest Botanist in the World

Hipólito Ruiz was the unluckiest botanist who ever lived. But he was also the leader of the first European scientific expedition to Peru and Chile between 1777 and 1788, and so he ought to be better known, not least for his heroic endurance of possibly the worst luck suffered by any of the New World's colonial explorers.

Ruiz was a twenty-eight-year-old pharmacology student, who had not even graduated yet when he was chosen as leader of King Charles III of Spain's botanical research project to the Viceroyalty of Peru. But he was the favorite of the director of the Royal Botanical Gardens in Madrid, who took personal responsibility for training his protégé, and his youth was actually seen as an advantage, as so many died during the sea voyage to Peru, which could take between three and five months to cross the Atlantic, travel around the deadly waters of Cape Horn, and then sail several thousand miles up the Pacific shore of South America. The theory was he would be strong enough to survive, and that devotion to his king and country would ensure his more professional French assistant, Joseph Dombey, would be kept on a very short leash and prevented from sending information to the rival court of France. For although the Spanish monarch was one of the greatest supporters of the Enlightenment, he was also in competition with the other imperial powers of

Europe, in particular Britain and France, and his sponsorship of the expedition to South America had as much to do with discovering new commercial opportunities as with adding to the sum of scientific knowledge. A particular agenda was finding valuable medicinal plant cures for European and New World diseases, such as malaria, so Ruiz's pharmacological training was extremely relevant, and his top priority was to study Peru's cinchona tree, whose bark was used to produce quinine, which was then the only known cure for malaria.

Unfortunately, the timing of the botanical expedition coincided with the declining years of the Spanish Empire and the king's death, in 1788. The American War of Independence (1775–1783) took place almost precisely during the years Ruiz was in Peru and Chile, drawing the Spanish Crown's focus north, to deal with the challenge of keeping the Americans out of its territory. Closer to home, the Second Hundred Years' War against Britain drained the royal coffers further, while the French Revolution that erupted the year after Ruiz returned to Spain seriously compromised the publishing program of the expedition's results, further exacerbated by the fact that the dead king's son and successor, Charles IV, preferred hunting to botany and had zero interest in scientific discoveries.

It was hardly surprising then, that by 1801 a new director of the Royal Botanical Gardens in Madrid cancelled the funding for Ruiz's ten-volume magnum opus, originally written in Latin as *Flora Peruviana et Chilensis*, so that only the first four volumes were ever published during his lifetime. Significant portions of his papers and the botanical illustrations made to accompany them were also secretly sold to private collectors and museums throughout Europe by his research partner José Pavón, to cover his personal debts. This has inhibited a proper evaluation of the expedition's discoveries, as well as due recognition for Ruiz himself; though the bulk of his work was, in fact, lost during the original decade-long project, so assessing the value of his contribution to science has always been virtually impossible. Thus an English translation of Ruiz's personal account of his voyage was not published until the twentieth century, and the bulk of his scientific writing remains in Spanish or Latin only, of more interest to historians than modern botanists and vastly overshadowed by the magnificent achievements of Alexander von Humboldt and Charles Darwin.

But while the overall historical context for Hipólito's expedition was very unfortunate, his run of disasters in South America beggars belief, and it is a miracle he did not lose his mind, like so many other Hispanic explorers who merely faced disease, getting lost, or poisoned arrows. If he had known what was coming, he would surely have found a reason to stay in Madrid, but misfortune took two years to find him during what was planned to be a four-year expedition to Peru alone, and things went really well at first. Together with his French and Spanish assistants and two botanical draftsmen, Ruiz not only discovered many new plant species but also recorded and illustrated a vast amount of new information regarding the cinchona tree, including collecting dried specimens and live plant samples that were carefully packed in crates to be shipped back to Spain. But that was the occasion for the first disaster, because the ship carrying two years' worth of work was captured by British privateers who took their booty to London instead, where much of the material remains to this day, part of the great treasure trove that is the British Museum.

The Spanish king ordered his scientists to recover the lost work, which sent the travelers back into the Peruvian mountains, but they were almost immediately caught up in the murderous Túpac Amaru Rebellion of 1780, which left one hundred thousand Quechua and Aymara warriors dead by the time it was quashed by the Bourbon army, and their leader drawn and quartered, before being beheaded when he failed to die. Clearly, it was no time for Spanish botanists to be wandering about the Andes, and the objectives of the expedition had to be completely rethought. The life-threatening danger of continuing research in Peru forced Ruiz to sail south to Chile instead, though he wisely traveled inland to Santiago first, to gather as much information about the country as possible, before setting off to remote areas of interest in the Indigenous heartland of the Mapuche Nation. This region, too, was in danger of violent conflict due to the ongoing Arauco War between the Spanish and the only Indigenous army they had consistently failed to vanquish, ever since Pedro de Valdivia had first tried, as long ago as 1546.

More than two centuries later, the most recent peace accord had only been signed a decade before Ruiz arrived in Chile, but the danger of armed conflict was ever-present due to the colonial authorities' persistent failure to respect agreements made with their official Mapuche and Huilliche counterparts as well as settler encroachment on lands legally forbidden to them. Travel by *huincas,* as European foreigners were known, through Indian territory south of the Bio-Bio River was therefore barely tolerated when Ruiz was there between 1782 and 1783, and certainly never welcome. But his immediate challenge on arrival in Chile was disease rather than war, as a major cholera epidemic not only kept Ruiz in Santiago for much of his time but also sidetracked his French assistant, Dombey, who chose to use his medical training to work in a hospital in the southern city of Concepción for a year.

Ruiz used his time based in Santiago to explore the Andes and coastal mountains of central Chile and, mindful of the king's interest in economic opportunities for Spain, he also surveyed Chile's mineral resources and flora and fauna, reporting on gold and copper mines and on the commercial properties of trees and plants used for construction and as dyes. For example, he noted that the crushed bark of the Quillay tree was used to make a foamy soap that was good for washing clothes and even for cleaning silver and gold, and to fix dyes. Of the many plants that were used for dying textiles by the Indigenous people, he reported that the native Fuchsia shrub was used to make black dye, which is an important color for

Mapuche clothing, along with red. He also noted that the fruit of the Chilean coco palm is used to make a very sweet honey (it is still popular to this day). Altogether slim pickings though, considering his royal commission was by now vastly overdue and incomplete.

The Spanish king's focus continued to be on the commercial possibilities of quinine, however, and so the Ruiz expedition was ordered back to Peru in 1783, as soon as it was deemed safe to travel into the tropical regions of the Andes Mountains again, to gather more cinchona specimens and study their medicinal properties. The original four-year mandate was officially extended, despite the fact that Ruiz and Dombey had fallen out by now and the Frenchman had been given permission to return to Europe, though he was obliged to leave his work at Cadiz to prevent him from preempting the publication of the official expedition report due from Ruiz. This was just as well, because another shipping disaster struck the expedition, and two years' worth of collections gathered in Chile sank in a shipwreck off the coast of Portugal, leaving only Dombey's impounded crates to await review, at some uncertain point in the future. Yet the most mind-blowing calamity of all was still to come, during the final three years Ruiz spent working in Peru.

Even today, the journey by road from coastal Lima to the central-eastern mountain town of Huánuco (1,898 meters) takes over eight hours, but it must have taken an eternity on horseback in the late eighteenth century, when the Ruiz expedition traveled there. Nevertheless, it was the designated area for their research, because the steep cloud forests perched above the jungle on the eastern side of the Andes were once the natural habitat for the many different species of cinchona trees and shrubs they were required to find.[1] Thus, based at the remote Mácora Estate, Ruiz and his companions cut paths through endless wet and muddy ravines to record and collect the botanical specimens they needed to examine.

According to the records, Ruiz was plagued by illness and fatigue the entire time and petitioned the king for permission to return to Spain. Eight years had passed since he had left Madrid, after all; but another two years went by before his request was processed and, in the meantime, he just had to get on with it. The subtropical environment and basic living conditions on the farm must have been miserable. But when the local manager accidentally burned down the farmhouse containing the scientific results Ruiz and his colleagues had so arduously worked for, his spirit was utterly broken. In his personal recollection published much later, he wrote, "The fire burned down whatever clothes and luggage I had taken to Huánuco for my use; all the natural products collected on those mountains for two months; the diaries of three and a half years; botanical descriptions of four years among which there were some 600 observations recorded in previous years, as well as additional notes recently corrected."

The loss was incalculable and also included all his plant pressing and drying equipment, valuable scientific reference books, and his entire research record of his years in Chile. The personal disaster was undoubtedly crushing, but the weight of responsibility as official expedition leader must have given him nightmares that were in no way relieved by the fact that he was not personally responsible for any of the failures that had mounted up over the years. Luck just was not on his side, but at least he did live up to the official hope he would survive the ardors of the expedition, unlike one of his botanical draftsmen, who may well have died of shame for not being at the farm the day it burned down and dropped dead of a heart attack aged just forty-one, before he could return to Spain.[2]

The Royal Botanical Gardens of Madrid eventually received 150 new genera of plants and 500 botanical species new to science as a result of the Ruiz expedition. But the fifty-three crates containing eight hundred original illustrations, dried plants, seeds, resin, and mineral samples resulting from the two years of research carried out in Chile were claimed by the ocean; the vital early research diverted to London by British privateers remained forever out of reach; and the collections that went up in smoke in Peru must have haunted Ruiz for the rest of his life, as he tried to write up his manuscripts from the tiny portion of personal papers he had managed to salvage from his eleven years in South America. Not surprisingly, the expedition's results were eclipsed by those of others, who were lucky enough to return to Europe with more concrete material that allowed them to present a higher caliber of work, and Ruiz had to content himself with the minimal reward of being elected to the Royal Academy of Medicine in honor of his achievements. No royal pension or other forms of recognition were forthcoming.

Hipólito Ruiz lived another twenty-eight years after his return from South America, his only consolation in obscurity being that he did not have to endure poverty as well. Instead, he completed his degree and lived comfortably from the income generated by a pharmacy he inherited from his uncle, and no doubt he did his best to ignore the political turmoil and cruel fates that overshadowed his life. But at least he was allowed to live in peace, unlike his philistine sovereign, who was forced to abdicate by Napoleon in 1808; and unlike his French assistant, Joseph Dombey, who was kidnapped by British pirates in the Caribbean and died their prisoner on the island of Montserrat.[3]

19

September 11

September 11 has been a fatal anniversary in Chile for almost exactly five centuries, ever since Michimalonco's warriors burned down the first incarnation of Santiago on that day in 1541. But of course the most significant date for Chileans in recent times is September 11, 1973, when the democratically elected government of President Salvador Allende was terminated by military coup, to be followed by the murder of 3,227 citizens during the seventeen years of dictatorship that followed. According to the country's own truth and reconciliation report (known as the Rettig Report), 2,125 people were officially executed, while 1,102 are recorded as disappeared. But the suffering extended to many more people, not least the 28,459 acknowledged victims of torture but also to the friends and family of each and every one of those individuals, who have had to live with the traumatic legacy of their lost or damaged loved ones. The costs of this horror include damaged relationships, because plenty of people have never been able to heal their psychological and emotional trauma, destroying the fabric of countless Chilean families.

The other side of this reality comprises the many thousands of people who were employed in the systemic violations of human rights between 1973 and 1990, from torturers to cleaners, drivers to gravediggers, caterers to prison warders; not to mention the combined personnel of the army, navy, air force, and police. If you consider that Chile today only has about nineteen million inhabitants, it is probably fair to say there is no family that does not carry some kind of scar or dark secret relating to that history, but very few are able or willing to talk about it.

For example, I know a man in his sixties who was taken away and tortured when he was fifteen, yet he has never had a conversation with his parents about it. Other family ties have been permanently damaged by political exile, which affected an estimated two hundred thousand Chileans, and even those who have come back to Chile since the return of democracy have found true homecoming an unattainable mirage, for the country and ties they left behind no longer exist. The dream of recovering their lives has been shattered by the fact that Chile has moved on without them and their old stories are not always welcome either, because they are too upsetting, too difficult, or too inconvenient. Others, who have returned to offer their professional skills, have been rejected by an ugly combination of envy and resentment from those who lived through the dictatorship and didn't get the chance to obtain fancy degrees in Europe or the United States. Getting a job or even voluntary work has been a struggle for many returning exiles, and I know several Chileans who have given up and used their foreign passports to go back to where they came from with their hearts broken, yet again.

One of Chile's best-known folk bands is a case in point: Quilapayún (which means "three beards" in the language of the native Mapuche) were successful proponents of the left-wing New Song Movement prior to the coup. They found themselves stranded on tour in Europe in 1973 and were lucky enough to be offered immediate asylum in France. When it became possible to return to Chile, however, several band members found it impossible to rebuild their lives and went back to France and their French families. Today, there is a Chilean Quilapayún and a French Quilapayún, both still much loved, but the split was very acrimonious and fans have had to choose between two versions of one of their most important cultural treasures. The same has happened with the even more famous band Inti-Illimani, which, after surviving exile in Italy, succumbed to a nasty litigious split resulting in Inti-Illimani Historico and Inti-Illimani Nuevo, as well as countless bereft fans.

Honoring the past and letting it go is unfinished business in Chile, so I was astonished and glad to know an important effort to create a space for public ceremony takes place in Limache every year on the anniversary of the coup. The event is organized by the local branch of the Communist Party, and though the commemoration is not promoted in the public media, much less in the town's schools or colleges, my good friends Howard and Caroline are old stalwarts, and I felt honored when they invited me to join them.

According to local lore, the Limache Valley may well have been the birthplace of the military coup, for many here believe Allende's opponents met to plan their strategy at a country estate near the village of Quebrada Alverado. It is certainly true that the big landowners—including Agustín Edwards Eastman, who is known to be behind the involvement of the CIA in the coup—were staunch allies, not least because they had all lost substantial amounts of property under the agrarian reforms carried out by the socialist government. The Eastman estate, for example, reached from Limache all the way to the coast before the Allende regime confiscated large portions because they were not being cultivated for food production. Today, only the main house, known as the Casa Eastman, survives, with plans for its transformation into Limache's newest cultural center.

The possibility that networking barbecues (or *asados*, as they are called in Chile) between likeminded opponents of the Allende regime occurred in the Limache Valley is not at all far-fetched, considering that such gatherings are the most important way people get things done in Chile, to this day. For example, the father of my children spent five years taking his CV to universities in several cities, but he did not get a job until he met the wife of a decision-maker at

Figure 22. Playing at the gates of the former canning factory in Limache.

a local asado. Chileans call it a *pituto*, which literally means a connecting plug, though it is generally understood to connect people, and everyone knows it is the only way to get ahead. Who you know is much more important than your qualifications, and definitely the only way you will solve a serious problem, including an unpopular president, it seems. The notorious Chilean press secretary of the military junta, Frederico Willoughby, admitted as much, when he said he and his friends targeted potential supporters by inviting them "to go hunting together or share an asado," and he also admitted having several lunches with navy captains in Valparaíso, who were ferociously anti-Allende and may well have had something to do with the assassination of his naval aide Arturo Arraya Peters

Figure 23. Sharing memories of 1973 at the gates of the CCU.

in July 1973, before he could become the next rear admiral of the Chilean Navy and hinder their plot.[1]

This might also explain why the antenna of Limache's foremost radio station was the first to be bombed as early as July 26, before being completely destroyed at 4:00 a.m. on September 11, 1973, over seven hours before the presidential palace was attacked. The navy airbase is just down the road at El Belloto, and it was an easy matter for the plotters to take out Hugo Arellano's socialist propaganda tool to prevent any warnings being broadcast that might have ruined the *golpista* plans (*golpe* means hit/coup).[2] The navy sanatorium on the road between Limache and Olmué was also an important support base, which later doubled up as a detention center.

Figure 24. Bearing witness at the Limache cemetery.

You would never know anything terrible happened at the sanatorium today, just as there is no sign or indication of what occurred at the sites of the Parma factory and the CCU. Birds chirp, weeds grow, and abandonment cloaks the buildings in quiet oblivion. But a few dozen local inhabitants have stubbornly conducted their own memorial every September 11, beginning at the cannery, where I joined a small crowd of men and women old enough to remember what happened here almost fifty years ago. A Chilean flag and a large portrait of Salvador Allende were mounted on the peeling wood of the factory gate, while some participants inserted roses and carnations between the planks. Gradually, an intimate circle drew close around the gate to hear the testimony of one of the workers, who had been forced to witness the torture of his manager, Oscar Farías; this was followed by supporting speeches by local representatives of the current socialist and communist parties in Limache. But the most moving moment was the impromptu appearance of a young man with a violin, who turned out to be the grandson of Jorge Villarroel Vilches, a truck driver from neighboring San Pedro who disappeared in 1974. The boy and his brother had come to offer a musical tribute, which drew spontaneous applause, followed by much hugging.

People reconvened at the other end of town, outside the locked gates of the CCU, where a bow-legged old man was helped to stand before the crowd and share his memories of arrest and torture, as well as his belief that the stress and fear of those years were to blame for his daughter's untimely death. Again, there were flowers and flags and Allende's framed portrait to cover the desolation of the physical space, but there were also smiles along with the tears, expressions of gratitude for the precious chance to share spontaneous stories, and open declarations of common humanity. Strangers embraced in acknowledgement of their mutual history, and it was touching to be welcomed among them to bear witness.

Finally, a long cavalcade of cars proceeded to the municipal cemetery, where the flower sellers were ready with spectacular bouquets or fragrant individual roses for the self-appointed guardians of memory, who gracefully made their way to Oscar's tomb for the final speeches on this special day of remembrance. I felt sorry for the family trying to bury a loved one nearby, who suddenly found their ceremony dwarfed by a flag-bearing crowd, but there were no complaints. For once, an aura of respectful goodwill outshone stony civility and I know I wasn't the only one who came away with a deep sense that I had taken part in something profoundly important and worthwhile.

In fact, one local couple was so moved by the young man's impromptu violin performance that day that they decided to contact the Memory Museum in Santiago to help create a lasting public memorial for the victims of the dictatorship in Limache, and thus the Residencias de la Memoria project was born. The idea the museum came up with was inspired and financed by a German organization dedicated to identifying the homes of victims of human rights abuses, for the purpose of installing paving stones in their memory there. But in the right-wing political context of Limache that was a very tall order indeed, requiring two years of hard diplomacy and research by Waldo García and his wife, Verónica González, who not only had to find out where the town's known victims used to live but also negotiate with their families and the people who live at those addresses today. The museum nominated Waldo as the official memory ambassador of Limache to give him formal credibility, but it was still an uphill struggle to sweet-talk town councilors and, most importantly of all, to persuade local residents at four specific addresses to accept a memorial plaque outside their front door. Worries about opening old wounds and dividing the community were a problem, but so was understandable fear at the four homes, whose inhabitants did not relish the idea of having their privacy invaded or becoming targets of vandalism. Meanwhile, Verónica took on the delicate work of tracing the families of the deceased or disappeared, which was also very challenging, because not everyone wants to be found, much less take part in public ceremonies with people they blame for what happened.

But Waldo studied law and Verónica was a social worker, so between them they had just the skills needed to make this project work and, on January 19, 2018, local dignitaries and representatives of the Santiago Memory Museum, alongside friends and families of the four Limachinos officially known as victims of the dictatorship, gathered to see four circular memorial stones set into the town's sidewalks.

"Truth and justice has been honored today," said the regional governor.

But the most memorable words that day came from Amanda Rojas, the wife of Carlos Vargas Arancibia who, prior to Verónica's research, had been one of Chile's official *detenidos desaparacidos* (detained and disappeared), whose last known address happens to be right in front of Limache's new police headquarters, at Calle Prat 395.

"I have to admit," she said, "that I have lived with a deep bitterness these past eighteen years." She continued, "I thought he had abandoned me and my two-year-old baby. I was just a young woman and believed all the lies I was told about his disappearance. So I am eternally grateful to each and every one of you, because this project has created a permanent memorial for us. And I am also grateful you have helped us know the truth."

For without Verónica's painstaking research, the witness who saw Carlos executed at the naval airbase at El Belloto would never have been found, nor persuaded to come forward with information that proved Amanda and her child were not abandoned for another woman. Instead, he had been taken from her by her complicit father's navy colleagues. A different horror to live with, but at least one based on facts.

20

House of Shame

Domestic Violence

A woman I know in Santiago remembers standing outside the bathroom door when she was about five years old, listening to her father raping her older sister. She remembers her sense of impotence and fear, knowing something bad was happening but not knowing what to do about it. But she also knew it was not something to talk about. When she was a little older, she remembers her father holding her head as he did unspeakable things to her. By the time she was seventeen, she ran away to make a life as far away as she could get. On her return, two decades later, she discovered all her sisters shared similar memories of their father, who was dead by then. They decided to confront their mother, but she insists to this day that she knew nothing, though I sense her own need for sanity and peace has always blocked her path to the strength she would need to face her daughters' violation by the man who fathered those girls in her own bed. It is too terrible to contemplate, not least because there is an inescapable element of collusion. The silence of a lifetime can never hide the fact that she must have known about the abuse in her bones.

What happened to those sisters is terrible on any scale, but what is truly horrible is to discover how common their fate is in Chile. I have met many other women of all ages who have been sexually abused at some point in their lives but have never felt free to do anything about it. In fact, as recently as the 1970s, women were obliged to obey their husband's will by law, and sexual abuse or violence within the family was simply not a matter for the courts. A popular phrase you will hear fathers saying to their children to this day is "*¿Quien manda?*" (Who's in charge?), and no doubt they say the same to their partners in the privacy of their own homes. A man I worked with even admitted as much, when he told me that while he regretted hitting his wife, he felt she had given him no choice, because she refused to do what he wanted. However, when she finally left him, taking their children too, his strongest emotion was self-pity, and there were plenty of people who thought he had every right to that feeling.

Incredibly, while it was traditionally a woman's duty to be faithful to her husband in every way, a man could only be found legally guilty of adultery if he was caught with another woman in his own home. Sex outside the marital home did not count and was nobody's business, either, an attitude that persists and makes for a thriving industry too, because the ubiquitous motels you see along every highway in Chile are not hotels as such but sex refuges, where couples go to enjoy themselves in private. Brothels exist as well, of course, but they are a minority business in a country where illicit sex is so normal. One sex hotel in Santiago, which was even immortalized in Isabel Allende's novel *The House of the Spirits*, was still the most desirable place to go for a sexual adventure when I first lived here, and some couples even openly chose it for their wedding night. In real life, it was called the Hotel Valdivia, and its claim to fame lay in the Hollywood-movie-style rooms, each a magnificently mirrored world of anything from an Egyptian palace to a tropical hideaway or Chinese fantasy, with real fountains and naughty hot tubs to go with the porn and discreet parking enclosures to protect identity. When it closed down in 2013, there were many nostalgic sighs, and it even made the news on the BBC World Service.

Sexual and physical violence exists everywhere, of course, but in Chile it has such a long history of being condoned by the Catholic Church and the law that it is deeply ingrained in society. Only recently has it been openly challenged.

"Sex outside marriage is a sin, except if it is between a priest and a boy," read a recent placard at a protest march.

The statement is designed to shock and provoke, but the sting in the tail is that court cases have proved it accurately reflects what has been going on behind closed doors all over the world, including in Chile. So the agony is not just a female experience either but has affected young men from all walks of life. In fact, my friend's theory about her father is that he himself was raped as a young schoolboy and that his pedophilia was the result of a censored experience that poisoned his soul. She could be right. Certainly there are far more male victims of sexual assault than official records will ever show. The shame of it is simply too much for most people, especially in a country where men are supposed to be virile pillars of strength and authority.

Some people call it machismo, though that fails to adequately reflect the fact that homosexuals, as well as anyone else whose identity and sexual orientation does not fit traditional norms, are at risk of private attack and public humiliation. So it is not just an offensive attitude; the problem goes much deeper, in a society where gender relations have historically been organized according to supposedly God-given physical differences between men and women. This is why, for the longest time, the law and the Catholic Church confirmed men as the natural authority of the family unit, because they were stronger, with women being seen as simply the "weaker sex."

It is a concept that has such a powerful tradition even women believe it and take pride in their silent suffering and endurance. It is their badge of honor, and those who rebel are traitors to their sex, which means there are still plenty of women of all classes and backgrounds in Chile who will have nothing to do with feminism of any kind, because it feels "unnatural" and threatens their sanctified role as long-suffering survivors. They are proud of their sacrifices and stoically give up their freedom to deal with whatever calamity comes their way, be it the result of their daughter's unwanted pregnancy or poverty from being abandoned by their husbands. To question their choices is to undermine their entire reason for being, and they proudly denounce young rebels as weak scroungers who don't have what it takes to be real women. This even extends to sexual abuse, which far too many women still consider to be a fact of life they have to put up with; they are just as liable as the local police station to blame the victim, if she dares to make a public statement about her experience.

Academics recognized this phenomenon long ago. It was described best by Jo Fisher, in her book *Out of the Shadows*: "The female equivalent of *machismo*, known as *marianismo*, refers to the exalted respect women command as mothers and has sometimes led to the misconception that countries such as Paraguay and Chile are 'matriarchal' societies ruled by women."

But young women in Chile today don't want to suffer in silence. They don't want to suffer at all, and it is notable how many Chilenas under the age of thirty prefer to become single mothers rather than to burden themselves with a husband or partner. This is not because they don't like men but because the deal they get in the gender role game just isn't fulfilling. But it is still a tough choice to make, because very often they do not have support from their own mothers or other female relatives and must stand alone. The Limache Valley is full of young single mothers, for example, as well as countless women of all ages who no longer have a male partner for one reason or another (usually because the men have either left or died). The poverty and loneliness they suffer is horrendous, especially among the elderly, who rarely have access to social networks.[1]

The shame of it is that single women of all ages are expected to put up with their lot in silence and in private, and there is huge pressure to simply stay out of sight and out of society's mind. This particularly applies to women over fifty, who are regarded as past their sell-by date and as people who should ideally disappear altogether if they don't have unpaid child-minding roles to fulfill for someone. It is bad form to make a spectacle of yourself by trying to have a social life or enjoying yourself in public, and when you are that age, married women make very sure not to invite you for dinner, in case you try to steal their husband. But the sad fact is their husbands are probably already unfaithful and, if truth be told, so are they. Sexual fidelity is a rare thing here, as I know from countless raucous conversations around "witches" bonfires where women gather to let their hair down and enjoy some female solidarity.

I certainly find the Chilean capacity to laugh in the face of adversity inspiring, but I can never get over the very real suffering that so many women endure here. The statistics speak for themselves. According to the Educación Popular en Salud (EPES), one of the leading public health organizers in the country, fifty women were the victims of femicide in 2020. Many more suffered violence, which includes financial threats as well, because these not only have a direct impact on their ability to survive and take care of their children but also cause huge distress and are a form of bullying and humiliation.

In fact, according to one investigation, an additional 151 attempted femicides failed in 2020, which is the highest figure recorded for the previous eight years and is undoubtedly directly related to the social unrest and global pandemic. Every one of those numbers represents someone's personal horror story, but I have no doubt the statistic is just the tip of an iceberg of suffering and discrimination.

There is one woman in particular I can never forget, and she was the mother of three who decided to set herself on fire on the plaza in Limache, one autumn evening in 2015. A shocked bystander tried to smother the flames with his coat, but she died a horrible death anyway. The next day, I went to buy the local newspapers to discover what had brought this young woman of thirty-two to such a level of desperation that she would commit such a horrible act on herself, but there was nothing, not a single word.

Instead, I went to spend a silent moment at the place where she burned herself to death, to remember a human being who was not newsworthy but whose passing I felt ought to be marked by more than the patch of blackened grass and paving that was already being eradicated by park maintenance workers. It was heartening to find I was not the only woman who felt that need, and our little group of four stood silently, shy smiles acknowledging our common need to bear witness.

Nothing marks that spot to this day, but I think of her every single time I walk that way to the weekly market and wish there was at least a flowering bush or flowerbed to remember Janet López Carrasco (as she was later identified by the regional press). I do not know what suffering led her to end her life and leave three children without a mother. Some say she suffered from depression, but to imply mental illness is always an easy explanation when women fail to behave in the manner expected of them.[2]

21
Robinson Crusoe Island (Juan Fernández Archipelago)

Brian Keenan and John McCarthy called their Chile book *Between Extremes*, which was undoubtedly related to both their experiences as hostages and free men and the nature of the country they chose to travel in as tourists, and it is indeed an apt title. But Chile is not just extreme in all the obvious ways of geography, politics, and culture; it also evokes extremes of emotion, in terms of both sorrow and sheer joy. For many of the foreigners who live here, that emotional roller coaster comes from their friendship with the intensely complex people, but for me it is the dramatic landscape and the infinite opportunities for solitude in nature that provide a never-ending inspiration and addictive challenge.

I love the unpredictability that comes with finding myself alone in nature, which may or may not be welcoming, and am entranced by the potential of being thrown on your innermost resources of physical and mental stamina as you attempt to reach a summit or a distant lake. It fulfills my deepest competitive urges to prove myself against a challenge I have always set myself but which often takes on unexpected dimensions and difficulties. In truth, much of that applies to any situation or relationship, but I prefer the comforting illusion of control when I am the one choosing the destination. Others have often marveled at what they think is my courage, but nature is far less terrifying than people, as far as I am concerned, and nothing offers me a deeper peace.

Of course solitude is only fun or meaningful if you have a choice. In any other circumstances it is a punishment few can stand, and being banished has always been the most terrible fate of all, reserved for political enemies, criminals, and those with incurable infectious diseases. But the drama of survival and endurance makes for great stories, of which perhaps the most famous is the fictional story of Robinson Crusoe, written by Daniel Defoe almost exactly three centuries ago.

In the novel, the island Robinson Crusoe finds himself on is tropical. However, the island the real-life person who probably inspired the story ended up on is part of a jagged volcanic trio, 362 nautical miles off the coast of central Chile. Officially, it is called the Juan Fernández Archipelago, though the main island was renamed Robinson Crusoe in the 1960s, to attract tourists.

Much closer to the mainland than Easter Island, these islands are nevertheless far more remote and difficult to reach, because the tiny planes that go there are usually full of islanders and the changeable ocean weather often makes it impossible to fly at all. A plane went down as recently as 2011, with no survivors and no explanation, though a Chilean pilot friend told me it was probably the victim of treacherous air currents that can take inexperienced pilots by surprise on the approach to landing on the very short runway set on a rare piece of flat headland jutting out to sea.

Passengers need quite a bit of courage, and not only because of the notoriously dangerous airstrip but because landing by air is not the end of the journey. Upon arrival, travelers have to brave an open boat for an hour, to reach the only settlement where they can stay, at the grandly named Cumberland Bay. That is where the Scottish privateer Alexander Selkirk was marooned at his own request in 1704, and even though he instantly regretted his decision and signaled desperately for his shipmates to come back, his captain was glad to get rid of him and carried on, out to sea.

For the young Alexander Selkirk was famously cantankerous and had been in trouble for fighting his entire life, beginning with beating up his own brothers, back in Scotland. Becoming a professional seaman and officially sanctioned as a pirate to harass the Spanish fleet on behalf of the British Crown was therefore the perfect job for him. Except he could never get on with his superiors either, it seems, and hence his rash decision to choose abandonment over continuing on a ship he considered unseaworthy was accepted with indecent speed, though his captain did leave him with a musket, hatchet, knife, cooking pot, a Bible, bedding, and some spare clothes, which was a pretty good start for a castaway.

Selkirk had the means to shoot the feral goats left by Spanish seafarers as a source of protein for passing ships, and he also drank their milk. When his ammunition ran out, he found other ways to hunt the goats, and when his clothes and shoes wore out, he used their skins to make himself a new set of clothes. He also made fishhooks and caught spiny lobsters, which are the most famous export from the island to this day. So life was not that bad, and certainly a lot better than the experience awaiting his captain. For Selkirk had been right about his vessel needing repairs, and it sank off the coast of Colombia, where survivors were immediately taken prisoner by the Spanish authorities and sent to Peru, to spend miserable years in Lima's dungeon.

Of course Selkirk had plenty of accidents and mishaps and suffered deep loneliness, by his own account, which all made for perfect material for the famous novel *Robinson Crusoe* (published in 1719), written by Selkirk's contemporary, the English author Daniel Defoe, who added his own inventions to suit his story. There was never a "Man Friday" in real life, for example, nor is the Juan Fernández Archipelago tropical; and there are no sandy beaches for mysterious footprints, only rocky volcanic shores with thousands of sea lions and fur seals. In fact, the only humans Selkirk spotted from his famous lookout were Spanish sailors, from whom he needed to hide, because they would have taken him prisoner.

What bliss it must have been to spot a British privateering ship on February 2, 1709, after four years and four months left to his own devices; and the crew, which included people who knew of his marooning, must have been utterly amazed to see him too. By all accounts, he enjoyed being a celebrity for his miraculous survival and lived life to the full, whenever he was back in London. But he also wrote that he never again found the "tranquility of solitude" he had known on his island outpost, and he spent the rest of his life as a professional sailor, until dying of yellow fever off the coast of Ghana aged just forty-seven.

Many others have been left to rot on the Juan Fernández Islands over the centuries, beginning with the Spanish royalists who found themselves on the wrong side of the Chilean War of Independence and, most recently, criminals and political prisoners of Pinochet's military dictatorship. But that part of the islands' history is well and truly over now, and what they are most famous for today is being a unique UNESCO World Biosphere, with more endemic species than even the Galapagos Islands, where naturalists and divers can find species no other place on earth can offer.

The statistics themselves are stunning: 80 percent of the fish species are native to this tiny spot on the globe, and nowhere else; and the island forest is a staggering 100 percent endemic, made up of tree species that only exist here. The incredible variety of ferns as you walk on the steep trails of the deeply crevassed mountain landscape is also amazing. Some look more like trees with an elegant umbrella of filigree fans than the ground-level greenery you would expect. The moist world of the forest is also home to a long list of unique birds, of which the most exciting is a red humming bird aptly called the Juan Fernández firecrown. Another unique bird that prefers the treeless headlands overlooking the ocean is the pink-footed shearwater, which is also desperately endangered because it nests in burrows on the ground that are vulnerable to invasion and damage by other animals, like rabbits or goats.

Sadly, the negative statistics are also stunning, because of the 131 unique plant and animal species found only on here, many are threatened with extinction from invasive species that were imported by humans over the centuries. The earliest imports were the goats and rabbits, but three species of rat also hitched a lift on those early galleons, and their descendants now eat up to 40 percent of the seeds in the native forest. Another disaster are the invasive plants that are suffocating the local flora, in particular the strawberry myrtle (*ugli molinae*) that can grow up to three meters tall, and the wild blackberry that has created impenetrable thickets all over the island of Robinson Crusoe, where only 20 percent of its unique forest currently survives. But they are just the most obvious threat, because there are no less than ninety-five introduced species on the islands that not only outnumber the local flora but will ensure their complete destruction if nothing is done to prevent it.

Distant Selkirk Island still has twice as much native forest as the other islands, but a scientific survey carried out as recently as 2018 found that unless drastic action is taken, most of the unique flora and fauna on the archipelago—including the red hummingbird—will disappear from the face of the earth in less than a century. Such drastic action has already been taken, as when the entire rabbit population of the smallest island, Santa Clara, was eradicated using poison, though how that was safely done is a mystery to me. But it was a success, and the endangered shearwaters, for example, increased their breeding pairs by almost 40 percent in just three years.

The fur seal colony is another success story, which has gone from the brink of extinction to a colony of over a hundred thousand, and one of the most exciting experiences on the islands is to snorkel or scuba dive in the company of these playful animals. The real Robinson Crusoe Island may not be tropical, but the pristine underwater world is still as magical as it ever was, as the natural murals created by thousands of mollusks, corals, and sea urchins are fanned by undulating seaweeds and the eternally moving ocean brings wave after wave of a miraculous cast of sea creatures.

22

Chile Rising, or the *Estallido Social*

Sunday, October 27, 2019
2:45 a.m.

I go to bed with the sounds of a thousand voices screaming for a better Chile; I wake up with the roar of the crowd reverberating around my skull. Day and night, for a week now, I keep hearing the sound of the crowd and the slogans being called up and down the country:

¡Renuncia Piñera! (Resign Piñera!) is one of the most common.

¡Pacos culiaos! (Fucking police!) is another one.

And then there are the many individually scrawled signs crowding my mind's eye:

Thank you for having the courage to do what we have been too scared to do, these thirty years—though Chile's military dictatorship ended, many of its undemocratic measures persisted.

I am demonstrating for my auntie, who cannot pay her medical bills—referring to the massively inflated price of many drugs.

I am here for my child, who has no future without a decent education—only those with money can afford a halfway good education in Chile, and even the private schools are often below the standard of a mediocre European school.

I am more scared of my ex than you!—referring both to the

extreme brutality of the police, who have not hesitated to beat, arrest, and humiliate ordinary citizens at peaceful demonstrations, and to a culture where men still feel free to abuse women.

It's not a drought, it's robbery—referring to the fact that Chile's water is a privatized asset and to a decade-long drought that has led the big landowners to divert rivers and groundwater to their avocado plantations, even while entire villages are without drinking water in the central region, where most of the population lives.

I step outside to catch what is going on in my little country town, only to find the eerie silence of the curfew we have lived with for almost a week, since the president of Chile brought in the military to reimpose public order and enforced strict rules on our movements and right to assemble in public. A state of emergency and a curfew were declared in Santiago on Saturday, October 19. By Monday, it included all of central Chile, where I live.

As a foreign resident, I do not have the legal right to attend protests against the state, even while I have the right to vote and must pay taxes, like every other Chilean citizen. If I or my sons are arrested and deemed to be acting against the interests of the state, we can be deported and lose everything we have—the life we have made, our home, our friends. (This is based on a law passed by General Pinochet in the 1970s that has never been repealed.)

The shock of the absurdly violent response to legitimate protest has been one of the most disturbing experiences of this past week: Water cannons attacked handfuls of stone-throwing youth in my country town of no more than fifty thousand people. Armored tanks and iron-grilled police vans stood guard at our picturesque train station. Gas canisters were shot at men, women, and children I see every day, going about our business on the high street. Young men and women my sons know as friends have been beaten up with truncheons and are covered in black-and-yellow bruises. Receiving those released from custody has become a new morning routine this week.

But there are those who have not been released, and whose

whereabouts and condition are not known. Disturbing lists of women are circulating, including their names and ID numbers, and the date and time they were last seen. I learned a new word this week. *Desnudizacion*: to force someone to get naked, which is a common humiliation tactic at detention centers.

The shadow of the 1973 military coup in Chile casts a heavy pall over the confrontation between ordinary people and the state today. The genuine fear in the bones of every Chilean over fifty is palpable. They lived this as children, saw their loved ones taken away, never to be seen again; were conscripted against their wishes; saw bodies floating in rivers; and were tortured and humiliated. No wonder people here don't like to speak their mind, much less complain in public. In this context, what is happening in Chile now is almost unbelievable. Only the untainted courage of youth can explain it.

A moment of joy this week came from the spontaneous concert of banging pots echoing throughout my neighborhood on the first evening of the curfew. A series of known rhythms matched each other across the barrio, and there was a sense of solidarity in the air that was extremely heartening. Meanwhile, our streets were an eerie ghost town, where fugitives ran from tree to tree and police cars cruised silently to catch them out.

The bravery needed to step up for what is right in Chile is of a whole different order than that needed for others living in a so-called democratic country. The criminalization of even peaceful protest is a trend throughout the world, but in Chile it has a long history, and no one walking the streets here can ever forget it. But the schoolchildren and students leading this massive wave of civil unrest were not even born in 1973. The events from that time are just stories to them, even if they are the stories of their aunts and uncles, mothers and fathers, grandparents and old neighbors. But, unlike them, they don't care.

The reason this *estallido social* (literally a social eruption or explosion) cannot be stopped with even grotesque violence on the part of the state is that young Chileans know they have no future the way things are. They have nothing to lose except their lives and the profound nihilism born of their situation and this Latin culture we live in means a bullet in the head is not the worst that could happen. The worst would be living in fear and knowing you are permanently excluded from the wealth of this land. Even on a good day, a Chilean will tell you there is no point worrying about your safety. If it is your day to die, you will. If it isn't, you won't.

The spark that lit this powder keg was an increase in the price of metro tickets, in a country where those on a minimum wage have to spend between 15 and 20 percent of their monthly income just to get to work and even those earning an average wage in Santiago city see up to 12 percent of their income swallowed up by public transport. But this conflict is about so much more, most especially the fact that the cost of a week's shopping at the supermarket is about the same as it is in Europe or North America. Yet half of all working Chileans earn less than $575 per month; 70 percent earn less than $750. Hence the slogan "It is not about 30 pesos, it is about 30 years," referring to the neoliberal economic model imposed by Pinochet's government. While that model has been the basis of Chile's economic growth, it has also created a shocking imbalance of income opportunities across society and income inequality has hovered between 53 percent and 56 percent since the 1980s, which puts Chile among the world's top ten most unequal countries for income distribution. In practice this means a school teacher, for example, knows it does not matter how hard she works; she is unlikely to get a mortgage to buy her own home or be able to pay for her children to go to a good university. The same goes for the majority of Chileans, while the wealthy minority, who almost all live in the exclusive Santiago neighborhoods of Lo Barnechea, Vitacura, and Las Condes are almost literally enclosed in another world, protected by armed guards and electrified fences, to which only maids and those with prior appointments can gain entrance.

I oscillate between the elation of the new community spirit and the courage of the crowd—which increase with every day—and the fear and paranoia of becoming a target. Much worse, I am afraid of losing my precious sons in this storm that has already cost a classroom full of lives. Over twelve thousand Chilean troops have been deployed against their own people.

Today, on Sunday, October 27, the state of emergency has been lifted, and last night there was no curfew, for the first time in a week. How strange it already feels to be allowed to walk out in the evening. But this battle is not over. It is just a lull. There is too much at stake for everyone involved, as indicated by President Piñera's astonishing public turnaround, in which he asked forgiveness from the Chilean people and offered immediate increases to their pathetic wages and pensions. But words are cheap and so was his offer. People want action and genuine change, and they want it now.

Sunday, November 3, 2019
3:00 a.m.

A headless monster is fighting a one-eyed cyclops in Chile right now, and the outcome is far from clear. The fury unleashed after three decades of repressed anger and hate harbored by people trapped in a straitjacket of inequality and incensed by the unanswered questions of what happened to so many of the tortured and disappeared during the military dictatorship is awful to behold. The peace and prosperity that has made Chile one of the wealthiest and most highly developed countries in Latin America has come at a terrible price to natural and human resources, and people literally can't take it anymore.

The older generation, who lived the coup and survived the dictatorship, never dared to think a popular uprising like this could happen in Chile, even if they secretly wished for it. For them, it was enough to defeat Pinochet in 1989 with the famous "No" campaign against continued military rule. The fact that Pinochet's constitution and the privatization of everything from public services to natural resources continued after his departure was simply the price for peace. No one over fifty today seriously thought anything could be done about it, even while they agreed that life here is monstrously unfair. How could it be that politicians earn *forty times* the minimum wage of those they are supposed to serve? The monthly salary of Chilean parliamentarians ($23,000) is vastly higher than that of even any of their European colleagues.[1]

When we emigrated to Chile in 2006, it seemed obvious that political violence would erupt one day, given most ordinary Chileans had no hope of ever sharing in the benefits of their country's wealth and progress—a fact we discovered early on, when we tried to find a state-run school for our young sons.

Massive personal debt is the order of the day in Chile, and paying for the shopping at the local supermarket by credit card is normal. But the interest rates are much higher than in England, and personal debt is a terrifying shadow for a huge number of people, even if they do try to make a joke of it.

"If I owe the bank a hundred thousand, I can't sleep," someone once said to me. "But if I owe a hundred million, the bank can't sleep!"

Our intention to escape a class-based society and rampant consumerism in Britain to build a more meaningful life in Chile was soon laughable. Except it wasn't funny, and despite my profound gratitude for the material advantages we have been able to enjoy here these past thirteen years, our privilege has never sat well with us. We did not come to Chile to be trapped in the values of nineteenth-century Britain, where people still doff their caps to their betters and the rich treat their staff like throwaway contact lenses.

My sons quickly learned Spanish and to move in the different worlds of both their privileged classmates at the private Waldorf School and their skater friends on the town square from humbler backgrounds, but in the context we find ourselves in now, it is terrifying indeed to be the "rich bastards in the big house" living on a street where, higher up the hill, there are those still living as illegal squatters with a dirt floor and no running water.

Thankfully, the raging mob has focused on corporate symbols

of wealth, attacking supermarkets, municipal buildings, and the now famous metro stations in Santiago. But I know property not far from my home was indeed attacked, and the owner's car parked on the street was burned. The postman tells me this is more likely to do with a drug vendetta and that I have nothing to worry about. People know us, and I am grateful for my sons' street credibility and my own intermittent participation in the local neighborhood association. Despite being an outsider, I am an acknowledged member of the community, which I feel protects us—at least from most of the local haters.

But the hate and violence is real, and the most horrible thing about this past week has been the news that (according to legal researchers at the University of Chile) thirteen women have disappeared since the start of the civil unrest, just over a week ago. Meanwhile, the Chilean Prosecutor's Office states twenty-three people have died throughout the country; and so far 437 gun-shot injuries have been officially recorded at hospitals, although everyone agrees there are likely to have been far more in reality. Another statistic that makes me shudder is the 127 people who have lost one or both eyes from being shot in the face with rubber bullets, and whose sight could not be saved because the local state hospitals don't have the materials they need to do their job. Medical students have been complaining about the lack of even basic facilities like rubber gloves for some time, but no one was paying much attention to them till now.[2]

One of the most moving images in the news this week was the crowd of victims with bandaged eyes standing in silent protest, arms raised in the air, in front of the capital's central police headquarters. Another was the silent march of women dressed in black to mourn the dead and remember the disappeared. Silent candlelit vigils have also been held on squares throughout Chile, and most Chileans will tell you they are profoundly disgusted by the violence that has occurred on both sides of the conflict. People are especially sorry for the small independent businesses that have been caught up in the looting over the past two weeks, whose owners have neither the means nor the insurance to begin again.

Many lives are on hold right now, with public and private institutions either closed or working intermittently. Vast numbers of self-employed people have been unable to earn a living since Chile came to a standstill, two weeks ago. Even big business is suffering, and the country's prestige took a huge blow when President Piñera cancelled the forthcoming World Trade Summit and the Global Climate Conference (COP25) in December. A scientist friend of mine told me her university paid three million Chilean pesos (about three thousand dollars in US money) for her to attend the climate conference, money they are not at all sure will be returned. Meanwhile, hotels and restaurants will stay empty and the economic consequences for the entire country are severe. Yet I only know of one person in my large circle of friends and acquaintances whose focus is on her personal loss rather than on the greater good we are all hoping for. There is a huge desire for real change. No one wants this brutal moment in Chile's history to have been for nothing.

I learned another new word this week: *sororear* (literally "to sister"), which I heard at the first women's forum held in my town square. Up and down the country, in every town and village and city, people are coming together to learn the political facts and skills they will need to be part of the solution in Chile. Over half the population failed to vote in the last election, with the younger generation a particularly notable absence. But now everyone, especially the young, know that being part of the political process is a fundamental step toward peaceful change, even if it is beginning to dawn on people that it will be excruciatingly slow.

"This won't make a difference to my life," said the local postman the other day. "I will still get nothing but a miserable pension. But hopefully my son will have a better chance."

A lot of talk revolves around the constitution written by the military government, but the facts of life that really bother people—the

Figure 25. Limache protest during the estallido social in 2019, © Aulikki Pollak.

compulsory pension scheme, the privatized healthcare, the education system—are governed by specific laws that have nothing to do with the constitution. So how to change that? Academics are coming to the fore to offer free popular educational seminars, and social workers are meeting in neighborhood meeting halls and in parks to give people the basic information they lack. Even the vocabulary is strange: What is a *cabildo*? What is the difference between a popular assembly and a parliamentary vote? Where is the power? Many people have no idea, but suddenly everyone wants to know, while the official government continues to trail behind the spirit of the times, with officials from the president down making speeches that convince no one. The mass demonstrations continue.

These public acts of protests have no leaders (hence I call them a headless monster). Each one is unique and called into being by the wildfire that is social media. And yet there is a recognized routine—a

Figure 26. Shrine to the victims of political violence.

place where marches begin and where they end, though the details in between can spontaneously vary. I join a march convened by my sons' skater friends. We wait beneath the clock tower by the train station for enough people to gather, all uncomfortably aware of the red eye of law hanging above us, filming everyone. These cameras have sprung up all over Chile in recent years, proudly announced as effective security measures, but few people are convinced. They are surveillance tools and the police freely admit they are gathering material to hunt down ringleaders as soon as the country gets "back to normal." I pull my hat further over my face and try not to look up, but of course it is far too late for that. We have been identified long ago, just going about our daily lives, as we have been filmed entering shops and banks, crossing the street at major junctions, or taking the metro. There are security cameras everywhere these days, and in some villages they have even cut ancient trees to clear the view, an act of municipal vandalism that has upset even the local fascists, who love their beautiful town squares as much as the next person.

The march sets off at last—a noisy but peaceful crowd banging pots and drums and shouting the familiar slogans:

¡El pueblo unido jamas será vencido! (A people united will never be defeated!)

Meanwhile, a couple of policemen on motorbikes redirect the traffic ahead of us. The crowd spontaneously heads up a side street and we all snake past nervous shopkeepers and more timid residents clapping discretely by their front doors. Not everyone has found the courage to march in public, even now.

We end up at a major road junction on the edge of town, where we are encouraged to lie down on the hot tarmac, completely blocking the traffic. But drivers are so used to these events by now that they simply wait patiently or honk in support. Amazingly, the armored police van we can see a block away keeps its distance, and it is not long before we are on our feet again and marching toward the bridge leading over the river and toward the town hall. But again the crowd wrong-foots the police and turns off onto a road doubling back to the train station, and their roadblock is left redundant. I realize with a sinking heart we are heading for the local police station instead, where I had already seen men with riot shields and heavy armor standing at the ready.

"Don't go there," I beg silently, but the crowd moves steadily toward the shotgun-clutching riot police.

Our young leaders wave their arms to silence us, and we advance like a herd of nervous antelope. Hundreds of men, women, and children come to a standstill within spitting distance of people wearing helmets and bulletproof vests. We raise our arms in a vulnerable gesture of peaceful intent and my heart beats for my son, steps away. Fear sits heavy in the air. A mistake on either side could turn this into a disaster, and I try not to picture the potential bloodbath.

Instead, someone walks the narrow space between the police and the crowd and harangues the force staring us down.

"Give me your name," shouts the protester.

"We want to know who you are!"

"You belong to this community! What are you doing, beating us?"

But the armored barrier standing at the ready remains silent and unmoving and the standoff ends with the protesters turning their backs on the police, singing and chanting. The crowd heads off up the high street and the relief we all feel twists our guts, but I am so grateful and proud to have been part of this moment. It could so easily have gone badly, but it didn't!

¡El pueblo unido jamas será vencido! the crowd shouts defiantly, as I peel off toward the safety of my home, where I can hear the music and drumming for several hours more. The most famous song people are singing at these protest marches is one by Victor Jara, murdered during the coup in 1973. The refrain is *el derecho de vivir en paz*—the right to live in peace—and it brings tears to my eyes every time.

A few hardy people decide they must march the ninety-two kilometers from our town to the capital, to protest in Santiago itself. It is a tough hike that involves crossing the coastal mountains and walking along the dry and dusty Pan-American Highway, but they arrive in less than twenty-four hours. A hundred cell phone cameras record the unfurling of homemade banners in front of La Moneda, and also the water cannon and teargas that is quickly used to disperse this harmless band of walkers. The people are not welcome at the presidential palace and the repressive response to their protest symbolizes the gulf between ordinary Chileans and those in power. People say the reason the police in our small town have not acted with the same aggression as in the capital is because their families live here and everyone knows each other. The fear is

Figure 27. Papier-mâché eyeballs strung up over Pio Nono Bridge.

on both sides here, whereas in Santiago the forces ranged against protesters have no personal connection and feel free to shoot into the crowd with impunity. It is an "us and them" situation, and the crowd is the enemy.

"We are at war," President Piñera said during the first week of this uprising, in an eerie repetition of an identical phrase used by Pinochet after his coup.

But this time the statement was immediately repudiated, even by Piñera's own military generals. It does, however, belie the attitude of many politicians, and the Chilean government shows no sign of genuine willingness to change.

Figure 28. The Virgin of the Barricades.

Sunday, November 24, 2019

The grinding routine of daily demonstrations, violence, and destruction is taking a heavy toll on people's nerves. Meanwhile, Amnesty International has officially confirmed what many feared: that the Chilean security forces are carrying out a policy sanctioned by the president of injuring demonstrators "in order to discourage protest, even to the extent of using torture and sexual violence."[3]

23
Paradise Valley

Valparaíso

Valparaíso's faded charms are best enjoyed from a distance and with the lights low, though the truth is it was never lovely, much less a "Bay of Paradise." Instead, it has always been something infinitely more interesting: a place of dreams and broken hearts where you might find every kind of thrill you ever wanted or die trying.

Once upon a time, during its brief golden age in the second half of the nineteenth century and up to the opening of the Panama Canal in 1914, the port boasted huge warehouses filled with goods from all over the world, from the finest Scottish whisky to French corsets, and the bars and cafes were awash with big spenders and colorful women, even while the barren hills above were crammed with the slums of the working poor, whose only consolation for slogging up the steep ravines to their rickety wooden homes was the stupendous view of the Pacific Ocean. Some things never change.

Back then, at a safe distance from the pungent aromas of fishy garbage and urine around the port, Joshua Waddington and his associates made a killing selling prime lots on the central promontory overlooking the shore that is now the historic heart of the city. Known as Cerro Concepción and Cerro Alegre, these adjoining barrios are what tourists come to see today and, as in the past, they are a world apart from the rest of the city: a beautiful island rising above an ugly sprawl of urban dereliction and crime. The mostly British and German families that once lived there have long gone, though it is very much a foreign enclave once again, ever since the city's elevation to a UNESCO World Heritage Site in 2003, which attracted massive investment to restore what was once a quietly decaying residential neighborhood. The tourist boom unleashed by that event has been amazing and fortunes have been made and lost, just as in the past.

Initially, there was no public access to this haven of mansions and picturesque streets illuminated by gas lighting. But in 1883 the first rack rail elevator—known as Ascensor Concepción—was inaugurated, and the numerous versions of this first marvel of invention are still one of the great thrills of exploring Valparaíso. To climb into the fragile wooden cabin mounted on its oily rail and be noisily hoisted above the port at an almost vertical angle is both terrifying and exhilarating. As far as I know, not a single one of the city's historic elevators has ever fallen, but you can't help wondering if your ride will prove the exception to the rule, and it is always a huge relief to step onto firm ground. The difference between the exhaust-choked thoroughfares at sea level and the breezy cobbled streets of Cerros Concepción and Alegre is also a revelation that never fails to get cameras clicking. Here are the famous rainbow-colored mansions coated in corrugated iron against the notorious horizontal rain, with their beautiful marbled entrances and immaculate polished wood. Here, too, are innumerable beautiful and charming cafes and restaurants, where you can eat some of the best seafood dishes anywhere in the world and enjoy sunset drinks from all kinds of creative perches, ranging from the cool terrace of Hotel Fauna to the historic black-and-white diamond patio of the Brighton, or the glassed galleries of the magnificent Hotel Gervasoni.

To come to Chile without enjoying a mouthwatering dish of grilled razor clams in parmesan sauce or a hearty slice of pan-fried conger eel with sautéed potatoes while enjoying the ever-changing

Figure 29. Classic tourist shot of Valparaíso.

scenery of Valparaíso's bay is unforgivable; and you do not need to be wealthy to give yourself this pleasure either. If the immaculate version of the city is too much, head down to the countless restaurants frequented by locals near the port or, even better, hop on a bus to the seaside neighborhood of Chacabuco and find a plastic table with the same divine food and equally fine views at Caleta Membrillo.

Of course the gentrification of a few limited sections of the city has not been achieved without the usual controversies and clashes of interest between local residents who have been priced out of their homes and newcomers who pay silly prices for almost any ruin. It has also magnified the horrifying social inequalities of the city, where thousands on the many hills and escarpments still live without basic municipal services and transport and remain almost entirely excluded from any urban regeneration plan. The ever-present dangers caused by deprivation and poverty are therefore no surprise and go a long way to explaining the long history of protest here. Add a volatile population of over one hundred thousand university students and the cauldron of rebellion is always hot.

One of the unique features of the city that was born out of the protest movement, however, is the striking graffiti and street art, and interest in this aspect of Valparaíso has spawned an entire tourism sector of its own. Certainly for me, no tour of the city is complete without a look at some of the streets adorned with the best and most colorful murals left by artists from all over the world. Some building owners have even paid for the designs on their houses and the art form is far beyond what some might think of as vandalism. Others have simply installed their own creative statement. My absolute favorite was an old television set painted with the slogan *apaga la tele, vive tu vida* (turn off the TV, live your life), which no longer exists, though the t-shirt derived from it does. Others I adore are the house-sized mural rising above the terrace of the Belgian Hotel Café Via Via at Dimalow 166, and the bizarre design on a building facing toward the Customs House near the container port, which bears the stylistic mark of Inti Castro, one of Chile's most famous urban street artists. There are literally countless others, and not just on Cerros Concepción and Alegre either. The vertiginous street of Hector Calvo climbing up to Pablo Neruda's house on Cerro Bellavista, for example, is an urban art gallery all on its own and also passes a side street to the open-air museum of murals known as Cielo Abierto (open sky), which is simply another residential street that was transformed as long ago as the 1990s.

Despite all of its horrendous problems of urban decay and inequality, Valparaíso continues to be one of the great cosmopolitan cities of the world, which is why the flow of visitors and newcomers is never-ending, though the warnings not to stray into the narrow staircases and alleyways alone should always be heeded. Those who ignore that advice are liable to be picked off by professional thieves who spend all day scanning the famous hillsides with their binoculars for unwary tourists strolling off the beaten track.

Of course fleecing foreigners is a local sport that began with the earliest shipwrecks, and the impact can be devastating for the victims, even if they usually get away with their lives. But there are plenty who have lost everything, or at least a very substantial part of their savings. For example, I knew a Canadian woman who bought an old house to restore, only to discover that it needed to be completely demolished. Or take the European couple who came to create their dream boutique hotel, only to find the access road blocked by roadworks for two years and levels of crime that simply took the fun out of trying to make a life. It does not help either that Valparaíso's tourist zones are now so overflowing with hostels, bars, and restaurants that it is impossible to earn a living, a problem that has been magnified a thousand times by the shocking violence and destruction the city has experienced since 2019 and by the pandemic that erupted in 2020. The city is in urgent need of life support.

Yet many people insist on clinging on to whatever life they have in Valparaíso, and it is certainly true that it is not only a city of survivors but also home to an amazing spirit of creativity and resilience that shows itself in an infinite variety of artistic expressions. Santiago may well be more sophisticated and glamorous these days, but Valparaíso is irresistibly fun, a place where people know how to laugh in the face of misfortune and party like nowhere else in Chile (the closest North American equivalent would be New Orleans). The biggest and most famous of those parties is of course New Year's Eve, with its unforgettable firework display over the huge bay that arches from Valparaíso all the way to the upscale resort of Reñaca, sixteen kilometers to the north. Only Sydney can rival the pyrotechnic explosion that fires off from half a dozen boats anchored offshore, and to witness that display is to experience one of the most exciting spectacles you could ever see.[1]

The city oozes life at its most raw and has an addictive quality you either feel or you don't. There is no middle ground. So while it is not the place to come if you are offended by the filth, poverty, and deplorable lack of urban planning, Valparaíso speaks to anyone with a romantic or creative spirit. Its outrageous shapes and colors and impossible living conditions are the very thing that inspire artists, whether they are painters or photographers, musicians or poets, and the well of stories is endless. It has captured the imagination for generations, from the famous Chilean cartoonist universally known as Lukas to the quirky French printmaker Loro Coirón, whose intricate black-and-white artworks are sold in any self-respecting tourist shop, and many others besides.

Sadly, when we first went to Valparaíso with our young sons, I was firmly told, "Mummy, don't ever bring us here again!"

But then we had made the beginner's mistake of thinking we could have our lunch on a park bench at the city's historic Plaza Echaurren down by the port, where we were quickly surrounded by the most derelict people imaginable. Trying to eat our fish and chips with a dozen bleary eyes on us was no fun at all, but the killer was the woman who decided to defecate under a nearby tree. That really did put us off our food and we retreated inland, just as quickly as our feet could take us to the metro station without actually running.[2]

I learned to enjoy Valparaíso's adult pleasures without my sons and have been back many times since that first stressful visit, not least because I am still looking for the grave of my ancestor who came to renew his fortunes in Chile and died here in 1880. Circumstances and limited information have made it hard to trace his movements, but I know he was granted a commission to lay the first underwater telecommunications cable between Peru and

Chile in 1877. What ship did he arrive on? Where did he live? What caused his death? I have no answers to any of those questions as yet, only a faded photograph and a folder full of documents relating to his adventurous life in Europe, where he abandoned his debts, his wife, and a dozen children.

Charles Samuel Scott-Stokes was my grandfather's grandfather and a black sheep in the family best not mentioned. But of course I have every intention of discovering his story one day, if I ever get the chance, and, in the meantime, his mystery adds spice to my explorations around Valparaíso's famous lanes. His death occurred within a year of the War of the Pacific, with Peru and Chile on opposing sides, which not only made his cable project extremely controversial but may well have had something to do with his untimely end. Was he, in fact, killed? There is no record of him in the local newspapers of the time and no report of his death, either. A Chilean friend has suggested the lack of a death notice might indicate he was really a spy who was spirited away by the British secret service. But that story is for another time. In the meantime, the only thing I feel certain of is that his fate was sealed by a "clash between expectations and reality," which is the essential experience of Valparaíso no visitor is spared. Some would say that applies to any encounter with Chile, and perhaps they are right. It is a country where you must think on your feet, whether you like it or not, because you will surely sink without trace if you don't—just like my ancestor.

24
The Right to Live in Peace

For me, a fascinating aspect of the estallido social is the vigorous debate it has inspired among my community of foreign friends, many of whom have lived here for decades. They range from scientists to journalists to eco-feminists to family therapists and social justice campaigners; they also include a good smattering of medical professionals, businessmen, translators, and academics. Their political spectrum is as diverse as their backgrounds and ranges from old-school socialism to neoliberal libertarian, but what brings us together is the love of a lively conversation, which is as likely to be about the best recipes for empanadas as the latest novel or political developments. Many have married into Chilean families and have a deep understanding of the historical context to the social uprising, as well as direct working relationships that cut across all class barriers.

"But you are not telling the whole truth," one wrote, after I shared my response to the shocking events of October 2019.

"You do not reflect the violence and destruction that happened throughout the country, the continued and sustained attacks on the metro system that suffered $400 million in damages . . . the fire-bombing and looting of supermarkets, factories, and hotels."

A third of Chile's supermarkets were made inoperative as a result of the attacks that began after October 18, 2019. According to a Reuters report from October 29, 2019, Chilean business lost more than $1.4 billion as a result of the riots. Soon, boarded up shops could be seen on commercial thoroughfares up and down the country, including those owned by innocent and uninsured families who had the bad luck to be in the line of the mob's fire.

My friend's main issue is that I have not given enough weight to what appear to have been coordinated attacks throughout the country, including on municipal buildings, banks, and supermarkets. Who was behind them? It is impossible to know, though the looting clearly included opportunist criminals and anarchists, as well as protesters, and even undercover police officers. But that public order needed to be restored and that injuries were incurred on all sides is recorded fact.

"It's all very well to condemn the violence (and I don't like or advocate it at all), but peaceful proposal, lobby, protest has not changed the way this tiny elite runs things," observed a Santiago resident. "For our generation, defeating the dictatorship was, in some ways, enough. But this new generation refuses to live the way we have, to accept a system that legitimizes extreme inequalities in every sphere, and blames the victims when they don't make it," she continued.

Her statement was not an exaggeration. The inequalities really are extreme, especially in Chile's capital city, which is home to almost half the nation's population (approximately eight million people). According to the independent researcher and former Chilean exile Roberto Matta Lemoine, only around 551,000 inhabitants have an average life expectancy of eighty-eight and enjoy monthly incomes of $1,450 and over in Santiago. The rest can expect to live to an average of seventy-five, a substantial number of them surviving below the poverty line.

Many agree on the impossibility of peaceful change, even if they disagree wholeheartedly with the looting and destruction that has taken place of public services such as the transport system, and of commercial outlets, especially the supermarkets. Yet most targets of the looting and burning may be considered "sites of daily humiliation and symbols of subordination and exploitation," either because they are symbols of a consumer society most have no access to or because they operate on slave wages and insecure, short-term contracts that offer their employees very little in terms of job security or saving for a better future. Just as the looter in Concepción said after the 2010 earthquake, the corporate owners of these businesses rob the vast majority of the population of dignity and opportunity on a daily basis. The legitimization of inequality through rules and regulations does not make it just, and that is a key trigger to the ferocious violence now. Most Chileans sense that they are trapped in a system that will never give them a chance, no matter how hard they work.

"The *milicos* [military] are happy to teargas children and infants but stand idly by while disenfranchised people rip things apart," a friend in Valparaíso reported after a huge demonstration there.

"After 12 days of mass demonstrations, rioting and human rights violations, the government of President Sebastián Piñera must now find a way out of the crisis that has engulfed Chile," Kirsten Sehnbruch wrote in the *Guardian* on October 30, 2019.

But by what means? Meeting violence with even more violence is just escalating what many see as a genuine class war. The economic model imposed by Pinochet's "Chicago Boys" has excluded too many people for too long, and "expectations for a better and more secure life have outpaced the opportunities for social mobility," according to Sehnbruch. I think we all agree on that, if not on the means for change.

An intriguing question is why the government decided to escalate the confrontation with protesters and looters by imposing a state of emergency that brought the military onto the streets. Mass demonstrations and violence are virtually annual rituals in Chile and do not normally lead to national curfews and the other extreme measures we are living through now. Certainly for my sons, and many youth, the annual ritual of running the gauntlet of water cannons and teargas is almost a rite of passage, and when my son Rémi asked if he could go to Valparaíso to join the student demonstrations happening then (he was thirteen), we agreed to go together and the experience was as exhilarating as theater. Everyone knew the story, but it was how they played it that mattered. The crowd would advance slowly to the armored vehicles and police cordons around the national congress building, someone would throw a stone, and then the battle was on. My son and I found ourselves sheltering behind a convenient tree, but the clouds of tear gas detonated into the crowd reached us anyway, causing our eyes to stream and our chests to heave. Street vendors sell bicarbonate of soda and lemons on these occasions, because rubbing the mixture under your eyes is the best remedy for the effects of the gas. Obviously these annual battles have real casualties and the events that occur are often manipulated by very dark agendas on both sides of the barricades, and yet they are also a ritualized occasion for expressing the anger that runs in so many people's blood in Chile, and most days the vast majority get to go home with the satisfaction of having released some of the pressure. It is almost a way of saving face, even while the odds are vastly stacked in favor of the armed forces. Both sides come away claiming victory.

"The army isn't the right tool for controlling civil unrest—not what they're trained for," my friend and long-term Chilean analyst noted. She also reminded us that while it is easy to condemn the violence, it is not so easy to see how change will happen any time soon without it, given that legitimate protest has consistently failed to have any impact whatsoever. "Would we be talking about it [change] now if it hadn't been for the violence?" she asked.

"We were caught off guard," a veteran of the Allende years admitted to me. "Yes, we knew that Chile had become one of the most inequitable countries on the planet with 10 percent of the richest earning twenty-six times more that the poorest 10 percent. But folks had gotten used to low salaries, along with rising costs in the light and water bills, health care, education, and transportation because, after all, Chile was fast becoming a developed country."

National pride in Chile's progress could make up for a lot, she seemed to be saying, and the dream was that if you worked hard, your kids might get all the chances for a better life you never had. But Chileans' sense of themselves was eroded along the way, she observed: "What was once a country known for its solidarity is now characterized by rampant individualism."

But she also noted the marvel of the extraordinary peaceful mass demonstrations up and down the country that prove a huge number of people are still committed to a spirit of community and constructive paths to change. Over 1.5 million people marched in joyful protest in Santiago on October 26, 2019—the largest march in Chilean history—while one hundred thousand others, including families with children, walked from the coastal city of Viña del Mar to Valparaíso without incident, until they were attacked by water cannons and tear gas barring the route to the national congress building.

"Most analysts agree that what is at stake is Chile's neoliberal economic model," she stated.

Given that Chile's current constitution enshrines the Pinochet model, many believe the possibility for systemic change lies in formulating a new constitution that could establish the basic rights of a welfare state, including decent working conditions, health care, and education, and renationalize the country's natural resources that were sold off to private business during the dictatorship. But this analysis ignores the fact that many of the issues at stake are covered not by the constitution but rather by a framework of laws. The challenge is much wider than simply rewriting the constitution, even if that would be a hugely important step in the right direction. The symbolic power of such a rewriting would be incredibly significant too, because it would give Chileans a genuine reason to believe in a better future. Most national parties seemed to agree on this point and the government was shamed into signing the so-called Agreement for Social Peace and a New Constitution on November 5, 2019, which set the stage for a plebiscite on whether to write a new constitution and, crucially, who should be the authors, should the vote be positive.[1]

But while these philosophical discussions kept me busy via emails, a community of friends closer to my home became embroiled in a very different conversation that was much more personal and tied to people's individual responses to the economic crisis the violence caused. For it was not just small shopkeepers caught in the crossfire of looting whose livelihoods were inadvertently destroyed; the problem affected self-employed professionals and all the employees of shuttered-up businesses. Their jobs and workflow suddenly came to a standstill and many families suddenly had no income to cover the rent, their pensions, the car, the school fees, the food bill, and all the other trappings of their lives. The trauma was profound. Not everyone agrees that the means justify the ends in a conflict that has brought the country to a standstill and, in the meantime, the financial disaster is personal and very distressing.

"While people are banging pots and lighting fires and barricades to stop people going about their legitimate business of going to work or school, please bear in mind that 90 percent of my income has just been wiped out," stated one friend bluntly.

Meanwhile, the owners of wineries, restaurants, and hotels are facing disaster, as Chile has suddenly become off-limits to the precious tourist dollar, and my heart goes out to the couple recently arrived from Belgium who had only just finished restoring their new hotel in Valparaíso, in time for the new tourist season beginning in November. Their personal disaster is mirrored a thousand times all over Chile in the lost bookings for accommodation, restaurant meals, transport, and tours. The cancellation of the global climate change conference (COP25) that was to be hosted by Chile means ten thousand delegates are now not coming to spend money in Santiago, and local universities that have paid millions of pesos for a stand at that conference have little chance of ever getting a refund.[2]

It is not just a matter of personal income and small businesses facing bankruptcy either but also of institutional resources wasted. For example, an academic friend points out that, unlike in many other countries, Chilean universities have to pay value-added tax on any grants for research or materials they receive, which cannot be deducted from future "sales profits" as such. Incredibly, the tax on bringing new technologies purchased overseas into Chile is almost 40 percent, which might be great for the government coffers but is a disaster for scientific progress locally. The waste of time, effort, and money Chile's educators are facing is therefore appalling, and yet my friend claims they are mostly fully supportive of the protests that have shut down their schools and colleges, because they know better than most how hard their students have to struggle to complete even a basic education.

"But all of us pay the taxes that will be needed to repair the damage to metro stations, bus stops, traffic lights, pavements, and so on and cover all these reforms you are out there banging pans for," said another friend grimly.

"Violence just breeds more violence; hate and intolerance beget more hate and intolerance. Who is going to break that cycle in Chile?" she asked.

The issue of a new constitution is not a clear-cut matter, either. Will it alleviate poverty or provide better health care? Will it ensure human rights? Latin America is notorious for its endless rules and regulations coupled with a total failure to monitor or enforce them.

Se obedece pero no se cumple, the famous phrase goes, meaning national authorities duly set out the law, but no one complies. It is a concept that actually has a long history in this part of the world and was first established as a technical legal phrase during colonial times, as a means to alerting the Spanish king of potentially unjust decrees. According to the American scholar John Leddy Phelan, there was even a ritual whereby the local colonial authority would kiss the royal seal and invoke the phrase "I obey but do not follow" before presenting a formal proposal to the Council of the Indies for improving a suspended piece of legislation.[3]

Of course this has long since been perverted into a way of life all over Latin America, and society and the environment suffer for it across the region to this day. Hence there is a vast black economy and contacts matter far more than qualifications. Chile is absolutely part of that reality, no matter how developed it may look on the surface. The systemic changes needed to create a fair and just society will have to cut very deep indeed.

25 Crossroads

On reading the Chilean Constitution, I was astonished to discover that according to Article 19.2, men and women are equal before the law. Yet the dismal record of successful prosecutions of court cases relating to the abuse of women from rape or domestic violence says otherwise. Even more surprising, according to the constitution, the Public Ministry is responsible for ensuring the safety and rights of victims and witnesses of crimes, and it can also oblige the security forces to comply with any investigations relating to judicial processes. But this does not imply justice is done in reality either, as was yet once more proved by the Chilean Court of Appeal on December 3, 2020, when it absolved sixty former agents of Augusto Pinochet's secret police of having been involved in Operation Condor, which resulted in the disappearance of 119 citizens between June 17, 1974, and January 6, 1975 (even before Operation Condor was formally set up in November 1975).[1] Meanwhile, the family of the Mapuche activist Camilo Catrillanca was prevented from attending the court hearing that was set to pronounce on his assassination carried out by members of the Chilean police in 2018.

The powers that be are not merely reluctant to address crimes committed during the military dictatorship. In July 2020, for example, Chile's public prosecutor confirmed 466 police officers were under investigation for abuses against human rights committed during the October 2019 uprising. Yet only sixteen officers have lost their jobs after convictions of gross misconduct. The list of failed court cases is endless and includes the stories of ordinary citizens, like my friend Alejandra, whose family sued the manufacturers of the baby food that almost killed their disabled daughter and did indeed kill several other children. But after many years and huge expense, they lost their case. Concerned citizens who have pooled resources and invested enormous amounts of time to sue municipalities for failing to protect rivers or parks from illegal dumping or construction companies have also failed, achieving nothing more than a mountain of debts and much bitterness.

The reality gap between what is officially law and order in Chile and how citizens experience their rights in everyday life is huge, and that goes for many other aspects of how the country is managed, from environmental protection to building regulations, from education and healthcare to the right to drinking water or a living wage. No wonder so many Chileans are disillusioned with the democratic process. The country is a seething mix of contradictions, where you can experience the exhilaration of people power in action one day and extreme repression the next. So what the country's constitution says on paper has very little to do with life as we know it.

Of course the most important problem with the latest version of the Chilean Constitution is that it was written under the auspices of the military dictatorship and legitimized by a sham plebiscite that was carried out under strict censorship and limits on freedom of movement. The fact that it was massively amended by the democratically elected government of Ricardo Lagos in 2005 could not remove that moral stain, and to this day there are some glaring omissions, such as a complete failure to acknowledge the country's Indigenous population or their land rights. It simply won't do and the population has long shown its disgust by failing to vote at all. Hence my builder said, "I don't vote, because it makes no difference. They will do what they want anyway." And that is precisely why the huge popular protests have been so important, because they have tangibly moved the goal posts of Chilean democracy and forced the government to agree to a plebiscite on a new constitution that will not only enshrine the rules by which the country is run but also have the legitimacy of popularly elected authors.

As a woman interviewed by local media on the street said, "I have never felt like I was part of a community before . . . but now we're remaking the social fabric that was destroyed both by the dictatorship and thirty years of neoliberalism."

An important aspect of remaking Chile's social fabric is a formal rejection of the political class that has failed to make significant improvements to ordinary people's lives. The million-dollar question is, however, whether a new constitution written by popularly elected authors will improve access to better health care, education, and fair pensions. Will it provide social justice or ensure environmental protection? Inexperience and lack of funds may leave independent candidates out of the process anyway, bringing us back to the old game of professional politicians, lawyers, and power brokers; and while the achingly slow wheels of constitutional change grind on, the country is bound to suffer political, economic, and social uncertainty.

Indeed, according to the Peruvian academic Patricio Navia, writing in the *Americas Quarterly* in March 2020, there is a real risk that this process will kill the proverbial goose that laid the golden egg (of Chile's economic success). He also stated, "I am worried that Chileans' overwhelming support for a new charter may reflect tragically misplaced expectations."[2]

For the truth of the matter is that Latin America in general is famous for its leviathan bureaucracy and obsession with legalized documents that have never yet resulted in a respect for human rights or equitable development. There is a real risk, therefore, of ending up with more of the same, but with an even angrier well of potential violence.

If the terrible injuries and ongoing sacrifices of millions of Chileans are perceived to have been for nothing in the end, the trouble ahead will be unimaginably worse than anything the country experienced in October 2019, because you just can't eat moral victories. People need genuine systemic change that will make life worth living now and in the future. That means not only reforming the unfair tax and pension systems and developing an equitable national education and health care service but also enshrining a genuine commitment to environmental protection and mitigating the impacts of climate change, ensuring the impunity of the armed forces is a thing of the past, and guaranteeing a fairer distribution of incomes. But a new constitution alone will not do any of that, because it is only a blueprint for change.

In any case, reaching the promised land of an equitable society is dependent on such intangible factors as political will, Chile's place in the global market, the whim of foreign investors, and even the weather. And, in the meantime, antidemocratic authoritarian measures continue to threaten and intimidate those who are trying to mobilize popular action, though the brave creative responses of individuals are truly inspiring. Among my favorites are the brother and sister team of light artists known as Delight Lab, who have been beaming huge provocative protest slogans onto the glass pillars of corporate power in downtown Santiago despite constant threats and harassment from the authorities.

Chileans have been living with the proverbial curse "may you live in interesting times" since time immemorial, yet the groundswell of community action and grassroots organizations throughout Chile as a result of the estallido social is inspiring. No matter how huge the odds against success, millions of ordinary people have turned their backs on apathy and fear and come together to be part of the solution to Chile's problems in countless different ways. Famous communitarian traditions, such as the soup kitchens and political embroidery workshops in poor neighborhoods, have massively expanded, and so have voluntary activities like weekly river clean-ups and citizens' advice stands at the country's markets and in town squares.

Of course there are also some key nongovernmental organizations that have been working in the spheres of social justice and environmental protection for decades, ranging from famous international charities to local campaigning forces. One of the most famous Chileans among these activists is the recently deceased priest Mariano Puga, who renounced a life of ease based on his family's substantial wealth and spent his life living and working in humble neighborhoods, not only sermonizing and carrying out his priestly duties but also getting his hands dirty carrying out back-breaking manual labor to help build much-needed homes for the poor. His example was a huge inspiration, but there are plenty of others who have dedicated their lives to improving the quality of life in Chile. One of the finest examples is EPES, which has been at the forefront of public health initiatives like banning tobacco in public spaces but also has dedicated regional centers where ordinary people can get help accessing everything from advice on health issues to dealing with domestic violence or learning about constitutional assemblies.

It could be argued all these efforts are just balms for a country dying of an extreme case of neoliberalism; that what Chile (and the rest of the modern world) really needs is an entirely new and sustainable socioeconomic model, which is precisely what my dear friend Howard Richards has been pondering for decades, long before fashionable authors like Yuval Noah Harari and others started writing best-selling books about how best to shape our future in an antidemocratic, capitalist world. As the great guru of corporate management Charles Handy wrote in his book *The Second Curve*, "It is one of the paradoxes of growth that it can end up as a recipe for perpetual dissatisfaction." But developing applicable alternatives is not easy.[3]

Nevertheless, the route to a more meaningful and just way of organizing society is what is at the heart of the "dialogues" Howard Richards has been promoting in conjunction with a highly distinguished international group of other academics, and the most exciting thing about it is that Limache residents have had the opportunity to be at the heart of a global debate that shares the insights of social scientists and activists from as far afield as Palestine, India, and South Africa with interested Chilean individuals and experts in their field, on subjects ranging from economics to philosophy, religion, and permaculture. The fact that his work has failed to reach a mass audience is not his fault, though the Internet is a wonderful tool for reaching out, and anyone can now discover more at his website, http://chileufu.cl.

The fundamental premise that social justice is incompatible with the needs of capitalism is addressed on the basis of the conviction that accumulation of capital for its own sake is at best pointless and at worst inhumane; and that a world where investors' money is more important than human rights and the environment not only causes hardship and injustice but is also destroying the planet, especially in the Southern Hemisphere.

These are not new ideas, but they are gaining more and more currency, and not just among social justice campaigners in Chile but at the highest levels of international policymaking and national governments. The idea that *enough* might be better than ever-expanding circles of economic growth and profits, and that national markets should be based on locally produced and manufactured goods, is no longer the preserve of alternative thinkers. But as Harari explained in his bestselling book *Sapiens*, putting the genie of the capitalist system back in the bottle is virtually impossible. The world's international corporations are not about to renounce their power, and modern trade agreements are designed to lock nations into destroying their own human and natural resources for the sake of multinational profit margins.

And yet, millions of people all over the world are demanding massive structural changes to how our globalized economic world is managed, not least because of the catastrophic impacts of climate change that are there for all to see, like the huge wildfires in California and Australia. Meanwhile, Chileans have set their own country on fire and it remains to be seen if they can break the economic and social mold they have been forced to live in.

The outcome for Chile is extremely uncertain, but it is inspiring to witness the courage and energy that is being put into moving from destruction to creation in the face of consistent obstruction and intimidation from the authorities and those who would rather protect their own advantages in the short term than provide a future for the next generation. There is no doubt, however, that what more and more people are dreaming of is nothing less than rewriting their destiny, not just the constitution, and that idea is just as powerful as Milton Friedman's and will not return to the bottle under any circumstances.

26

Water

The ingenuity of South American irrigation canals is a marvel. All over the continent humans have used the natural declivity of the landscape to feed their agricultural settlements, be they tiny homesteads in remote Andean valleys to entire cities on the desert coast of Peru. Beginning high up in the mountains, the annual snowmelt, glacial streams, and natural springs are redirected along the contours of the landscape to reach distant crops, and their routes have also often doubled up as long-distance footpaths. In fact, in Chile, there is a traditional rule that paths along irrigation canals must be the same width as the water course itself to allow easy access to clear weeds and debris each spring. Cut off the water and you kill your opponent, which is exactly how the Inca soldiers were able to defeat the much more sophisticated coastal cultures in their orbit, including Chan Chan in northern Peru, once the largest pre-Columbian city in South America.

Preconquest Chile never had great urban cultures or a population large enough to warrant the complex network of irrigation systems you can find elsewhere, and no wars were fought using water as a weapon, but the original pastoralists of the Quillota Valley in central Chile certainly found ways to divert the rivers coming off the Andes Mountains, just ninety kilometers away, and use them to their advantage. The most important river in this area is the Aconcagua, named after South America's highest peak, whose rounded summit is easily recognized, even from my local La Campana mountain.

A few centuries later, the wealthy investors who came to the agricultural haven of the Limache Valley certainly knew about the vagaries of drought and the importance of regular water supplies, and that is how the Waddington and Ovalle irrigation canals came into being in the mid-nineteenth century, built using a combination of ancient techniques and modern engineering to guide water to all the major country estates between Quillota, Limache, and Olmué. My Quinta, too, was once connected to this network via the Loreto canal extension that follows the highway into Limache from the main Ovalle branch, and the gush of water to every corner of my land via our own network of channels was a wonder to behold. Using nothing more than the incline of the property, open waterways were designed to reach almost every fruit tree, and where that wasn't immediately possible, there was a large tank that filled during our designated irrigation day, whose water could be directed to every last tree using a series of underground pipes and standing taps.

For eight months each year during the growing season, from September to April, water from the distant Andes and Aconcagua River would come coursing onto our land, providing life-giving sustenance to our six varieties of avocado trees, three varieties of peaches, plums, and apricots, as well as the seven grape arbors and many other fruit trees, ranging from figs to pomegranate and apples to cherimoya.

In the early years, I was as happy as a child, loving the sensation of the ankle-deep water gushing over my bare feet as my sons and I directed the flow by opening and closing the many wooden sluices that allowed pools of water to collect around each tree, until it was time to close off the flow and take it elsewhere. Of course it was not just a matter of opening and closing sluices but also of back-breaking work with hoes to clear the eternal leaves and debris that could block the water, and whenever we were not quick enough, unforgiving floods immersed entire footpaths and even entered our house through the front door on one occasion. It took years of trial and error to develop a good routine without the benefit of the generational knowledge of locals, but I learned a lot from my gardener and by the time my sons were young adults we were totally professional. In fact, by then, I was very grateful to let them take over, and it filled me with pride to see them calmly working together.

Attending the annual general meeting of the local irrigation associates was my job, however, and it was an experience that became more tedious and depressing with every year, but especially from 2013 onward, when our meetings came to be dominated by interminable discussions of the drought that threatens Chile to this day. It was not helped either by our legal representative, a man of towering self-importance who loved the sound of his own voice so much we were obliged to listen to him read out the minutes of last year's meeting before we could even get started. Not once, however, did we receive a written record of our meetings, much less verifiable accounts. Everything was run on trust in Señor Eugenio Castellaro, who never hesitated to regale us with the story of how he found the bank account of the Limache water community empty when he took over, and how he had single-handedly built up funds and infrastructure ever since. Conveniently, his predecessor was dead and unable to tell his side of the story, and we all nodded in grateful appreciation of his efforts and insisted he continue to manage our water rights whenever he broached the option of electing someone else. But every year without fail, we would go through the motions of being told how hard it was to manage the funds and maintenance of our section of the irrigation system, and how much he would like to hand over to someone else. On one occasion, he even suggested I should take over, which was enjoyably absurd to everyone including me, and we quickly confirmed our complete faith in the man who clearly knew best and meekly accepted whatever quota he decided we each needed to pay for the privilege of receiving water once a week between September and April.

It was a privilege that doubled in cost over my first decade in the association, not least because we went from nineteen associates in 2008 to six in 2018, as more and more members sold or subdivided their properties during an unprecedented boom in house prices, in no small part due to the success of the local Waldorf School. But the costs of maintaining the irrigation system still had to be paid by the remaining contributors and the sharp rise in the price of materials and labor after the 2010 earthquake only made it worse. Nevertheless, I could not help noticing that the section of the canal to supply my property was rarely given more than a perfunctory sweep, and once the neighboring nunnery stopped paying its dues after selling half their land to a construction company, maintenance came to a complete standstill. From then onward, our canal days became much harder, because someone always had to spend many hours sieving leaves and debris out of the water entering the property that threatened to block not only our channels but also the water tank. It was not just organic matter either; there was also a great deal of plastic garbage and even dead cats and other animals. Rats were another problem, and we all made sure to wear boots and wash any skin exposed to canal water because of the risk of Hantavirus and the incurable disease it causes. It also became very obvious over the years that our irrigation water was contaminated by agricultural chemicals from the big industrial farms farther upstream. Sometimes our water was a milky gray, making a mockery of our organic practice.

Finally, in the 2018 to 2019 season, we received no irrigation water at all and the hydrographic deficit for our Valparaíso Region was estimated to be 92 percent. The local reservoir, like many others, became a dustbowl, and the inhabitants of Olmué and surrounding villages were forced to buy expensive water from commercial truck deliveries. Lucky for us, that has never been the case in Limache, but everyone worries that the day will come when domestic taps run dry here too.

"If you have a well, it's time to start using it," I was told, but I had neither the resources nor the contacts to revive our ancient well, even though it was comforting to know I owned the rights to do so.

For ever since the military dictatorship in Chile, ownership of the land does not automatically give you the right to use the water underneath it. Instead, those resources, and even entire rivers, are deemed separate property, which means someone who owns the rights to them can come onto your land, whether you give permission or not, and start extracting water to irrigate their plantation next door, and this is exactly what has happened all over Chile, where impoverished farmers have been persuaded to sell their water rights to large multinational companies, who have covered the land in massive avocado or commercial tree plantations fed by wells reaching up to a hundred meters underground. Increasingly, Chileans have found their water resources threatened as a result, and while the impacts of climate change are a factor, the real reason for the severe water shortages and drying up of entire lakes and rivers is Chile's privatization of water, creating a situation where springs and ground water can be diverted to provide each avocado tree with around sixty-six liters of water per day, while humans dependent on water transports are only entitled to fifty liters each, which is just half the amount deemed necessary for domestic needs by the World Health Organization to maintain a minimum standard of health and hygiene.

Nevertheless, the green gold that is the avocado has completely transformed the landscape over the past twenty years, including in the Limache Valley, as multinational companies have taken advantage of juicy government subsidies to develop their monocultures and nothing and nobody has been allowed to stand in their way. Those who have tried have been bullied and threatened, even to the extent of receiving death threats, as happened to the mayor of Petorca and a local water activist in January and February 2021, 220 kilometers north of Santiago, where over half the population is dependent on water lorries because local sources have been diverted by huge commercial avocado farms. Becoming dependent on private commercial water deliveries is bad enough, but the problem is not just financial; it is also a matter of health, because there is no efficient quality control system in place and the drinking water villagers receive has been found to contain heavy metals, impurities, and even feces. I have seen these water lorries fill up at roadside riverbeds myself, so I am not surprised.

A terrible irony is that the second largest foreign shareholder in Chilean water companies is a Canadian pension fund for teachers, people who live in a country where citizens have successfully lobbied against the private ownership of water resources and where the suffering of villagers in Chile would be an unacceptable scandal. But North America's and Europe's fashion for eating avocados is a multimillion-dollar business that is actively subsidized and protected by the Chilean state, which has so far felt free to ignore the environmental cost and human suffering it causes and has even actively promoted the destruction of native forest to make way for more avocado plantations.

Obviously, none of this information is on the menu in the fashionable restaurants of the world's top avocado eaters, like at the super hip The Avocado Show, which serves nothing but avocado dishes to Instagram disciples in Amsterdam, Madrid, and Brussels. I went to the one in Amsterdam, while visiting a friend, and was stunned by the inventiveness of the menu that offered everything from avocado fries to peanut butter and avocado ice cream. It was dazzling and beautiful, but the price is literally too high.

"When you eat an avocado that comes from Chile," the well-known local campaigner Rodrigo Mundaca has said, "think about the fact that the water used to produce it is water that homes in the country's humblest communities now lack."

Thus our irrigation water went from being supplied once a week during the growing season, to every two weeks, to once a month, to nothing, and we are now living in a situation where only 5 percent of Chile's entire water consumption is for domestic use, while 77 percent of water resources are used by commercial farming, vastly more even than by all the mining operations up and down the country.

Of course my personal disappointments are hardly a tragedy, and unlike those living in rural areas that have officially been declared *zonas de catastrofe* by the Chilean Ministry of Agriculture, we not only continue to have municipal piped water supplies but I also have the professional and financial resources to adjust to new realities (such as paying to irrigate using tap water). Meanwhile, 350,000 others do not even have enough water to wash their hands, according to CNN Chile, which is a national scandal. But it is the one close to home that hurts me the most. It turns out the man we paid and trusted to manage our local irrigation community sold our water to a private water company (Esval) behind our backs and there is nothing we can do about it, because in a slick maneuver to persuade just four attending members including myself to dissolve the historic irrigation association of Limache by a "majority vote" in 2018, he ensured there is no one left to challenge his actions.

"We always trusted Señor Castellaro," a long-term resident told me. "His family has been here for generations."

But she could not remember ever being told that he was also the director of the private corporation of shareholders of the Canal Ovalle, which clearly meant he never had our best interests at heart, despite all his protestations of working himself into the grave on our behalf. Supposedly, we were all going to get shares in the Canal Ovalle that would secure us a more cost-effective supply of irrigation water. But the legal paperwork never materialized and I discovered the half share I was supposedly going to get would not have entitled me to attend annual general meetings anyway.

No es sequía, es saqueo, as they say in Chile: It isn't drought; it's robbery.[1]

27
The 2020 Plague Year

January to June

In Chile, the year begins in March. That is when the academic calendar begins and millions of children and students start another learning cycle. In many ways, the rest of society is getting back to business as well, because the entire country virtually shuts down for the hottest months of summer, which are January and February. Nothing important ever happens then, not even fighting for a better future. Santiago was virtually a ghost town in February 2020, as almost everything shut down and people who could afford it headed to their holiday homes in the south or on the coast. Mass demonstrations also came to a halt as students and school children returned to their families or looked for summer jobs.

Except for on New Year's Eve, the battle was temporarily on hold, and many people were grateful for that, not least the Chilean government. The first big date for retaking the streets was International Women's Day, on March 8, followed by a national strike the next day. And what an exhilarating return it was. An estimated two million people filled the emblematic Plaza Dignidad (officially it is called Plaza Baquedano, but it was colloquially renamed for its role as the epicenter of the most recent protest movement).

It was a glorious, joyful day of legitimate feminist protest and creative solidarity, and also a very clear declaration of intent. The estallido social was not over; not in Santiago, and not in the rest of the country either. Every single town and city the length of Chile organized a demonstration and it felt good to walk proud and loud with my women friends in Limache and also to show Chile does not revolve around the capital alone. We in the provinces carry the torch with equal passion, and it was especially satisfying to see how many young teenagers participated.

"What does today mean to you?" I asked a lovely fifteen-year-old girl with a ring through her nose.

She explained violence against women was an issue for her and her friends, and that they also wanted to stand up for equal pay between men and women.

The summer heat had not cooked people's brains and made them forget their commitment to the cause of social and economic justice or to the many victims still waiting for medical treatment for their terrible injuries sustained over recent months. Their suffering was surely not going to be in vain and, in fact, the only event I went to in Santiago over the summer was a fund-raising concert for the twenty-seven-year-old medical student Diego Lastra, the first person to lose an eye to a tear gas canister, in the early hours of New Year's Day. No one had forgotten a thing. *Ni perdón ni olvido*, as they have been saying here for thirty years already (No forgiving or forgetting). It was a deeply moving event, not least because it was located a stone's throw from where Diego lost his eye, in the battered heart of the city.

The walls of the iconic GAM (Gabriela Mistral Cultural Centre) on the city's main artery leading to Plaza Dignidad had been transformed into a magnificent mural of witty, gruesome, and beautiful art works consisting of everything from blood-spattered school blazers to poems, prints, and framed oil paintings; necklaces of gas canisters, plastic flowers, and even strings of papier-mâché eyeballs. The explosion of creativity was astonishing, and I was not the only one moving in silent contemplation from one icon to the next, honoring the spirit of the uprising and its many victims. There was an inescapably spiritual atmosphere along that wall, and indeed many artworks were of the newly divined Virgin de las Barricadas (Virgin of the Barricades).

It was shocking to see the extent of destruction in downtown Santiago. Pavements had been transformed into rubble where demonstrators had hacked entire concrete blocks out of the sidewalk to throw at armored police vehicles; every single building was covered in graffiti and street art; and the entrance to the closed Baquedano metro station on the city's central plaza had been transformed into a monument to protest, with everything from Mapuche flags to the ubiquitous reference to eyes, as well as abandoned helmets and personal items, including shoes and even a pair of crutches. A human body lay insentient below a slogan that read, "The Police Kill Children in Chile," and I hoped he was just sleeping off the night before. But the most piercing slogan said, "Baquedano Station: Transfer to 1973." As if to confirm that distressing reference, unidentified individuals obliterated the entire GAM mural with white paint under the cover of the nightly curfew, just weeks after my visit.

The national strike called for Monday, March 9, was ignored by many who feared losing their jobs, but the propaganda machine on social media was in full flow, and the government was left in no doubt at all that an overwhelming number of their citizens' hearts and minds were set on not giving up the fight begun in October. The national plebiscite for a new constitution was due in April, which was hopefully going to be a huge vote for systemic change, and a great deal of effort was being put into awareness programs to increase participation in the democratic process. It was sorely needed, because huge swathes of the Chilean population, especially those under forty, have turned their backs on voting in recent years. Less than 40 percent of Chile's eligible voters under the age of forty bother to vote, according to the government's own electoral services.

But the first recorded case of coronavirus infection in Chile was March 3, and by March 18 President Piñera had declared a ninety-day state of emergency, which allowed him to call on the army to join the police on the nation's streets and also to ban all public events of over fifty people. National air, land, and sea borders were closed except for repatriation, and the authorities now also had the right to coopt private property or even requisition it. A week later, the president ordered a complete quarantine for seven of Santiago's municipalities, an order immediately condemned for favoring the rich and middle-class neighborhoods, and the government's premise that selective quarantines could effectively prevent the spread of the virus was almost immediately revealed as a failure. The army of workers crowding into packed public transport from outlying neighborhoods quickly spread infection all over the city, while the privileged carried it to their beach house communities farther afield.

By March 22, the entire country was put under curfew from 10:00 p.m. to 5:00 a.m., though most towns and cities remained free of compulsory quarantine. Incredibly, the major urban conglomeration of Valparaíso and Viña del Mar, with a combined population of well over six hundred thousand people, was not put under quarantine until June 19, by which time Chile's infection rates per capita were among the highest in the world. According to *Bloomberg*, "poverty, overcrowding and a massive off-the-books workforce" whose daily food depended on going out onto the streets to earn a living meant staying home just wasn't an option.[1]

The academic year did not recommence at the beginning of March, and schools, colleges, and universities were forced to either cancel the year or come up with an online teaching program for some 3.5 million students. But they quickly ran in to problems, not least that an estimated 380,000 school-age children in Chile live in areas with deficient Internet connections. The dark side of life here was also revealed in *La Tercera* newspaper the following month, when it pointed out that many children had been safer at school and were now trapped in unsafe environments at home, exposed not only to mental and physical abuse but also to hunger, because thousands of Chilean children get their main meal at school.[2]

The pandemic changed our lives so quickly, it was difficult to adjust. Suddenly, fear and danger no longer had anything to do with the social uprising. An entirely new context to do with contagion and death appeared out of nowhere and, all of a sudden, it was not even safe to embrace or visit your nearest and dearest. Just walking to the supermarket might turn out to be fatal, and I found myself holding my breath whenever another person passed me on the street. Crazy, surely? But even though I had no television and consciously avoided scaremongering news, the barrage of conflicting advice on how to deal with the new risk forced its way into my consciousness. How long could the virus survive on any given surface? Should you wear gloves as well as a mask? Should every item of shopping be disinfected as soon as you got home, or could you just leave it standing in the sunshine for a few hours instead? Did you need to have a shower and put all your clothes in the wash after every time you walked the dog? The questions and answers covered a huge range, and deciding where the dividing line between bizarre and crazy and sensible precaution lay was not at all easy.

My own inclination to resist any advice protected me from the extremes of behavior some of my friends felt drawn to, but the unease was inescapable nevertheless, soon joined by sorrow and loneliness. The silence of my empty home and the pointlessness of my daily life were overwhelming, even for someone used to solitude and the self-discipline of working from home. There were far too many hours to fill, and sometimes fear, regret, and melancholy got the upper hand. Practicing gratitude for my good fortune often felt very lame. I was uncomfortably aware that "trauma porn and reactionary solidarity" just wasn't good enough, but it wasn't easy to see how impotent guilt could be turned into constructive support, so I was delighted when a local solidarity fund was set up. It was also heartening to see other spontaneous community projects appear, including a time bank where members gave each other hours of their time in whatever capacity required, without cash involved. Many other creative support groups emerged as well, ranging from exchange markets for goods to advice on growing your own food and making cheap meals. Delivery services exploded, and it felt good to support local businesses and stay away from the supermarkets, especially once they began pointing temperature guns at their customers and cashiers hid behind plastic shields. Yet I was grateful for the little pots of disinfectant for my PIN finger.

As the weeks and months passed, I found purposeful activity and meaningful routines (like writing this book!), and the ten pounds I gained by June just didn't matter. What was weight or looks if no one was going to see you anyway? But even with life reduced to the isolated, private world of my own home, it was impossible not to also develop a growing sense of unease, because the grim stories on social media were unrelenting. For example, on April 24 in Santiago, a compassionate sign offering food and goods to anyone in need who rang the bell was answered by two truckloads of armed soldiers; on May 22, also in Santiago, Juan Vega died of COVID-19 on the street, twelve days after being sent home on public transport from the nearest hospital, because of a lack of facilities and an ambulance to take him home; on June 4, in the Mapuche community of Collipulli in southern Chile, Alejandro Treuquil was killed by an unknown gunman, strongly suspected to have been a member of the local police force, but since independent journalists were banned from onsite reporting on June 15, proper scrutiny of events is impossible.

Closer to home, my attempts at fitness were curtailed, not for lack of commitment but because I found the civilian men carrying heavy machine guns on the footpaths behind my house too ominous.

"What do you need that for?" I ventured to ask, but no answer was forthcoming, and I decided my dawn routine in the hills above Limache was not safe.

Enquiries revealed a construction firm has bought the land, which is a beloved natural sanctuary, to build apartment blocks, so the men are most likely private security. I was also shocked to find the derelict tomato factory four blocks from my house, which had just been part of an application to make it a national monument, was demolished overnight, without so much as a word in the local press; and what remains of the Limache River is being dug out and diverted into concrete piping to feed a private reservoir while potential witnesses and protesters are busy sheltering at home.

Meanwhile, the infection and mortality rates for the coronavirus are spiraling out of control because overcrowded homes make social distancing impossible; and millions of Chileans who were surviving in poverty before the pandemic are now so hungry there have been riots on the streets despite the quarantine, because vast numbers of citizens who have been unable to buy food since March are desperate, and the 2.5 million food boxes the government claims to have purchased are not reaching them.

I am not the only one tempted to think the mismanagement of the pandemic coupled with the massive increase in surveillance and curtailment of civil liberties is a purposeful government strategy to destroy the social uprising. Even in a small town like Limache, cameras have been erected at almost every road junction over the past year. But both the editor of the *Bloomberg Report* in Chile (Philip Sanders) and the former Chile correspondent for the *Economist* (Ruth Bradley) told me they believe the culprit is a fatal combination of political arrogance that saw the pandemic as an opportunity to show who's in charge instead of as a health emergency; and ignorance of the facts on the ground, as personified by the government's disgraced health minister Jaime Mañalich, who admitted during a television interview "there are areas of Santiago where I had no awareness of the magnitude of the poverty and overcrowding."

What we can all agree on is how the COVID-19 pandemic has revealed the true extent of Chile's divided and unequal society; and that very bad times are ahead.

July to September

As the months passed, and March turned into April, and May into June, isolation fatigue was such that we began to bend our own safety rules. Not because we no longer believed in them but because the need for social contact was stronger than our fear. It also felt reasonable to honor the trust inherent in our friendships, to start creating "social bubbles" where we could recover a semblance of our lost social lives. The rigid rules and regulations on freedom of movement and protective measures were definitely starting to feel offensive when compared to the statistics; and even though the 4,479 official fatalities from COVID-19 by June 2020 were deeply distressing, they represented a tiny 0.023 percent of the Chilean population. Also, in the context of the roughly ten thousand people who die of respiratory disease here every year, and the many more who die for other reasons, like never reaching their turn on the hospital waiting lists, the extreme paranoia ruling our lives was starting to feel very disproportionate.

It seemed something odd was going on, though it was by no means clear what. The extreme infectiousness of the coronavirus was beyond dispute. But why was it not being contained after all these months, despite the strict containment measures enforced by gun-toting military personnel? There were no satisfactory answers to these questions, but the inescapable conclusion was that we were not so much victims of a virus but of failed political policies that had allowed the disease to spread and prevented effective medical care reaching those who needed it.

Among my circle of friends, people began to establish their own rules of engagement, including on how to manage their social distancing and even whether to allow their children to go back to school. Official notifications were no longer sufficient parameters for decision-making. Instead, everyone was getting very personal, closing ranks within their communities and trusting their own people rather than either political or medical officials, who seemed to be acting on agendas that even they didn't fully comprehend or support.

I had my first lunch with friends four months after voluntarily self-isolating, as they had.

“This feels so weird!” we found ourselves saying.

Seeing each other in real life instead of in a Zoom meeting was extraordinary, and the extra frisson of breaking our own rules just added to the thrill. But, to be honest, the joy was short-lived, because that cherished lunch caused days of worry, in case we had somehow infected each other after all, despite the masks and the sanitized footwear. Did helping myself to salad with my own fork put my host at risk? Was she going to catch something from me, just by washing my dishes? It seemed unlikely, but it spoiled the memory and made me realize that standing up to fear is one of the hardest challenges there is.

Resistance to the constant barrage of bad news was definitely becoming a trend, at least among those whose immediate material needs were not endangered. But, at the same time, the suffering among those without that cushion was really becoming acute; so much so that the government was forced to set up temporary emergency housing (often in tents) for the many infected people who had no possibility of isolating themselves, due to their overcrowded living conditions.

Confusion was the order of the day, whether it was trying to keep up with the constantly changing government directives on freedom of movement or making sense of the variety of financial aid packages available, depending on your class or income. (There really was a *bono de la clase media.*) Inevitably, the vast black economy made coming up with verifiable income figures a tricky business up and down the social scale, and many people continued to fall through the net, including many of the so-called middle class. Borrowing money without any idea if paying it back was ever going to be possible became a matter of survival, and it was shocking to see how the government encouraged those kind of personal debt decisions, even to the extent of enabling the entire population to withdraw 10 percent from their miserable compulsory pension fund (a decree that was repeated several times, leaving many, including myself, with zero at retirement age). That decision alone proved once again that the biggest danger facing Chile still comes from a ruling elite that prefers short-term solutions to systemic change. Yet the issues that led to the social uprising of October 2019 won't go away, and nor will the violence. Further proof, though none was needed, that the Chilean government is more interested in the economy than human welfare came when the shopping malls were reopened to the public, but the country's national parks remained closed; and when quarantines began to be phased out, freedom of movement excluded weekends and bank holidays, forcing people to stay home unless they still had a job to go to. As Violeta Parra's brother Nicanor said as long ago as the 1990s: "*De vencer o morir se paso a vender o morir*" (To win or die has turned into sell or die).

October to December

October 3 is an important anniversary in our family. It is the day we left England for our new life in Chile. But from 2020 onward, it will only ever be the day I remember a sixteen-year-old boy being grabbed from behind by a policeman and pitched headfirst off downtown Santiago's Pio Nono bridge, in broad daylight, in front of countless witnesses. The concrete channel of the Mapocho River was ankle-deep at the time, so the boy was lucky to survive, but the shock that a policeman felt free to act as he did without any semblance of trying to hide his crime filled me with dread for the runup to the plebiscite on the new constitution due on October 25, 2020.

Over the months, social media had already spread news of the way the Chilean government was abusing the special dispensations of the state of emergency, as well as the antiterrorism laws invoked in October 2019, to use them against Mapuche land rights campaigners and also against social justice campaigners in general. Now it was very obvious anyone could be a victim of the impunity of Chilean state forces, and the possibility that President Piñera might use the pandemic or civil unrest as an excuse to cancel the plebiscite felt very real.

"But if he does that, the shit will really hit the fan!" said many, but that hardly diminished my foreboding.

To be sure, the *Guardian* reported the Chilean police had racked up eighty-five hundred allegations of human rights abuses over the past year and the government's lack of enthusiasm for democratic processes was undeniable, even in the face of massive popular demand.

The day of the plebiscite I was awake by 6:30 a.m. and ready to be first in line to vote. Peaceful birdsong accompanied my morning stroll to the polling station an hour later, and I felt a tense thrill walking past navy personnel with their dark blue berets and matching facemasks, and police in their olive-green uniforms. But the only people in the polling station were dozens of citizen voting assistants awaiting instructions. The booths and paperwork were not even ready yet, and I could not help smiling at the thought that the democratic process was an hour late in Limache.

"This is Chile," said a polling agent with a shrug, and we both settled in to wait for the ballot delivery.

It felt odd being the only one in line. I had arrived early to avoid the queues, but there were none.

"People don't like to arrive early, in case they get coopted as compulsory polling assistants," the agent explained.

Voting is all very well, but few people anywhere want to spend all day on it.

The news from around the country was of a peaceful vote, which was a relief; and by nightfall the result was clear. Chileans voted in favor of a new constitution: 78.27 percent nationally (78.12 percent in Limache). As to the mechanism by which it should be drafted, 78.99 percent of voters chose that it should be written exclusively by constitutional members popularly elected.

"I waited forty years for this to happen," a dear Chilean friend told me. "Didn't think I would live to see it."

The resounding rejection of Pinochet's constitution imposed during the dictatorship and the allowance of current parliamentarians to formulate a new one was indeed astonishing.

By 9:00 p.m., Chile was ringing to the sounds of honking cars taking victory turns around every plaza, and I took to the streets once more to join the crowd on ours. I found men, women, and children jumping up and down in euphoria, flags on sticks and poles waving above our heads in a jubilant frenzy of color, and my ears rang to blasts from a giant Mapuche horn, a lone bagpipe player, massive beating drums, and plenty of individual pots being banged by spoons. Impromptu fireworks lit up the sky and the most extraordinary thing of all was the complete absence of armed forces. None. Not even at a distance, though I had seen a couple of policemen standing in the darkness of the locked and silent polling station as I had hurried to the rainbow of lights and color nearby.

Walking home, close to midnight and past the normal curfew hour that had been in force all year, I felt elated and also stunned. This was not my moment of truth. There were no memories of the military coup for me, or its aftermath, or of the famous plebiscite of 1988 that hastened Pinochet's personal removal from public life. Yet I could not help but remember the horror of just one year ago, when I feared for my sons' lives as they ran the gauntlet of gun-toting police and armored vehicles with water cannons.

"I could feel his breath on my neck as I ran," Sascha had told me of his closest encounter.

"We've got you now," the man behind him shouted.

They didn't, and my trembling mother's heart was spared. But the tension and the fear were all-encompassing and not improved by being physically safe. Knowing that others were not so lucky overshadowed everything during those days and weeks and months.

Yet, just one year on, it already all seemed so long ago. October 25, 2020, was indeed a new dawn for Chile—at least psychically. The complex work for the foundation of real change was still to come. But now there was hope where there had been none, and the conviction that a more equitable society *is* possible. How glad I was to be part of that.

December 14, 2020: Total Eclipse of the Sun

According to the Mapuche, the symbolic death of the life-giving sun during a total eclipse is a bad omen, especially this year, since 10 percent obscurity is set to be precisely over the Araucanía Region.

The belief is that when the earth is left in darkness, it not only produces a change in nature but also causes a spiritual and existential crisis for humans, which could arise from a pandemic or other kind of catastrophe. Of course the hope is that the destruction implied is of injustice and the old ways of being that no longer serve humanity, so it is also a moment of profound thanksgiving, and of paying heed to the urgent sign of an unbalanced nature that is manifesting as climate change and disease. Now, more than ever, it is necessary to honor the four cornerstones of an individual's duty to contribute to the common good, proceed with courage, cultivate wisdom, and act justly.

The eclipse portends that worse than the uprising and the pandemic is to come. The end of life as we know it is at hand, but a new cycle of life is about to begin. Most importantly of all, according to the Mapuche academic Elisa Loncón of the University of Santiago (who was later elected president of the first constitutional convention responsible for writing a new Chilean constitution), the eclipse is an invitation to acknowledge nature as an *actor* in our futures, alongside humanity—not an adversary but an ally.[3]

28

Cambia todo cambia

Everything Changes

I have lived most of my life on the premise that dreams are worth chasing and never to accept second best.[1] But dreams can turn into nightmares, and sometimes second best is the best there is. Put another way, I have learned that sometimes even your best is not enough, and that acceptance is not defeat but wisdom. It wasn't a lesson I wanted to learn, but it was forced on me over many painful years of trying to find a way for us all to live happily ever after in Chile.

Instead of the dream, I first found myself without the main man in my plan, and then in a home without a future I wanted to sustain on my own. The grief I endured on both those counts has marked me in every conceivable way and yet, strangely, it has also made me a happier and more peaceful person, much more flexible mentally and emotionally, and less obsessed with success. Today, gratitude is my strongest feeling, but it was a very long path indeed to find that peaceful place, which is not dependent on anyone or any location and enables me to say good-bye to my beloved Quinta, the only place I ever thought was going to be forever. But forever does not exist and I am so glad I found that out before it was too late to move on. I still have places to see and love to share, and I can't wait for what comes next.

In the meantime, however, change can hurt and the changes to my beloved hometown in Chile are very sad. Once upon a time, the Limache Valley was the wonder of Chile in microcosm: natural beauty, a wealth of agricultural produce, and a fabulous Mediterranean climate, all cradled within the protective embrace of the coastal mountains that gently spill their waters into the Pacific Ocean nearby. Some will tell you it is also at a profoundly important junction of spiritual lines that converge here, which is confirmed in the roots of the word Limache itself, which means "place of the *machi* or shaman."

The town was not just a pretty face either. Once upon a time, it was also a vibrant manufacturing hub that moved Chile's most famous historian Benjamin Vicuña Mackenna to dub it Limanchester; and while that was delusional, it nevertheless underlines the fact that many family-owned firms once produced everything from beer to iron products, canned fruit and vegetables, sweets and jams, and even loofahs. Today only the Merello sweet factory survives, which was founded by Italian immigrants in 1932. All the other manufacturing businesses were destroyed by the impacts of the military dictatorship, which puts the lie to the common perception that Pinochet's government saved the country's economy. In the case of Limache, he destroyed it, and only reconnection to the coast via the modern commuter rail in 2005 has brought new impetus, but it has been in the form of a devastating construction boom that is turning Limache into a dormitory town for people who work on the coast and even as far away as Santiago.

When we first came to live in Limache in 2006, however, the town seemed ideal. The nearest beach is just thirty-two kilometers away, where the Aconcagua River flows into the ocean at Con Con, and while we don't get the morning fog that hangs over most of Chile's coast every day, we do get the invigorating ocean breeze, and even the occasional seagull coasting high above. To be able to enjoy seaside and mountain pleasures within a short drive from each other, yet be close to the urban centers of Santiago and Valparaíso as well, is a luxury no other place in Chile affords in this way, and even now I can think of nowhere else I would rather be, if my personal circumstances had allowed it. But the combination of life's unexpected twists and turns and the fact that this treasure is being destroyed by humans who care nothing for the environment or the life of future generations breaks my heart, and I cannot bear to witness the incessant violation of the natural and urban landscape where, despite the energetic efforts of hundreds of people, the local authority has completely failed to protect the most picturesque urban skyline in Chile and continues to drag its heels against the construction companies who are threatening its official status as a protected *zona tipica*.

What was once a beautiful nineteenth-century garden town filled with orchards and boasting one of the country's finest tree-lined boulevards is now scarred by empty lots where its historic buildings have been demolished to make way for unimaginative concrete constructions. Over the years, I have witnessed the demolition of nine historic houses within a ten-minute walk from my home, and there are at least half a dozen others that have been left derelict by their owners, because there are no financial incentives to protect urban heritage. Of the many other nineteenth-century homes there remains no trace, except for the incongruous pairs of palm trees you see dotted around town, marking the location of grand entrances long gone. If I were to cross the Limache River to record the destruction on the other side of town, the figures would easily be tripled.

The unique tree-high skyline has been ruined by ugly apartment blocks and a new school, some of which seem unlikely to withstand the next serious earthquake, and the environs of the Limache River, which once had several popular bathing pools lined by lovely sandbanks and the shade of weeping willows, are now a garbage-filled sewer that brings shame to every citizen with a conscience. Even worse, the municipal authorities appear to have completely sold out to external financial interests, allowing the valley's groundwater to be sucked up by commercial avocado plantations and the river to be diverted into concrete pipes feeding a nearby dam that provides drinking water for the explosion of coastal conurbations between Con Con and Viña del Mar. To cap it all, plans to build a thermo-electric plant in neighboring San Pedro were only defeated after a very costly and exhausting environmental campaign that may or may not stand the test of time.

The fact that La Campana National Park, at the end of the valley, was declared part of a UNESCO Biosphere Reserve in 1984 appears to have had no influence in preventing the tide of urban and industrial development in and around its unsecured delineation, including a brand new necklace of high-tension electrical pylons that now stand over the valley like faceless metal centurions from another planet. The list of minor and serious infringements of environmental protection and urban planning is seemingly endless, and the sustained efforts of concerned inhabitants have achieved nothing more than delays and a great deal of distress as a result of peaceful protest becoming increasingly criminalized by the Chilean state. Truly, it is a sad situation that only genuine systemic change can fix.

To be part of the solution is the only honorable and conscientious position to take and that is in part my motivation for writing these tales. Because I have come to love this country, despite the heavy heart it has given me, and if my stories inspire debate and contribute to the demands for change that are sweeping Chile, I will feel I have done my best to bear witness, which is all I am entitled to do as an immigrant. It is not my place to offer solutions or insist on change. Only Chileans can do that and I sincerely hope they succeed.

But I can't help also being sad for what has been lost and can never return. I miss the thrill of canal water gushing to every corner of the Quinta to feed our fruit trees, even though my sons would be the first to remind me how stressed I used to get, trying to keep up with directing the exuberant flow. It was hard physical labor clearing

Figure 30. The fruits of my garden, once upon a time.

the channels and opening and closing the sluices for six hours on irrigation day, but how lucky we were. Chile's ten-year drought did not affect us too badly until 2018, when the irrigation water stopped coming and many trees died. Like others in the valley, I was forced to cut marvelous house-high avocado trees to stumps, to help them gather their strength to survive, and though the drastic measures have largely been successful, I feel the loss deeply. The extreme dryness of the climate and weakened plants have also increased the threat from insect plagues and disease, and although we did our best to learn sustainable techniques to manage our fruit trees, the challenge is overwhelming and requires resources I do not have.

The responsibility and physical strength needed to run the

Quinta is too much for me, yet I was not willing to leave my jewel to be destroyed by the construction companies running rampant in Limache, either. The solution I found is insane from the point of view of investment profits, but it made sense to me personally, and so one of San Francisco de Limache's last historic quintas was divided in two, thereby making each half too small to be of interest to the builders of apartment blocks. Another guardian was found to love and care for the nineteenth-century house and its surrounding gardens, and I am free to enjoy the remaining plants and trees without the burden of a huge home to take care of.

In many ways, I am returning to the freedom I have always loved, so even while many people have asked me how I could possibly give up the most beautiful property anyone could ever hope for, my answer is that life is for living and impermanence is second nature to me. Flying the golden cage that was once my home is liberation and today the Quinta is someone else's dream. I wish the new family well. It will break their hearts and bring them joy, but that is the definition of love.

Postscript

From the arrival of the first conquistadors onward, people have regularly not been happy with their lot in Chile, and even though the famous slogan of the 2019 uprising, "*No es por 30 pesos, es por 30 años*," was an accurate summary of the conflict, it really does not come close to describing the deep-seated depression of the Chilean people. Because the truth is, the issue of inequality and injustice has been a defining feature of their society, ever since the first Europeans arrived.

The end of colonial times did not improve the situation, according to the founder of the Socialist Workers' Party in Chile, Luis Emilio Recabarren (1876–1924), who noted on the occasion of the centenary of the independent Chilean Republic in 1910 that there was not much to celebrate for the majority of its citizens, who had no share in the country's wealth.[1] The same could have been said in 2010, and his insistence on making a connection between moral progress and material progress also seems fitting: In other words, a good education and cultural values need to go hand in hand with economic opportunity and social equity. Meanwhile, the aspirational middle class seem to get the worst of both extremes, combining the desire for status and material possessions of the wealthy with the nightmarish personal debt and complete lack of work security of the poor. The resentment is palpable.

The tragedy is that the descendants of those who have lived here for millennia could have shared how to live a purposeful life and enjoy economic stability, a long time ago. It is a simple wisdom that has been learned all over the world, again and again: that happiness is about giving, not taking; that peace is about justice, and prosperity is about serving your community and respecting the laws of your natural environment. Institutionalized religion, power, and financial profit have nothing to do with it.

This missing context of the fundamental need for humanity to respect its place in the natural order of the universe has long been studied in Chile, most notably by the revered ethnomusicologist and philosopher Gastón Soublette and his colleague, the ethnographer Ziley Mora. Both have repeatedly made the point that Chilean society's profound depression and potential fulfillment can be located in the very thing it has been so eager to deny: namely its mestizo culture's roots in Indigenous knowledge and customs.

While Chile's leaders have always accused Indigenous people, and specifically the Mapuche, of holding the country back with their stubborn insistence on fighting for obsolete land rights that stand in the way of profitable economic ventures, such as mining, forestry, and hydroelectricity, they have lost sight of the vital connection between a nation's spiritual identity and its worldly one, which in turn has led to a failure to cultivate not only the earth but also the human values so vital to a successful and vibrant society. At best, Mapuche cultural heritage and ancient wisdom have been treated as a quaint selling point for the tourism industry. More frequently, Chile's Indigenous groups have been despised as representing everything that is primitive, backward, and even violent.

Mora notes in his book *Newen* that a side effect of Chile's obsession with progress and maximum control of its mixed-blood people is to have created one of Latin America's dullest societies without even a national carnival.[2] There are plenty of local festivals, to be fair, but nothing to rival the famous parties throughout the rest of Latin America and the Caribbean. There is no joie de vivre. Modern Chile has sucked the life right out of this part of the world. True, some would argue the harsh climate of the Mapuche and Patagonian tribal homelands was never conducive to joyfulness. Life has always been very tough at the southern tip of the Americas and it is a romantic aberration to assume the natives lived in joyful bliss before the Europeans arrived.

Nevertheless, it is the country's stubborn aboriginal roots that hold the key to a more environmentally and socially sustainable society, and increasing numbers of Chileans are coming to the conviction that living in harmony with nature is not just for hippies and Indians but actually crucial to their own survival. Internationally respected scientific and philosophical authorities have confirmed this, including Chile's very own analyst Raúl Sohr, in his latest book, published in November 2020, *El Mundo será verde o no será* (The Earth Shall Be Green or Not at All).

Ziley Mora assures his readers there is every reason to be hopeful, because the immutable laws of nature, the "eco-moral and social code of mother earth" (or the *matria*) have endured, whether or not humankind has taken any notice. The opportunity for the authors of the new Chilean constitution and the country's leaders is therefore to rediscover this code and incorporate it into the foundation of a renewed and united society that has something to celebrate at last.

The May 2021 election results for the 155 seats on the first constituent assembly were a wonderful confirmation of Chile's historic opportunity to live up to the hopes and dreams of its citizens, not just in terms of the environment but also in terms of creating a constitutional framework based on inclusive and equitable principles. The news made much of the fact that Piñera's right-wing coalition only gained 24 percent of the vote and failed to secure the possibility to veto genuine structural change. Yet candidates representing the center-left coalition of the past three decades did even worse, gaining just 16 percent. Both sides of Chile's political establishment were rejected. Instead, ordinary Chileans voted for individuals much closer to their own realities: two-thirds of the people initially elected to write Chile's new constitution were aged forty-five on average and were educated in the state school system; over half were women; and 17 of the 155 constituent seats were allocated to Indigenous representatives. For the first time in the country's history, there was an opportunity to write a constitution based on principles of social equity and access to resources, and many hoped Chile might just go from being one of the most unequal countries in the world to a unique example of grassroots democracy on a national scale. As if to prove this exciting new era, the Mapuche academic Elisa Loncón was elected as the assembly's first president; and the resounding election of the country's young president Gabriel Boric on a promise to bury neoliberalism sealed the new dawn for many in December 2021. But things are always far more complex and unpredictable than anyone can imagine in this part of the world, and victory has a habit of evaporating as fast as any sunbaked riverbed.

**

As the poet Nicanor Parra provocatively put it in his famous poem titled "Chile," over half a century ago, "We think we are a country, but the truth is we are just a landscape" (*Creemos ser país y la verdad es que somos apenas paisaje*).

As much as anything, Parra was referring to the elite, who have always treated Chile as a natural resource for the extraction of wealth, while the majority of the population is treated like so much cattle, to be used and managed to the advantage of others. This essential truth continues to haunt and is starkly underlined by the World Inequality Database, which put Chile's income inequality, as recently as 2021, at 59.8 percent, ahead of both the United States (45.6 percent) and the Russian Federation (50.8 percent) for the same year. Only South Africa was worse (65.4 percent).[3]

Again and again the people living in the country we now know as Chile have tried to defend their land and claim a better share of the good life to be had, and again and again they have been defeated by the superior resources of those who would control them. Sadly, the most recent example of this cycle is what has happened in the aftermath of the estallido social and it is an important context in trying to understand the seemingly contrary facts that almost 80 percent of eligible voters voted for a new constitution, to be written by individuals popularly elected; and yet, just two years later, the draft constitution written by those ordinary citizens was overwhelmingly rejected by national plebiscite.

A subsequent plebiscite in 2023 elected predominantly extreme right-wing candidates to oversee the writing of a new Magna Carta for Chile, retaining only a minority of representatives from the original movement for a more representative and inclusive society. Yet their version was also rejected after the final national vote on December 17, 2023, with the result that there will be no change at all and the running of the country will continue to be based on the constitution written by General Pinochet's men—an indescribable blow to those who dreamed of a new, more just, and progressive Chile, and to all those who died or suffered life-changing injuries during the uprising in 2019. Social media was soon awash with the view that it would have been less trouble to just pay up the thirty-peso increase on the Santiago metro fares!

The seeming contrariness of the Chilean electorate regarding a new constitution does have a hugely important context, however, and that is the drastic social and economic changes brought about by the pandemic and two years of unexpected hardship, which completely changed many people's priorities from dreaming about progress and social justice to simply trying to survive physically and economically. Political idealism and innovation suddenly felt like a luxury no one could afford, least of all in a country so dependent on not scaring off the corporate capital and foreign investment that keeps its economy afloat. That, combined with the inevitable rise in crime during desperate times, and the huge influx of refugees from Venezuela, which increased by an astonishing 162 percent between 2016 and 2020, according to the Chilean National Immigration Department, made the conservative press campaign focused on patriotism, stricter immigration controls, public order, and national security seem like a very good idea compared to radical changes with unpredictable results for the future of the country. Better the devil you know.

The shock and despair among the millions of citizens who really believed they would win out this time cannot be overstated. But the hard fact is that those brave few millions were always outnumbered by the silent majority, and the outgoing President Piñera left the new government of Latin America's youngest ever president with a very clever poison pill, making the vote for the plebiscites obligatory for the entire population of eligible voters, whereas the presidential elections had been based on voluntary participation. So even though the same number of people voted for a new constitution as elected Boric, they could not compete with the entire Chilean electorate, including prisoners, dragged to the polls against their will, who used their forced vote to protest in the only way open to them: to vote *no* on an issue they felt no connection to. Without a doubt, several other important factors played a role as well, especially the attempt to enshrine controversial or inappropriate statutes, such as granting a parallel justice system for Indigenous Chileans or the protection of specific plant and animal species that should be addressed by the legislature and not a constitution. A significant number of Chileans did not feel the most recent draft they were voting on represented their best interests, and the promise of amendments later was simply not good enough. But the compulsory vote was a killer.[4]

The *rechazo* (rejection) of 2022, as it is known in Chile, was not just a rejection of a highly problematic draft constitution written by people who got bogged down in a process they were not equipped to manage but also a rejection of being obliged to vote at all. This, combined with a profound lack of faith that politicians have the people's best interests at heart, kept voters in a very dark place, where they were easy prey for the massive media campaign of fear and negativity that bombarded them daily via television, radio, social media, and the printed press, which is predominantly owned by right-wing corporate business interests. A demonstration of the huge disparity between media resources for opposing arguments regarding the draft constitution was shown by the sums donated toward opposing camps: According to the Chilean newspaper *La Tercera*, 144,773,400 Chilean pesos was given to the *rechazo* campaign by private political donors, while the *apruebo* or accept campaign could only muster 771,363 Chilean pesos.[5] According to the Chilean academic Marcelo Casals, the press has also been very successful in rebranding the estallido social as a "criminal outburst," rather than a legitimate social justice campaign.[6]

The practice of false news and misinformation has been transplanted to fertile ground and recent research has shown that Chileans perceive themselves to be living in a far more dangerous environment than they really are. For example, the multinational market research company Ipsos reported in March 2023 that 85 percent of those interviewed believed public safety had declined over the past twelve months, with home invasions, assault, and robbery and urban delinquency being listed as the main perceived causes of the decline.[7] They also agreed it was the government's responsibility to solve the problem, which played straight into the hand of the ultraconservative parties, which promised to restore security and public order.

Yet Chile does not even make it into the top twenty most dangerous places to live in Latin America, according to the Spanish investigative media organization Público, which has stated Chile ranks twenty-second on the homicide index for Latin American countries and thirty-first for criminality globally (www.publico.es). Nevertheless, fear and prejudice are alive and well, which serves not only political extremists but also those determined to corral the population into ever-tighter boundaries, where they can be controlled and managed without interfering with the important business of making vast profits from Chile's privatized natural resources.

On the other hand, living in Chile since 2006, I have learned that nothing works in less than a minimum of three attempts, so there is still room for hope. A concerted grassroots campaign of voter education and convincing arguments that can reach into the heart of Chile's many distant communities, who feel excluded from the machinations of the capital city, could just put the brakes on the country's tragic destiny of total exploitation. Also, as Marcelo Casals has so cogently argued, "the simplistic and sometimes unfounded criticisms of republican egalitarianism" need to be reformulated into a less patronizing discussion of what kind of state the citizens of Chile want and how they wish to achieve it.

In any event, however, it is worth remembering that a constitution is just a road map. It is not where laws or policies affecting people's lives are made. The opportunity to build a more inclusive society and protect Chile's magnificent landscapes endures. The hope is there. But it won't be enough without an enormous leap of faith to jump over the fires of division.[8]

TALES FROM THE SHARP END

Notes

Introduction

1. See my book of traveler's tales from Central America, titled *Chickenbus Journey: False Paradise in Guatemala* (Norwich, UK: Remsasch Press, 2006).
2. The Indigenous population of Chile is just 13 percent, of which the Mapuche of southern Chile are the largest surviving group of peoples. And so Native food and craft markets are much less present than in neighboring Peru or Bolivia, for example, where traditional Native culture and people still make up a substantial part of everyday life.

Chapter 1

1. Ever the opportunist, Barrientos hired himself out to guide Almagro's party back to Peru.

Chapter 2

1. These towering plants are close relations to the San Pedro cactus, so they are famous not only for their flowers but also for the psychedelic mescaline you can cook out of their trunks.

Chapter 3

1. Chile's first constitution was a far cry from the ideals enshrined in the US Constitution, but then the Chilean elite were never motivated by democracy—a trend that continues to this day.
2. Meanwhile, her poor father was stripped of his assets, including the family estate, and exiled to the Juan Fernández Islands, despite always staying loyal to the Spanish Crown. The same islands were later renamed the Robinson Crusoe Islands, in honor of the novel inspired by their most famous castaway.
3. *La Nueva Aurora de Chile*, no. 4, June 2010, published by the Instituto

de Investigaciones Históricas General José Miguel Carrera, Santiago de Chile.

4. David Jewett (1772–1842) was a naturalized Argentinean, and later Brazilian, who played an important role in the original conflict between Argentina and Britain over the Falkland Islands in 1820, before offering his services to the Brazilian Navy.

Chapter 4

1. I have climbed the 1,880-meter/6,170-foot mountain four times now, and though the view of the Andes is superb, I have only seen the sea once. It needs to be a very crisp spring or autumn day.
2. Rudolf Steiner (1861–1925) was an Austrian philosopher and educationalist whose school system is represented by the international community of Waldorf Schools. He is also the father of anthroposophy.
3. Democracy officially returned to Chile in 1990, after a plebiscite on Augusto Pinochet's continued leadership led to the famous *no* vote, ending almost seventeen years of dictatorship.

Chapter 5

1. *Revista Chilena de Nutrición* 47, no. 2 (April 2020).
2. See *Con mi humilde devoción* by C. Mercado and C. Rondón, whose original book was published in Santiago in 2003 by Carlos Aldunate del Solar Editions, and which you can view online for the wonderful photos at Memoria Chilena: Biblioteca Nacional, https://www.memoriachilena.gob.cl.
3. See M. Carrere and V. Romo, "Chile: 416 concesiones para salmonicultura están en áreas protegidas," *Mongabay Latam*, March 17, 2021, and related articles at *Mongabay: News & Inspiration from Nation's Frontline*, https://www.mongabay.com.

Chapter 6

1. Edward Davis spent most of his time plaguing Spanish galleons in the Caribbean but also led some very successful raids along the South

American Pacific Coast, where he sacked La Serena and other ports between 1686 and 1687.

2. Miguel Gallo Vergara was twice mayor of Copiapó and also a Liberal deputy in the Chilean government, until his death in 1852. Today, his fabulously rich Gallo-Goyenechea clan is remembered in many ways, including as a street name in one of Santiago's glitziest neighborhoods, popularly known as Sanhatten for its modernist buildings and superb restaurants: Isidora Goyenechea Avenue in El Golf.
3. My source is an obscure Chilean history book by Carlos María Sayago, whose *Historia de Copiapó* (1874) is a collector's item in Chile.
4. The Diaguita make up 3.2 percent of Chile's Indigenous population and were only officially recognized in 2006, after a ten-year campaign to confirm their historic land rights. In the upper Huasco Valley, according to Chilean geographer Raúl Molina, that translates into twenty-four villages representing 262 families.

Chapter 7

1. By comparison, the 1994 California earthquake measured "just" 6.7 on the Richter Scale.
2. Oficina Nacional de Emergencia del Ministerio del Interior y Seguridad Pública.
3. "Tsunami paso a paso: Los escandalosos errores y omisiones del SHOA y la ONEMI," *CIPER Chile*, January 18, 2012.
4. *El Mercurio* (Saturday magazine), March 6, 2010.

Chapter 8

1. Caroline Richards is the author of *Sweet Country* (New York: Harcourt Brace Jovanovich, 1979), which was inspired by the events surrounding the military coup in Chile and later made into a Hollywood movie by Michael Cacoyannis. Howard Richards published many books and articles over the past fifty years and was active in several Chilean grassroots community organizations; he died in 2024.

Chapter 9

1. A cogent challenge of old theories for Rapa Nui can be found in T. L. Hunt and C. P. Lipo, *Ecological Catastrophe and Collapse: The Myth of Ecocide on Rapa Nui* (Honolulu: University of Hawaii Press, 2009).
2. While people with one of the thirty-six surnames officially recognized as Rapanui can trace their ancestry back to one of the ten tribes (*mata*) that once existed, it should be noted there are no islanders left who are 100 percent Indigenous, as miscegenation took place from the very first time visitors came to Rapa Nui.
3. See Riet Delsing, *Articulating Rapa Nui* (Honolulu: University of Hawaii, 2015), and also the International Work Group for Indigenous Affairs reports published in 2012 and 2019 that provide excellent context to the problems facing the island today (available at the International Work Group for Indigenous Affairs website, www.iwgia.org).

Chapter 11

1. As far as I know, the Chilean Air Force has only ever been deployed against its own citizens. At any rate, the Limache bomb was probably dropped by aircraft from the nearby naval airbase at El Belloto.
2. It has been confirmed by a Chilean court that the manager of the CCU factory, Jaime Aldoney, was thrown from a helicopter into the ocean after being tortured to death in 1973. Retired navy captains Sergio Mendoza Rojas and Pedro Arancibia Solar were convicted for the crime in 2011, though both had their prison sentences commuted to nothing more than regular reporting to their local police stations.
3. In fact, the purchase and sale of that quinta was the subject of a scandal, because Pinochet sold it to a state agency at a 230 percent personal profit in 1980. For more on his shady financial dealings see Heraldo Muñoz, *The Dictator's Shadow: Life under Augusto Pinochet* (New York: Basic Books, 2008).

Chapter 12

1. To be fair, the urban version of the cueca, known as *cueca brava* or "fierce cueca," is more in tune with modern times.
2. If you understand Spanish, see YouTube for the excellent short presentation on the tapestry titled "Lectura de arpillera 'Contra la guerra' de Violeta Parra por Jorge Montealegre" (2017).
3. Andrés Gómez Bravo, "La última carta de Violeta," *La Tercera,* July 13, 2019.
4. *El Mercurio* magazine, September 3, 2016.

Chapter 13

1. I find it fascinating to note this conversational custom has its roots in the traditional exchanges between Indigenous Mapuche chiefs and their messengers, which always begin with a ritual questioning regarding health and the well-being of the animals and nature, before the issue at hand can be considered.
2. Chile's government spends less than 3 percent of GDP on pensions, compared with an average of 8 percent in the OECD, according to a *Financial Times* report from November 2020.
3. Excellent sources of information (in Spanish) regarding the scandalous systemic inequality in Chile, and in particular the issue of labor relations and pensions, can be found at FundaciónSol, www.fundacionsol.cl.

Chapter 14

1. See C. Bonelli, "Visions and Divisions in Pehuenche Life" (PhD diss., University of Edinburgh, 2013), available at https://era.ed.ac.uk/bitstream/handle/1842/8275/Bonelli2013.pdf?isAllowed=y&sequence=2.
2. A superb source of information and references on the dam projects is Lorenzo Nesti's article "The Mapuche-Pehuenche and the Ralco Dam on the Biobío River: The Challenge of Protecting Indigenous Land Rights," *International Journal on Minority and Group Rights* 9, no. 1 (2002): 1–40. To learn about the Pehuenche sisters, see Alejandra

Toro's wonderful documentary in Spanish, *Berta y Nicolasa, las hermanas Quintremán*, available on YouTube.

Chapter 15

1. See articles published by Centro de Investigación Periodística at www.ciperchile.cl.
2. See *Elmostrador*, at www.elmostrador.cl, for January 11, 2019.

Chapter 16

1. Kuki Gallmann, *I Dreamed of Africa* (London: Viking, 1991).

Chapter 18

1. Sadly, due to slash-and-burn agriculture, road building, and human encroachment, Peru's national tree is now an officially endangered species that can only be found in the country's northwestern region of Piura, on the border with Ecuador.
2. The quote and story are used by kind permission from Chilean historian Rodrigo Moreno, who wrote an introduction for the private edition Agustin Edwards had made from original manuscripts in his possession for the Roxburghe Club in London, for which I was the translator.
3. An interesting footnote to Dombey's history is that he was on a mission to bring metric weights and measures to the United States, at the request of Thomas Jefferson, in 1793. But his death meant metrication was delayed until the mid- to late nineteenth century. See Keith Martin, "Pirates of the Caribbean (Metric Edition)," National Institute of Standards and Technology, *Taking Measure* (blog), September 19, 2017, https://www.nist.gov/blogs/taking-measure/pirates-caribbean-metric-edition for the full story.

Chapter 19

1. See the undated report by Esteban Bucat Oviedo, published by the Chilean Study Centre for Democracy and Civil Defense in March 2013, at https://coyunturapolitica.files.wordpress.com/2013/03/cedec_prep_marina.pdf.

His book (only in Spanish) is also of interest: *El general* (Madrid: Punto Rojo Libros, 2016).

2. A wide-ranging report on censorship and the role of radio media in Chile in the 1970s and '80s can be found in Eva Herrera and Katherine Reyes, *El rol de las radios opositoras frente a la censura instaurada durante la dictadura cívico-militar en Chile* (Santiago, Chile: Documentation Center of the Museo de la Memoria, 2018). The report can be found via their website, https://cedocmuseodelamemoria.cl.

Chapter 20

1. See "Share of Births Outside of Marriage," OECD Family Database, https://www.oecd.org/els/family/database.htm, which lists Chile as the leading nation for children born outside marriage: 75 percent at last count in 2018.
2. The work of the Chilean Anti-Violence against Women Network can be found at www.nomasviolenciacontramujeres.cl. My published sources for this chapter include the work of EPES (https://www.epes.cl) and M. Segovia and G. Perez Campbell, "Femicidios no bajan a pesar de reformas y políticas contra la violencia de género: 131 víctimas entre 2018 y 2020," *Centro de Investigación Periodística*, March 7, 2021, https://www.ciperchile.cl/2021/03/07/femicidios-no-bajan-a-pesar-de-reformas-y-politicas-contra-la-violencia-de-genero-131-victimas-entre-2018-y-2020/.

Chapter 22

1. For gross monthly salaries of congress members in Latin America see, for example, "Gross Monthly Salary of Congress Members in Latin America in 2018, by Country (in U.S. Dollars)," Statista, accessed March 31, 2024, https://www.statista.com/statistics/1075333/latin-america-congress-members-salary-country, where you can discover the shockingly high income of Chilean members compared to other countries.

2. By December 2019 Chile's National Institute of Human Rights officially put the number of victims of eye injuries since the beginning of the Chilean uprising at 352. See *La Tercera*, December 7, 2019.
3. See "Chile: Deliberate Policy to Injure Protesters Points to Responsibility of Those in Command," press release, Amnesty International, November 21, 2019, https://www.amnesty.org/en/latest/press-release/2019/11/chile-responsable-politica-deliberada-para-danar-manifestantes/.

Chapter 23

1. Sadly, the continuation of this annual spectacle is in doubt, in our post-COVID, politically turbulent world.
2. One of my sons and I walked through the square as recently as 2023; the only change was that this time a woman was peeing freely on the sidewalk, without even bothering to take down her pants.

Chapter 24

1. The plebiscite was originally set for April 2020, but postponed to October 25, 2020, because of the COVID-19 pandemic. A third and final plebiscite took place on December 17, 2023.
2. They did not, an academic friend confirms.
3. See J. L. Phelan, *The People and the King: The Comunero Revolution in Colombia, 1781* (Madison: University of Wisconsin Press, 1967).

Chapter 25

1. For more, see Giles Tremlett, "Operation Condor: The Cold War Conspiracy That terrorized South America," *Guardian*, September 3, 2020.
2. Patricio Navia, "The Politics of Chile's New Constitution," *Americas Quarterly*, October 26, 2020, https://www.americasquarterly.org/article/the-politics-of-chiles-new-constitution/.
3. Charles B. Handy, *The Second Curve: Thoughts on Reinventing Society* (London: Random House, 2015).

Chapter 26

1. My sources for this chapter include the book by Tania Tamayo and Alejandra Carmona, *El Negocio del agua* (Santiago: Random House, 2019); the Terram Foundation
(https://www.terram.cl); and El Desconcierto (https://www.eldesconcierto.cl).

Chapter 27

1. *Bloomberg,* June 16, 2020.
2. According to a report at https://www.cooperativa.cl from March 11, 2019, over 358,000 school-age children were not attending any school, even before the pandemic, so it may well be that up to a third of all children eligible for the public school system in Chile are living in conditions of socioeconomic risk.
3. My source is an article by Marco Fajardo, "La visión filosófica mapuche del eclipse que vivirá La Araucanía en diciembre," *Elmostrador,* July 10, 2020, https://www.elmostrador.cl/cultura/2020/07/10/la-vision-filosofica-mapuche-del-eclipse-que-vivira-la-araucania-en-diciembre/.

Chapter 28

1. "Todo cambia" is a South American song made famous by Mercedes Sosa, but for Chileans the version by Julio Numhauser, the exiled founder of Quilapayún, is most meaningful.

Postscript

1. Note his party became the Communist Party of Chile in 1918 and has nothing to do with the Socialist Party of Chile, which Salvador Allende cofounded in 1933.
2. Ziley Mora, *Newen* (Santiago: Ediciones Urano Chile, 2019).
3. See World Inequality Database, https://wid.world, data for 2021.
4. For more information on this topic see, for example, Matthew Malinowski and Valentina Fuentes, "Why Chile's Draft Constitution Has Come under Attack," *Washington Post,* September 4, 2022.

5. See Luciano Jiménez, "Aportes monetarios de campaña del Rechazo superan en casi 200 veces al Apruebo," *La Tercera*, July 26, 2022.
6. For his analysis of the failure of the Chilean left, see "Chile Has Entered Its Thermidorian Period," *Jacobin*, May 10, 2023,https://jacobin.com/2023/05/chile-thermidorian-period-far-right-constitutional-council-election.
7. Ipsos Report Number 16, March 2023 (https://www.ipsos.com).
8. Thanks to the actor Jim Carrey for saying it first: "Hope walks through the fire, and faith jumps over it." (commencement speech, Maharishi International University of Management, Fairfield, Iowa, May 30, 2014).

Select Bibliography

History and Biography

Bonnefoy, P. *Terrorismo de estadio: Prisioneros de guerra en un campo de deportes*. Santiago: Ediciones Liberalia, 2023.

Bressan, D. "Climate, Overpopulation and Environment—The Rapa Nui Debate." *Scientific American*, October 31, 2011.

Cayuqueo, P. *Historia secreta Mapuche*. 2 vols. Santiago: Catalonia, 2017, 2020.

Collier, S., and W. Sater. *A History of Chile 1808–1994*. Cambridge, UK: Cambridge University Press, 1996.

Contreras Painemal, C. "Los Tratados celebrados por los Mapuche con la Corona Española, la República de Chile y la República de Argentina." PhD diss., University of Berlin, 2010.

Cordingly, D. *Cochrane the Dauntless*. London: Bloomsbury, 2007.

Cunninghame Grahame, R. B. *Pedro de Valdivia: Conqueror of Chile*. Reprint. Westport, CT: Greenwood Press, 1974.

Feinstein, A. *Pablo Neruda*. London: Bloomsbury, 2004.

Hunt, T. L., and C. P. Lipo. "Revisiting Rapa Nui (Easter Island) "Ecocide." *Pacific Science* 63, no. 4 (2009): 601–16.

Kerschen, K. *Violeta Parra: By the Whim of the Wind*. Albuquerque: ABQ Press, 2010.

Mackenna, V. *Doña Javiera de Carrera*. Santiago: Guillermo E. Miranda, 1904.

Mann, C. *1491: New Revelations of the Americas before Columbus*. New York: Vintage, 2006.

Mount, G. *Chile and the Nazis: From Hitler to Pinochet*. Montreal: Black Rose Books, 2002.

Onetto Pavo, M. *A Passage to the World: The Strait of Magellan during the Age of Its Discovery*. Santiago: Autonomous University of Chile, 2019.

Rojo, G., and J. Hasset, eds. *Chile, Dictatorship and the Struggle for Democracy*. Gaithersburg, MD: Ediciones Hispamérica, 1988.

Ruiz, A. *Stella Díaz Varín*. La Serena, Chile: Universidad de La Serena, 2017.

Sánchez, G. *La caravana de la muerte: Las víctimas de Pinochet*. Barcelona: Contrapunto, 2001.

Souhami, D. *Selkirk's Island*. London: Phoenix, 2001.

Spooner, M. H. *Soldiers in a Narrow Land: The Pinochet Regime in Chile*. London: University of California Press, 1999.

Torre Barca, J. *Pequeña Inglaterra de Chile*. Valparaíso, 2011 (purchased from the author on the street).

Tromben, C. *Crónica secreta de la economía chilena*. Santiago: Ediciones B, 2016.

Politics, Society, and Culture

Agosín, M. *Tapestries of Hope, Threads of Love: The Arpillera Movement in Chile*. Lanham, MD : Rowman and Littlefield, 2007.

Barros, J. P. *Mira tú*. Santiago: Editorial Hueders, 2018.

Beckett, A. *Pinochet in Piccadilly: Britain and Chile's Hidden History*. London: Faber and Faber, 2002.

Bonelli, C. "Visions and Divisions in Pehuenche Life." PhD diss., University of Edinburgh, 2012. https://era.ed.ac.uk/bitstream/handle/1842/8275/Bonelli2013.pdf.

Chilean Pre-Colombian Museum. 2016. *The Art of Being Diaguita*. Santiago: Chilean Pre-Colombian Museum.

Constable, P., and A. Valenzuela. *A Nation of Enemies: Chile under Pinochet*. New York: Norton, 1993.

Delsing, R. *Articulating Rapa Nui: Polynesian Cultural Politics in a Latin American Nation-State*. Honolulu: University of Hawaii Press, 2015.

Dinges, J. *The Condor Years: How Pinochet and His Allies brought Terrorism to Three Continents*. New York: New Press, 2005.

Dorfman, A. *Other Septembers, Many Americas: Selected Provocations, 1980–2004*. London: Pluto Press, 2004.

Durston, J., ed. *Pueblos Originarios y sociedad nacional en Chile*. Santiago: UNDP, 2013.

Fisher, J. *Out of the Shadows: Women, Resistance and Politics in South America*. London: Latin American Bureau, 1993.

Follegati Pollmann, R. *Pequeñas historias íntimas*. Quilpué, Chile: Werken, 2020.

———. *Valparaíso entre la utopía y la realidad*. Quilpué, Chile: Werken, 2020.

Franceschet, S. *Women and Politics in Chile*. London: Lynne Rienner, 2005.

Garcia Espinoza, F. *Pinceladas a la historia limachina*. Limache: Impr. Creación Gráfica, 2003.

Guerriero, L., ed. *Extremas*. Santiago: Universidad de Diego Portales, 2019.

Handy, C. *The Second Curve: Thoughts on Reinventing Society*. London: Random House, 2015.

Hora, E., and D. Meyer. *This America of Ours: The Letters of Gabriela Mistral and Victoria Ocampo*. Austin: University of Texas Press, 2003.

International Work Group for Indigenous Affairs. *The Human Rights of the Rapa Nui People on Easter Island*. Report no. 15, Copenhagen, 2012. https://www.iwgia.org/images/publications/0597_Informe_RAPA_NUI_IGIA-Observatorio_English_FINAL.pdf.

Matus, A. *Mitos y verdades de las AFP*. Santiago: Penguin Random House, 2017.

Mora, Z. *Newen*. Santiago: Ediciones Urano Chile, 2019.

Nesti, L. "The Mapuche—Pehuenche and the Ralco Dam on the Bíobío River: The Challenge of Protecting Indigenous Land Rights." *International Journal on Minority and Group Rights* 9, no. 1 (2002): 1–40.

Palet, A., and P. de Aguirre. *Desiguales: Origines, cambios y desafíos de la brecha social en Chile*. Santiago: UNDP, 2017.

Richards, H. *The Evaluation of Cultural Action*. London: Macmillan, 1985.

———. *The Nurturing of Time Future*. Lake Oswego, OR: Dignity Press, 2012.

———. *Repensar la política*. Santiago: Universitas Nueva Civilización, 2016.

Richards, P. "Of Indians and Terrorists: How the State and Local Elites Construct the Mapuche in Neoliberal Multicultural Chile." *Journal of Latin American Studies* 42, no. 1 (2010): 59–90.

Rivano Fischer, E. *Chileno Callejero: Street Chilean Spanish*. Concepción, Chile: Universidad de Concepción, 2005.

Routledge, K. *The Mystery of Easter Island: The Story of an Expedition.* London: Hazell, Watson and Viney, 1919.

Salazar, C. *Urbatorium* (blog). https://urbatorium.blogspot.com.

Sehnbruch, K., N. Agloni, W. Imilan, and C. Sanhueza. "Social Policy Responses of the Chilean State to the Earthquake and Tsunami of 2010." *Latin American Perspectives* 44, no. 4 (2017): 24–40.

Sohr, R. *El mundo será verde o no será.* Santiago: Random House, 2020.

Solimano, A. *Chile and the Neoliberal Trap: The Post-Pinochet Era.* Cambridge: Cambridge University Press, 2012.

Soublette, G. *Manifiesto: Peligros y oportunidades de la megacrisis.* Santiago: Ediciones Universidad Católica de Chile, 2019.

Štambuk, P. *Rosa Yagán.* Santiago: Pehuén, 2011.

Tamayo, T., and A. Carmona. *El negocio del agua.* Santiago: Random House, 2019.

Wright, C. "La Peña de los Parra: The Power of Song." *Iowa Review* 22, no. 1 (1992): 46–77.

Travel and Memoir

Agosín, M., and J. Levison, eds. *Magical Sites: Women Travelers in Nineteenth Century Latin America.* Buffalo, NY: White Pine Press, 1999.

Allende, I. *My Invented Country.* New York: Harper Perennial, 2004.

———. *Paula.* London: HarperCollins, 1995.

Boylston, H. *Hay locos.* N.p.: Kaye Productions, 2011.

Bridges, L. E. *Uttermost Part of the Earth: A History of Tierra del Fuego and the Fuegians.* London: Hodder and Stoughton, 1948.

Camus, A. *American Journals.* London: Spear Marlowe, 1995.

Clissold, S. *Chilean Scrapbook.* New York: Praeger, 1953.

Cooper, M. *Pinochet and Me: A Chilean Anti-Memoir.* New York: Verso, 2001.

Dixie, F. *Across Patagonia.* New York: R. Worthington, 1881.

Graham, M. *Journal of a Residence in Chile during the year 1822; and a Voyage from Chile to Brazil in 1823.* London, 1824.

Jara, J. *Victor: An Unfinished Song*. London: Jonathan Cape, 1983.

Keenan, B., and J. McCarthy. *Between Extremes*. London: Bantam Press, 1999.

Montecino, M., and C. Montecino. *Irredimible: Diario 1973*. Santiago: Ocho Libros, 2011.

Silver, K., ed. *Chile: A Traveler's Literary Companion*. Berkeley, CA: Whereabouts Press, 2003.

Swale, R. *Back to Cape Horn*. London: Collins, 1986.

Wheeler, S. *Travels in a Thin Country: A Journey through Chile*. London: Little, Brown, 1994.

Flora and Fauna

Darwin, C. *Voyage of the Beagle*. London: 1839.

Echenique, A., and M. V. Legassa. *La flora chilena en la mirada de Marianne North, 1884*. Santiago: Pehuén Editores, 1999.

Hipolito Ruiz: A Botanist at the Ends of the Earth. London: Santiago, Agustin E. Edwards private edition for the Roxburghe Club, 2017.

Hoffmann, J., J. Watson, and A. Flore. *Flora Silvestre de Chile: Cuando el desierto florece*. Vol. 1. Santiago: Fundación Claudio Gay, 2015.

Jaramillo, A. *Birds of Chile*. Princeton, NJ: Princeton University Press, 2003.

North, M. *Recollections of a Happy Life*. London, 1892.

Payne, M. *Marianne North: A Very Intrepid Painter*. London, Kew Publishing, 2011.

Schell, P. A. *The Sociable Sciences: Darwin and His Contemporaries in Chile*. London: Palgrave Macmillan, 2013.

Schultes, R. E., and M. J. Nemry von Thenen de Jaramillo-Arango, trans. *The Journals of Hipólito Ruíz: Spanish Botanist in Peru and Chile 1777–1788*. Portland, OR: Timber Press, 1998.

Steele, A. R. *Flowers for the King: The Expedition of Ruiz and Pavon and the Flora of Peru*. Durham, NC: Duke University Press, 1964.

Poetry and Literature

Allende, I. *The House of the Spirits*, London: Jonathan Cape, 1985.

———. *Inés of my Soul*. London: Harper Perennial, 2007.

———. *Of Love and Shadows*. London: Jonathan Cape, 1987.

Berlin, L. *A Manual for Cleaning Women*. New York: Farrar, Straus and Giroux, 2015.

Cerda, P. *Violeta and Nicanor*. Santiago de Chile: Planeta, 2018.

Coloane, F. *Cape Horn and Other Stories from the End of the World*. Pittsburgh, PA: Latin American Literary Review Press, 2003.

Donoso, J. *Curfew*. New York: Weidenfeld and Nicolson, 1986.

Emar, J. *Amor*. Santiago: n.d., 1925.

Escritores Indigenas: A photographic and literary project to introduce Indigenous Chilean writers and poets to a wider audience. https://www.escritoresindigenas.cl.

Gander, F. *Pinholes in the Night: Essential Poems from Latin America*. Port Townsend, WA: Copper Canyon Press, 2014.

Hughes, B. *Folk Tales from Chile*. New York: Hippocrene Books, 1999.

Le Guin, U., trans. *Selected Poems of Gabriela Mistral*. Albuquerque: University of New Mexico Press, 2003.

Lemebel, P. *My Tender Matador*. New York: Grove Press, 2003.

Maturana, A. *No decir*. Santiago: Alfaguara, 2006.

Meruane, L. *Seeing Red*. Dallas: Deep Vellum Publishing, 2016.

Parra, N. *Poemas y Antipoemas*. Santiago: Nascimento, 1954.

Parra, V. *Poesía*. Valparaíso: Universidad de Valparaíso, 2016.

Rojas, M. *Hijo de ladrón*. Santiago: Nasciamento, 1951.

Russel, D., trans. *The Araucana* [epic poem by Alonso de Ercilla y Zúñiga, originally published in Madrid in 1574]. N.p.: Amazon, 2013.

Sepúlveda, L. *The Old Man Who Read Love Stories*. London: Souvenir Press, 1993.

———. *Patagonia Express: Apuntes de viaje*. Barcelona: Tusquets Editores, 2011.

Chilean internet sources relevant to human rights abuses during the 1973 military coup and subsequent dictatorship

Archiveros sin Fronteras. http://www.archiverossinfronteras.cl. Independent archivists dedicated to preserving archives in Chile and promoting public debate.

Archivo Nacional de Chile. https://www.archivonacional.gob.cl. The Chilean government's public national archive.

Archivos Chile. https://www.archivoschile.com. An investigative journalism site, run by the Miguel Enríquez Research Center, based on information recovered from public records using the Chilean Transparency Act.

Arzobispado de Santiago. Fundación Documentación y Archivo de la Vicaría de la Solidaridad. https://www.vicariadelasolidaridad.cl. Archbishop of Santiago's Foundation for Documentation, including the Archive for the Solidarity Vicariate, which was a vital Chilean aid organization during the Pinochet dictatorship.

Cantos Cautivos [Captive Songs]. https://www.cantoscautivos.org. A deeply moving musical archive of songs composed or sung by political prisoners in Chile's detention and torture centers between 1973 and 1989, recorded by survivors and compiled by Katia Chornik, the musicologist daughter of Chilean exiles in Britain.

Centro de Investigación Periodística [Centre for Investigative Journalism in Chile]. https://ciperchile.cl.

Cornejo, M. "Historias de la dictadura militar chilena desde voces generacionales." *Psyche* 22, no. 2 (2013): 49–65. https://scielo.conicyt.cl/pdf/psykhe/v22n2/art05.pdf. Research paper published by the Pontifical Catholic University of Chile on oral histories of experiencing the coup and military dictatorship, with an emphasis on the construction of memory.

Expdedientes de la Represión. Archivo de Sentencias Penales. https://expedientesdelarepresion.cl. Published record of all Chilean court papers of criminal cases relating to the systematic human rights abuses committed during the Pinochet dictatorship.

Fundación Victor Jara. https://fundacionvictorjara.org. Dedicated to preserving the musical and political legacy of Victor Jara.

Marineros Constitucionalistas de Chile. https://www.marineros-constitucionalistas-chile.com. Website produced by the association of Chilean ex-navy personnel who were opponents of the military coup of 1973.

MemoriaViva. https://www.memoriaviva.com. A London-based research website on human rights violations and authoritarian impunity in Chile, with a huge amount of information, including the location of all detention and torture centers identified in Chile to date.

Museo de la Memoria y los Derechos Humanos. https://www.museodelamemoria.cl. Dedicated to all aspects of recovering information regarding the military dictatorship and human rights abuses, including witness testimonies and audio recordings of victim statements.

National Library of Chile. https://www.memoriachilena.gob.cl.

Pérez Guerra, A. "Los negocios de Pinochet & familia." Santiago, Centro de Estudios Miguel Enríquez, 2004. Available at Archivo Chile. https://www.archivochile.com/Dictadura_militar/pinochet/sobre/DMsobrepino80018.pdf.

Servicio Nacional del Patrimonio Cultural. https://www.patrimoniocultural.gob.cl. Chilean government website for national archives, libraries and museums.

Tremlett, Giles. "Operation Condor: The Cold War Conspiracy That Terrorised South America." *Guardian*, September 3, 2020. https://www.theguardian.com/news/2020/sep/03/operation-condor-the-illegal-state-network-that-terrorised-south-america. This is not a Chilean website and the article is not only about Chile, but it is 100 percent relevant. Operation Condor was convened on Pinochet's order in 1975 and institutionalized impunity across six South American nations with the full knowledge of both the United States and European governments.

Universidad Alberto Hurtado. Centro de Derehos Humanos. https://memoriayderechoshumanosuah.org. A resource guide to all archives dedicated to preserving historical memory and human rights in Chile, published by the University of Alberto Hurtado in Santiago de Chile.

Villa Grimaldi. https://villagrimaldi.cl. Museum and educational center dedicated to the memory of all those who were incarcerated and tortured on this property in the Peñalolén suburb of Santiago, which was the most notorious detention center run by the Chilean secret police during the dictatorship.

About the Author

Natascha Scott-Stokes is the author of *Tales from the Sharp End: A Portrait of Chile* and has been a renowned independent traveler and author for over three decades. She established herself as a pioneering traveler in 1989, when she became the first woman to travel the length of the Amazon River alone, from its Marañon headwaters in the Peruvian Andes to the Atlantic off Brazil. Soon afterward, she based herself in Guatemala, where she not only met the Quebecois father of her two sons but also coauthored two guide books.

After the fall of the Berlin Wall she was inspired to take a journey into history by bicycle, following an ancient trade route for amber through the newly accessible countries of Eastern Europe.

Scott-Stokes emigrated from England to Chile in 2006, but her family's connection with the country goes back to the nineteenth century, when her great-great-grandfather arrived in Valparaíso in 1873 with a contract to install the first submarine telecommunications cable between Peru and Chile.

Scott-Stokes has a Masters in Latin American history and archaeology from London University and is a member of various professional associations, including US-based Biographers International, the Chilean Translators' Association, and the Society of Authors in the UK. She has four travel books and a biography to her name, and she has also coauthored a number of travel guides.